Newcastle
City Council

Newcastle Libraries and Information Service

☎ **0191 277 4100**

Please return this item to any of Newcastle's Libraries by the last date
shown above. If not requested by another customer the loan can
be renewed, you can do this by phone, post or in person.
Charges may be made for late returns.

Also by Amanda Petrusich

Pink Moon

IT STILL MOVES

IT STILL MOVES

Lost SONGS, Lost HIGHWAYS, AND THE SEARCH FOR THE NEXT AMERICAN MUSIC

AMANDA PETRUSICH

ff

faber and faber

First published in the USA
in 2008 by Faber, Inc.
First published in the UK in 2009
by Faber and Faber Ltd
3 Queen Square London WC1N 3AU

Designed by Charlotte Strick
Interior artwork by Hatch Show Print
Printed and bound in the UK by CPI Mackays, Chatham ME5 8TD

Grateful acknowledgement is made to the editors of *Paste* magazine and
Pitchforkmedia.com, where portions of this book appeared
in slightly different form

A CIP record for this book
is available from the British Library

ISBN 978–0–571–23420–2

2 4 6 8 10 9 7 5 3 1

FOR MOM, DAD, ALEX, AND BRET

A place belongs forever to whoever claims it hardest, remembers it most obsessively, wrenches it from itself, shapes it, renders it, loves it so radically that he remakes it in his image.

— JOAN DIDION

CONTENTS

AUTHOR'S NOTE

Throughout the construction of *It Still Moves*, I consulted, parsed, quoted, and admired the work of countless published and unpublished authors, but *It Still Moves* would not have been possible without the research and insight of writers like Ed Cray, Joe Klein, Mark Zwonitzer and Charles Hirshberg, Peter Guralnick, Robert Palmer, Robert Gordon, Colin Escott and Martin Hawkins, Peter Goldsmith, Bill Malone, John Alexander Williams, and too many more to name.

The histories included here are intentionally episodic narratives and in no way represent the full lives or careers of these artists; likewise, there are many essential musicians whose work is not mentioned (or not mentioned extensively). Americana is a broad and varied beast—this is simply my understanding of its story.

IT STILL MOVES

Goodbye, Babylon

Where lies the boundary between meaning and sentiment? . . .
Between memory and nostalgia? America and Americana?
What is and what was? Does it move?
—Donovan Hohn,
"A Romance of Rust: Nostalgia,
Progress, and the Meaning of Tools"

✶ ✹ ✶

In October 2003, Dust-to-Digital, a fledgling Atlanta, Georgia–based record label, released a boxed collection of traditional Americana music titled *Goodbye, Babylon*. Founded in 1999 by a twenty-three-year-old Georgia State University radio DJ, Dust-to-Digital is dedicated to reconciling the past with the present by preserving and digitizing early American songbooks.

Goodbye, Babylon is Dust-to-Digital's flagship release. The box itself is lovingly constructed from cedar and measures about eight inches by eleven inches; the title and a crude drawing of ancient Babylon are etched onto the front in thick black lines. As the top cover of the box slides forward, its insides are slowly revealed in a shower of soft splinters.

Two of the four compartments are packed with unprocessed cotton flowers, lumpy white puffs riddled with bits of dirt and seeds. One houses a short stack of six CDs, each disc enveloped in a thick brown sleeve. The last holds a big, tightly bound booklet containing liner notes written by the renowned musicologist Dick Spottswood.

Each of the six discs included in the *Goodbye, Babylon* box pivots around a central theme: the first disc, which functions as an introduction to the entire set, is dedicated to the exploration of "death, joy, salvation, and the apocalypse." Appropriately, the title track, Reverend T. T. Rose and Singers' "Goodbye, Babylon," cites Revelation 14:8 (which roars: "And there followed another angel, saying, 'Babylon is fallen, is fallen, that great city, because she made all nations drink of the wine of the wrath of her fornication' "), and the song's lyrics ("I told you once, told you twice / You can't go to Heaven by rolling dice!") playfully mimic the Bible's staid counsel.

That primal opposition—sin versus piety—is slathered all over the *Goodbye, Babylon* box and has invaded nearly every other bit of popular American music recorded since. It is, in many ways, the most central American dilemma: We are an ostensibly devout country—one of the most religious in the world—that is also preoccupied with temptation. We are a nation of hell-fearers and heaven-hopers who still like to have a good time, and that tension seeps into nearly every cultural artifact we produce. From "Goodbye, Babylon" on, Americana music is dedicated to exploring that divide, to poking at and magnifying all of the different things that make us American.

Recorded in Grafton, Wisconsin, in April 1930, the Reverend T. T. Rose and Singers' version of "Goodbye, Babylon" is all spirit and very little sound: there's tape hiss and piano and wild, throaty warbles, but ultimately "Goodbye, Babylon" is, like all Americana music, the kind of thing that lives and thrives in the dark, gooey pit of your stomach—not in your ears.

It's half past midnight when I slip the first disc into my stereo. A taut piano melody rises stoically, pushing hard through a heavy curtain of tape hiss. Jerky but determined, the piano waddles on, commanding everyone within earshot to engage in some variation of sharp, heel-toe jigging. I dance, shimmying backward, ponytail swinging. A man starts shouting; his voice is weird and unwieldy, overemphatic, barky. A pack of women chime in emphatically, finishing his thoughts: "Goooodbye!" he yaps. "Babylon!" they holler back.

Goodbye, Babylon is so stoic an object, so unwavering and certain, it's hard to imagine it was constructed around an idea as nebulous and tentative as Americana. Collective notions of Americana tend to be both knee-jerk and bizarre: as an umbrella term, *Americana* is convoluted and sloppy, so overloaded with vague connotations and heavy-handed nostalgia that it's been rendered almost meaningless outside the faux-log walls of Cracker Barrel gift shops. Consequently, it's difficult to talk about without feeling like you're narrating the aw-shucks contents of a Norman Rockwell painting. The word invariably provokes a barrage of clichéd images (think waving fields of golden wheat, wind-rippled flags, and steaming apple pie), quasi symbols that made the grand, unflattering leap from emblematic to silly a long time ago. What does Americana look like? Is it a John Deere alarm clock? A wooden yo-yo? A peppermint stick? A tin of Virginia peanuts? What does it sound like? Does it move?

Historically, Americana music has had an awful lot to do with pawing unamplified instruments, employing minimal production techniques, and dropping at least a few lyrical nods to big southern rivers. Loosely, Americana music is traditional folk music, a symbiotic swirl of folk, bluegrass, country, gospel, blues, and classic guitar-and-vocals emoting. It is twentieth-century, indigent, mostly rural music that is often connected with poverty and usually written on an acoustic guitar. Narrative thrust is important, but it is not necessarily paramount (nor is it delivered exclusively through lyrics). Americana can be quiet or loud, pretty or cacophonous. It is always infused with the vitality of the landscapes from which it has sprung.

Consequently, most traditional Americana music is produced without much concern for its commercial potential—for the most part, there is no pressure for Americana musicians to concede to trends or pop-culture whims, because Americana music so rarely fractures the Hot 100 Billboard charts. There are a handful of notable exceptions: in 2001, the T-Bone Burnett–curated *O Brother, Where Art Thou?* soundtrack, which featured a healthy mix of plucky artifacts and modern Americana revivals, earned itself a mess of Grammys (including Album of the Year), sold more than seven million copies, and was instantly (and inadvertently) crowned America's Unofficial Rough Guide to Americana. The album's success was curious but apt, as quirky and unexpected as the music itself.

Lurking in the background of all that media hoo-ha was the vague sense that the record's galactic reception was actually rather logical. In retrospect it seems almost inevitable that a film soundtrack packed tight with ancient American folk songs would soar to the top of the pop charts in a year when nearly everything "American" was being challenged, threatened, and rearranged. Chalk it up to snappy marketing, snowballing publicity, or incessant NPR chat-ups, but something about that particular record sounded awfully good to a massive number of people at a time when nothing else in the cultural cookie jar (including the omnipotent Billboard stacks, which were piled high with prefab pop, Nashville country, and snarly rap-rock) seemed capable of satiating the public's cravings. For a brief moment, Americana music was sacred again, but more important, it was functional.

Almost all of the contemporary artists included on *O Brother*— Alison Krauss, Gillian Welch, Norman Blake, and others—are well-known and well-acclaimed keepers of the Americana flame. They proudly maintain the genre's warm traditions and staunch rules of conduct: they play acoustic instruments, pen earnest lyrics, ooze down-home humility, and permit only the tiniest of musical updates (most revivalists do ditch the front porch for the relative comfort of a modern recording studio). Theirs is a noble pursuit, and yet: it's so easy to be seduced by the plain, organic glamour of old America, to spin kitsch into commodity, to rank banjos over synthesizers, general stores over Wal-Mart. It's always simpler to spew nostalgic over what's passed than to put hard work into reimagining hallowed, spent traditions for a whole new world and to do so in a way that is just as meaningful now as it was when it started.

Witness, then, a handful of young, pioneering musicians, settled comfortably at obscure or semiobscure independent record labels, catering mostly to the twentysomething T-shirt-and-Pumas set, but playing a new, weird kind of Americana, punctuated by twittering Moog synths and prickly classical guitar, harp strums and free-jazz sax blows. These artists are as concerned with the future as they are with the past, unapologetically embracing the strange synergy of the organic and the synthesized, the beautiful and the hideous, the real and the imagined. The resulting sounds are the best possible reflection of the juxtapositions— factories perched on riverbanks, purple peaks interrupted by Shell stations—outside our windows.

Subverting the acoustic doctrines of folk music is not an entirely new phenomenon. Foundations of dissent have been in place since at least 1965, when Bob Dylan first wailed electric at Newport. Over the subsequent decade, avant-folk pioneers the Incredible String Band, bedroom saint Nick Drake, and the incomparable Captain Beefheart laid serious bricks, and now contemporary acts like Devendra Banhart, Joanna Newsom, Iron and Wine, Sunburned Hand of the Man, Six Organs of Admittance, Matt Valentine and Erika Elder, and the No-Neck Blues Band are twisting old folk habits into new (and sometimes unrecognizable) shapes.

"It's as diverse as it has ever been," says a smiling Jeff Green, the former executive director of the Americana Music Association, when we first meet in his CD-littered Nashville office. "And it's our responsibility to keep it that way. It's not just twangy, rockabilly, Texas terrain. We embrace everything from swamp to zydeco to Native American music. Americana has a pretty big definition," Green continues. "You have to be open-minded. [Americana] can still happen without the bustle of the Big Four record companies. Pro Tools and convenient, portable studios mean that it's a ball game where almost anybody can play, and thanks to CD Baby and Yahoo! Groups and Amazon, the tools for building a community and a fan base and to find management are there."

Even if traditional Americana has, ostensibly, slipped off the cultural and commercial radar, it is far from dead. The genre is slowly evolving, gathering new momentum, breaking out of museum basements and history textbooks, and taking another stab at relevance. And how and why this music has changed—into rock 'n' roll, into Nashville country, into alternative country, into indie-folk and free-folk—is just as much a story about how and why America has changed.

Ain't It a Pity,
I'm in New York City!

Here is a picture of the world: It is a vast globe or ball surrounded on all sides by a sky sparkling with stars. Its surface is divided into land and water. It has upon it two great Continents, five Oceans, many Seas, and Lakes, and Rivers, and Islands, and Mountains. The waters are inhabited by fish and the land is inhabited by man and animals; the land is also covered with trees, and plants of various kinds.
—Picture of the World, *lithograph, 1833*

* ✳ *

I live in Brooklyn, New York, in a gently gentrifying neighborhood called Boerum Hill, eight blocks east of the river and a fifteen-minute subway ride from downtown Manhattan. Last June, I moved to Brooklyn from Charlottesville, Virginia, tugging sagging cardboard boxes through summer swelter, squishing black ants with my flip-flops, balancing potted plants on sloping windowsills, nailing pictures to brick walls. Clawing open a crate of LPs and plugging in an old suitcase record player, I broadcast the hottest songs I could think of: thick, crackling Delta blues.

Brooklyn is removed from mass American culture in complicated

ways and consequently feels intensely foreign to the outsider, no matter
how askew your trucker hat, how immense your mental Rolodex of
dollar-PBR nights, how frequent your trips to the borough's lone Target.
Despite growing up only thirty-five miles due north of Times Square,
and having squirmed through graduate school at Columbia University, I
still feel unprepared for New York City every time I trip out my front
door, scrunching my nose to the smell of street-boiled, urine-soaked
trash, corking my ears with headphones, curling myself away from sirens,
body taut and defensively posed.

A year later, I'm still learning the mechanics of this new place, walking the streets, sniffing, gawking, searching. Today's incessant, soggy rain
does little to alleviate the city's inherent muck, and I think, again, about
how New York City is maybe the only place in the world that seems dirtier when it pours. Everything thickens: cigarette butts swell into tar-
kissed mush, brown puddles crowd the sidewalk. Rain might shine and
polish lesser cities, but here, water lands like shellac, leaden and sticky,
solidifying our mess. Afterward, the air bloats, becoming too thick to
breathe. It's hard not to hear My Morning Jacket's Jim James's high, desperate howl, and shiver: "All your life / Is obscene." But this is the same
story everyone tells: living in New York is serious business. It screams, it
stinks, it hurts; people push and shoot and kick and grab and yell and
dance and holler. The city stings. You are not welcome.

Luckily for me, Brooklyn is not all sludge. I do not miss parking lots
or driveways or property lines or cold, suburban isolation. As Ian Frazier
writes, "Like many Americans, I fear living in a nowhere, in a place that
is no-place; in Brooklyn, that doesn't trouble me at all." Here there are
magnificent bookstores, and too many rock clubs, and grain silos where
you can watch packs of theremin players congregate, zapping one another with sound waves. In Brooklyn, on the streets, there are fewer secrets, and I judge whole lives from my living room, chewing a pen and
listening to Ike Turner records, pressing my palms into dirty window-
panes, nose flat to the glass. There are people fighting on the sidewalk;

women carrying big, plastic shopping bags; men with newspapers; dogs on leashes of thin white string. Young professionals frown, trudging home from the subway, clutching overstuffed briefcases and sacks of take-out shrimp pad Thai, faces long and prematurely gray, juggling duffel bags stuffed with damp gym clothes, shifting their work from one arm to the next. They are tired. Women with toddlers and sacks of produce smile. The man in the beige trench coat smokes a joint, leans against a street sign, crosses his ankles.

On Friday nights, I fall asleep to Brooklyn Cable Access Television, where Lebroz James, a twentysomething white kid with a beard combed out past his nose, hosts my favorite program: an unpredictable variety show wherein James scrambles eggs, yaps about titties, lifts weights, and superimposes his dancing image over Gwen Stefani videos taped straight from MTV (complete with *TRL* pop-ups). In the afternoons, I buy chicken empanadas from street vendors, eating them with one hand, smearing excess grease on my thrift store jeans. I read back issues of *The New Yorker* on steaming subway platforms, my fingers sticking to the pages until I give up and slump over, fanning my damp face, silently commiserating with the woman in nursing scrubs pressing a bottle of Poland Spring to her forehead. I coerce old pals into packing peanut butter sandwiches and thermoses of lemonade and camping out for free concerts in Prospect Park; I huff over the Brooklyn Bridge, kicking at wayward boards with my sneakers, snapping group pictures for giddy tourists. I wander down Bergen Street at night, peeking in the windows of million-dollar brownstones, coveting crystal chandeliers and floor-to-ceiling bookcases. I smile at kids in huge shorts doing pull-ups on crosswalk signals, their white sneakers dangling, thwapping against the yellow pole. At the end of my block, I watch residents of Gowanus Houses, one of New York's largest housing projects, trickle into the street, slicing fruit and pumping hot summer jams, gathering around our local bodega, nodding their heads at passersby. It's trite but awfully true: Brooklyn is bloated with weird, magnificent life.

Regardless, possibly the biggest upside to living in New York is that nearly everywhere else in the country feels easier when (and if) you leave. Now I understand why New Yorkers make the very best travelers. Here outsider status becomes a perpetual part of the daily web of living. Suddenly, feeling a little bit misplaced seems comparably tame. The armor is already built-in; we hold our bags to our hips and keep our heads down.

In 1942, the Texas-born scholar Alan Lomax went "song hunting" in the Mississippi River basin, armed with a missive from the Smithsonian and the same five-hundred-pound portable recording machine that he first used with his father, the folklorist John Lomax, in 1933. Before his death in 2002, Alan Lomax recorded stacks and stacks of quasi-obscure regional folk songs, beginning with the American South and, eventually, stretching his net most of the way around the world. To some, Alan Lomax was an unapologetic imperialist, selfishly scouring foreign cultures for folk songs, making a career out of capturing and lionizing and publishing and picking apart indigenous anthems that did not belong to him—but Lomax also saved hundreds of folk songs from grim, untimely deaths, offering subsequent generations tiny, mysterious bits of art.

For many modern folklorists, a wariness of the Lomaxes' methods still lingers. (There is much mostly unsubstantiated fuss about the family's self-serving agenda, a controversy that began after John refused to sign over his part of the copyright to Huddie "Lead Belly" Ledbetter's "Goodnight, Irene"—which John recorded at a Louisiana state prison in 1933, and with which the Weavers scored a colossal hit in 1950— despite the Ledbetter family's continued impoverishment.) But both John and Alan Lomax understood folk songs; they felt them in their teeth. I admire their bone-deep fervor—the way they craved these songs—as much as I admire their bravery, and, to an extent, their nerve. The Lomaxes understood that America has always been a frontier country. One quick glance at an elementary school social studies syllabus makes the point—Daniel Boone, Sacagawea, Thomas Freeman, Peter

Custis, Zebulon Montgomery Pike, Stephen Long, Jedediah Smith, Nathaniel Wyeth, John Audubon. Pillage, claim, steal. Advance, acknowledge, apologize.

There is a famous black-and-white portrait of Alan Lomax, taken in 1941: The room is dim, and Lomax is perched in front of his typewriter, legs splayed. A box of typing paper, an ashtray, and a coffee press crowd a tiny writing table. He is wearing a shirt and tie; a cigarette droops out of the far left corner of his mouth. Blank-faced, Lomax gapes at his paper, hair mussed. I like to stare at his hands: each index finger is pointing straight out, poised to peck, taking careful aim at his keyboard. Along with his father, Alan Lomax is often considered responsible for the preservation and distribution of much of southern American music, and, subsequently, could arguably claim ownership for the past fifty years of rock 'n' roll. Still: here he is, typing with two fingers, like a little kid. Somehow, it makes his work seem less monumental, less intimidating, less dirty.

John and Alan Lomax might be America's most renowned songcatchers, but the notion of trekking into mountains and valleys, poaching and doting over and preserving ancient songs, was hardly a novel endeavor, even in the 1930s. Nor is it extinct. Scholars and academics still toil in libraries and archives and cornfields, rolling up their trousers and wiggling out of their corduroy blazers, tying cardigans around their waists, trying their best to help these songs endure. Part of that impulse comes from the preservationist instinct of people who read too many books; part is imperialist; part is love.

There is something about indigenous, rural music that invites myth-telling, that demands movement and discovery. Like so many other things, this is as much about the quest as it is about the prize. Where music comes from—the landscapes and faces and churches and industries and seasons that create and preserve certain systems of sound—is the real story. It is my perpetual and unmistakable failure as a music critic that I am infinitely more interested in personal details than in studio settings or guitar pedals or synthesizer type or whether or not something has been recorded in 3/4 time. I would rather discuss what the weather was like in Portland the month a band was recording, if the bassist's sister had her baby, what everyone ate for breakfast, or how hard it was to get off work. These are narratives that can't be parsed exclusively through song lyrics and chord changes and backbeats and bass lines.

So in order to get closer to the songs I love—Americana music, craggy, tottering, uncontrollable country, blues, and folk—to see where they started and what they've since inspired, to fully understand the ways in which these songs have been perverted and rearranged and revisited and reimagined in the decades since their creation, there was only ever one place for me to go.

Periodically, in interviews or conversations about American music, my counterparts will shift their eyes, lean close to my face, and whisper—voices deep, conspiratorial, hushed—a curt proclamation: "All great music comes from the South." If they are feeling particularly plucky, they will fold their hands and add: "And literature, too." A pause. "I mean, you know."

Precisely how and why the American South has shaped and nurtured so much successful art is something sociologists and anthropologists will still be bickering about a half century from now. All I know is that it is mostly true. That particular chunk of rock and water and dirt and kudzu, where people speak in warbles—voices stuck in perpetual song, all slow consonants and giggly cadences, singing, always—and eat too much pie and drink Mountain Dew with spoonfuls of sugar stirred in, bears wild and ridiculous fruit. This is why I decide to climb into my scratched-up Honda Civic and start driving, leaving New York City to learn more about where the songs I love come from and, when I am very lucky, why. My mission is relatively simple: How are our collective ideas about Americana changing? Where did they start? How are those notions preserved, celebrated, milked for profit? How do the places we come from—our hometowns, our regions, our city blocks—influence the

sounds we make? And, most important, how is Americana music transforming to accommodate the massive cultural and geographical shifts in
the American landscape?

I will chug eagerly (and haphazardly) through Virginia, West Virginia, Kentucky, Tennessee, Arkansas, Mississippi, and Georgia, zooming
up and down big highways and country lanes, shooting left and right,
going in circles, pushing down, down, down, following little lines on
maps, reading signs, squinting at blacktop—looking for music, and
looking for more roads. Because every good story about America is also a
story about the road.

I sometimes think that there is nothing more emblematic of America's base ideology—liberty and justice for all—than its indiscriminate,
empowering, hopelessly communal roads. Every day, America's populace
segregates and defines, marking neighborhoods and claiming territory,
but our highways remain inherently shared experiences, both in memory
and in present tense, all tax dollars and shit-spitting potholes. These
highways—thin red and blue lines etched into maps, scrawled onto napkins, shouted across gas station parking lots, tucked into wedding invita-
tions—unite us in perpetual motion. For the contemporary American,
the language of the road is satisfyingly concrete, unambiguous, and hard:
north, south, east, west. Interstate 81 to 64 to 29 to 10. Left at the dairy
stand, right at the split oak, straight past the McDonald's parking lot,
circle around the baseball field.

The notion of the American road as an unregulated gateway to freedom has been codified and repeated so many times throughout modern
American literature and history that road stories have practically become
their own genre. The stereotypical narrator is the lonely male (the man
on the road is the stuff of American legend; the woman on the road is the
stuff of teenage fantasy), preoccupied with achieving catharsis or reinven-
tion, desperately fulfilling an awkward, unnamed quest for authenticity. I
understand: Here, moving, shooting fast through the countryside, press-

ing my foot to the gas pedal, waving to the tractor driver, I am real, and my world is navigable. Driving is both freeing and clarifying; you are steering your own journey, controlling, in very physical and intellectual ways, your trajectory. The road contains the potential for change, for discovery, for adventure. It is the ultimate antidote to plain old life.

There is something deliberate about that kind of idolization—everyone knows that good road stories make the finest fodder for barstool rants, best barked with a cigarette sliding out of the side of your mouth, boots striped with dirt, voice thick and grumbly from sleep deprivation and too many cups of whiskey. It is shameful escapism, romanticized. See Mark Twain, John Steinbeck, Alexis de Tocqueville. See Jack Kerouac write, in 1957's seminal *On the Road*: "What did it matter? I was a young writer and I wanted to take off . . . Somewhere along the line I knew there'd be girls, visions, everything; somewhere along the line the pearl would be handed to me." Or, as William Least Heat-Moon explains, in 1983's *Blue Highways*: "A man who couldn't make things go right could at least go. He could quit trying to get out of the way of life. Chuck routine. Live the real jeopardy of circumstance. It was a question of dignity." Or, as the novelist Larry McMurtry admits, in 2000's *Roads*: "My destination is also my route, my motive only an interest in having the nomad in me survive a little longer."

These are lonely choices, which is also why they yield such rich stories. Driving a U.S. interstate is not a particularly social endeavor. It's possible to drive eight hundred miles without ever speaking to anyone, charging gas and wadding up the receipts, nodding to the convenience store clerk as he stuffs your Snickers bars and pretzels into a plastic sack, sleeping in the backseat, barely looking up from your book when the waitress refills your coffee cup. Driving this way, alone, it's easy to develop faux relationships with the cars around you, dreaming up adventures for their captains, squinting into rearview mirrors, trying your best to snag a glimpse of face. Who are they yelling at on their cell phones?

What brand of cigarette did she inch out of the pack with her lips? The graduation tassel wagging back and forth, the STEAL YOUR FACE sticker half-peeling off the bumper, the tire rims, the radar detector stuck to the windshield—where did it all come from?

Eventually, I find myself asking the same questions of our roads, and here is what I find out: In 1956, President Dwight D. Eisenhower, high on the post–World War II economic boom, scribbled his name on the Federal Aid Highway Act, guaranteeing federal funding for the majestic interstates (the government covered 90 percent of the net costs, with individual states ponying up the rest). The project's official name was the National System of Interstate and Defense Highways, and it was intended, at least in part, to facilitate the movement of troops and supplies during wartime (General Eisenhower had been impressed by the efficiency of the German autobahn). Rather than charging through, interstates are built to circle major metropolitan areas—the system's original designers understood that American cities could someday be bombed, which would inhibit the flow of essential interstate traffic.

The projected cost of the original federal interstate project was set at $27 billion, with sixteen years slated for its construction (thirty-five years later, in 1991, the estimated cost of the interstate system sat at nearly $129 billion, $114 billion of it covered by the federal government). In 2003, 702 billion miles were logged on interstate highways, more than doubling the 296 billion reported in 1980, but the capacity of the system stayed almost exactly the same. It's obvious to anyone who's ever spent any long, soul-crushing hours stalled in traffic: cars keep rolling up the on-ramps, even when there's nowhere left for them to go. Puttering through gridlock can be trying for the casual driver (even more so for the commuter), inviting loads of exasperated sighs, radio dial spinning, and the occasional burst of tears, but it has even drearier implications for commerce: essential shipments are lost or misdirected, employees arrive late, irritated, or not at all, and irreconcilable jams at the nation's ports lead to freight delays, complicating international trade agreements. And on and on.

In their defense, the system's designers had no way of anticipating the rise of suburbia, and were thus unable to predict the glut of cars now clogging their precious arteries. But the government is trying to fix it. In 2006, the National Cooperative Highway Research Program launched Project 20–24(52), also known as Future Options for the National System of Interstate and Defense Highways. Their work—developing "a strong, clear vision for the nation's future highway needs and options"—was declared complete in December 2007.

The interstate system may have been conceived at the height of romantic American driving, around the same time Kerouac began funneling his bearded brethren out of cities and onto highways, but today's interstates are simply not those kinds of roads: gargantuan and numbing, most contemporary incarnations of the interstate program are comically dull, peppered with fast-food huts and gleaming gas stations, framed on each side by huge slabs of tire rubber, cigarette butts, and crushed Coke cans. Witness nasty symptoms of mass homogenization: identical Wal-Marts, McDonald's, Pizza Huts, Exxons, Waffle Houses, and Burger Kings, colossal plastic signs poking up into the atmosphere, announcing the new regime.

Although it might sound obvious or naive, the easiest roads for me to romanticize—to love, to return to—are still the smaller, lesser-known passages. They are scrappy underdogs: dirt roads, country roads, unmarked roads. "Blue roads," Heat-Moon suggests, nodding to their designated tint on highway maps. I am entranced by America's scrawniest streets, admiring their postcard-pretty backdrops and unexpected quietude, pulling the car over to snap photographs and dip my toes in tiny, gurgling creeks, pretending that my entire life is actually transpiring on the countrified set of a Hallmark movie.

In his book *Off Ramp: Adventures and Heartache in the American Elsewhere*, the journalist Hank Stuever claims "Elsewhere"—the culture of on-ramps and off-ramps (read: big-box stores, frozen-yogurt huts, multi-plexes, auto body shops)—as his lifelong beat. "This is the kind of world where I look for ideas, for joy and loss and the marginal things, the funny quirks of what is bland and true," he writes. "Elsewhere offers what I con-sider to be true mystery and has taken me to places and events where I could draw connections . . . If I was looking, I could find the Lord, death, porn, destruction, tanning booths, and teriyaki chicken bowls." Stuever's love of Elsewhere is hardly typical. James Howard Kunstler, author of the brutal, sprawl-indicting *The Geography of Nowhere: The Rise and Decline of America's Man-made Landscape*, finds no romance in interstate spittle: "Eighty percent of everything ever built in America has been built in the last fifty years, and most of it is depressing, brutal, ugly, unhealthy, and spiritually degrading . . . the whole destructive, wasteful, toxic, agoraphobia-inducing spectacle that politicians proudly call 'growth.' "

Still, as most working critics know, judging anything in relation to glib signifiers like *authentic* or *timeless* is a precious, pretentious, and flawed process. Is Robert Johnson more authentic, any more real, than Britney Spears? There is just as much beauty and truth to be spotted in the monoliths, the sprawling, ugly, accident-prone, ten-lane interstates, the roads that carry many and carry fast, as there is in the modest two-lane country road. Ultimately, I am happy to drive them both. Maybe it is because I know, deep down, that the real action, the things that happen off-road, everywhere—the crying, the building, the singing, the sighing, the loving and hating and making and playing and recording—are still a million times more important than the streets that get you there.

I leave Brooklyn on a gray Tuesday morning—my trunk heaving with plastic bags crammed full of clothes, two crates of mixtapes, three pairs of sneakers, and four family-size tubs of animal crackers—and drive more than 1,100 miles to Memphis, Tennessee, where this particular story begins. Because, as the Smithsonian's National Museum of Ameri-can History so wisely notes: in the quest to identify the roots of Amer-ican music, all roads lead to Memphis.

Bluesland:

Beale Street, Memphis

Rolling southwest on Interstate 65, I move toward Tennessee, slicing Kentucky cave country, shirking doughy thunderheads. I readjust my side-view mirrors and pat my belly apologetically: Last night, at Louisville's famed Brown Hotel, I devoured my first Hot Brown, a sloppy, buttery, open-faced turkey sandwich with bacon, pimento, and Parmesan cheese, all soaked in a puddle of gooey Mornay sauce. Aside from burgoo, an opaque stew of mutton, lima beans, okra, corn, potatoes, and cornmeal that requires at least twenty-four hours of cooking time, the Hot Brown is Louisville's most famed culinary export. It is also a monstrous meal.

I-65 is an anonymous slab of highway, fat, well-maintained, and monotonous. Raindrops slap my windshield, splattering into bunches on contact. I'm less than three hundred miles from Memphis, and, outside my car, road signs streak by: HORSE CAVE, MAMMOTH CAVE, CAVE CITY, LOST RIVER CAVE. I pass the exit for Hodgenville, Kentucky, and Abraham Lincoln's birthplace, where a modest nineteenth-century log cabin is preserved inside an enormous white memorial tomb and fronted by an imposing set of fifty-six stone steps (which allow well-wishers plenty of time to contemplate the enormity of the spot toward which they're climbing). The cabin inside, tented by Plexiglas, is not actually Lincoln's, but a log home declared "authentic" to the period. The entire complex was erected on the land Lincoln's parents were farming when he was born. Which, I suppose, makes it close enough.

I steer with one hand, swatting at the radio dial with the other, trying to find voices. The landscape is static; Christian missionaries have achieved a monopoly on roadside billboards in western Kentucky, and their guiding aesthetic, and its ramifications, are clear. Canvases are washed in black and decorated with white or red block letters, recounting the Ten Commandments or distracting highway drivers with big, ominous questions (IF YOU DIED TODAY, WHERE WOULD YOU SPEND ETERNITY?). I stop in Bowling Green for coffee, peanuts, and gas; while crouched on the blacktop by the pumps, using a fistful of paper towels to scour flattened mosquitoes from my windshield, I realize I'm standing directly across the street from the National Corvette Museum. From the road, the museum is not terribly inviting: a colossal, flat gray expanse of concrete interrupted by a decorative bloodred peak, an uncomfortable mix of drab and violent. Appropriately, at least a dozen Corvettes sit diagonally in the parking lot, each four or five spots from the next car. On my way over, I watch two women on a green and yellow John Deere cart drive by, rolling wild at about fifteen miles per hour. It is a Thursday afternoon; the museum is big, awkward, and empty. Everything smells like truck exhaust.

Standing alone in the lobby and thumbing glossy brochures, I learn that Bowling Green has a population of around forty-eight thousand, houses a prominent General Motors assembly plant, and is the birthplace of the from-the-box baking guru and restaurant critic Duncan Hines (each August, the city hosts the Duncan Hines Festival, which features face painting, a Duck Derby, and performances by local cheerleaders). It is also one of the largest Bosnian immigrant enclaves in the United States. On my way out, I buy three Corvette postcards and stuff them in my rear pocket. I will sit on cardboard Corvettes the whole way to Memphis.

I ease back onto the highway and chase I-65 south, crossing the Kentucky/Tennessee border (and, at some point, swerving into the Central Time Zone, although I won't realize that until several days later) and following I-40 west to I-55, where I finally disembark at exit 5: Elvis Presley Boulevard. From there, I follow signs for Graceland. I am listening to Michael Jackson's *Thriller*, which I exchange for Neil Diamond's "Memphis Streets," and clap along with the chorus. Directly across the street from Graceland mansion is a tottering all-white construction with the words "Elvis Presley's Heartbreak Hotel" scrawled in white and blue neon, balanced neatly above a tiny heart fashioned from pink light. As I roll by the entrance, I hear a selection of Elvis songs piping proud, drifting into the parking lot from speakers hung low in the hotel awning. An endearingly battered pink Cadillac limousine (license plate: LONELY ST) is dispensing Hawaiian-shirt-sporting passengers at the front door. I am charmed, park, and wander inside for a room. The lobby is decorated with gold and purple couches and cardboard cutouts of the King, posters for Lisa Marie Presley's new record, and random bits of mod furniture. Around back, a heart-shaped swimming pool sits empty, attracting mosquitoes. A television set plays *Blue Hawaii* while Jungle Bar patrons mingle, their reflections sparkling off a wall of multicolored rhinestones. Behind me, two European men flip through an Elvis trivia set, guffawing over bags of popcorn and bottles of Bud Light. I book a room on the second floor, drop off my bags, and ask the receptionist how to get to Memphis's famed Beale Street, where the city's celebrated blues scene was born. She scribbles me a map: it is a ten-minute drive, following the barren eastern edge of the Mississippi River.

Founded in 1819, Memphis is the kind of city that feeds on collision and conflict, rubbing opposites together and making fire. Crammed in the southwesternmost corner of Tennessee and geographically isolated by a hundred-mile radius of rural farmland and Delta flood zones, Memphis has accepted disciples from every direction, geographic and otherwise: rich and poor, rural and urban, black and white, all eating pork sandwiches and bumping into one another on the sidewalk.

Between 1930 and 1969, the farm population in Memphis's surrounding environs—Tennessee, Mississippi, and Arkansas—cascaded from 3.7 million to 965,000, as agriculture was politely mechanized with tractors, picking machines, and herbicides, rendering most workers obsolete. Memphis, the only remaining possibility for freshly unemployed laborers, was packed with newcomers. As its population multiplied, Memphis's citizens instinctually followed preordained American rules about racial segregation, which meant, among other things, that blacks and whites could never visit the Memphis zoo on the same day.

Tonight, as I climb out of my car and trip past police barricades (for the most part, Beale Street is a pedestrian-only thoroughfare), the contemporary incarnation of Beale's infamous stretch seems big and stupid, littered with generic souvenir shops and oversize bars, more neon-razed food court than the nefarious birthplace of the blues. In the documentary *Deep Blues*, the Arkansas-born writer Robert Palmer, author of the indispensable blues history of the same name, gives Dave Stewart of the Eurythmics a tour through Memphis. They shuffle down Beale, Palmer wearing an overcoat and big brown eyeglasses, Stewart in Wayfarers and an unbuttoned black dress shirt: "The city considered [Beale Street] an eyesore, and [in the 1980s] came in and bulldozed it. And just left desolation for a number of years until they came in and built this stage-set, nineteenth-century mall-type thing, which doesn't look anything like what Beale Street used to look like," Palmer narrates.

I stop for a whiskey at Silky O'Sullivan's, on the corner of Beale and Third streets. Inside, a guy in khakis and a polo shirt is playing Marc Cohn's atrocious "Walking in Memphis" on a beat-up piano, and coeds wearing silly hats are drinking eight-dollar hurricanes out of giant plastic glasses. When the bartender tells me that there's another Silky O'Sullivan's on Bourbon Street in New Orleans, I'm not terribly surprised. Silky's reeks of spring break, of well-intentioned gentrification taken to stifling, theme-park heights. Beyond Beale, much of Memphis is desolate, run-down, and impoverished. In 2004, the U.S. Census Bureau ranked Memphis the fourteenth poorest city in the nation.

Beale Street does house a handful of saltier pseudothrowbacks: the Blues City Cafe, with its blinking BEST MEAL ON BEALE! and PUT SOME SOUTH IN YOUR MOUTH! signs, opened in 1991, quickly becoming the top-earning business on Beale and boasting an impressive client roster, from Ike Turner to Al Green to R. Kelly to Jerry Seinfeld. Blues City serves up giant platters of slow-cooked, hickory-smoked ribs, heaps of steak fries, squished, buttery slices of Texas toast, and plastic cups of sweet and peppery baked beans, all barbecued by the chef Bonnie Mack, whose grinning picture can be found on rack cards all over town. Tonight, Blues City is bloated with patrons who spill out onto the sidewalk, staring intently at menus, fervently discussing catfish versus ribs, and whether the sausage-and-cheese plate or the bowl of seafood gumbo makes for a better start. Down the street, at Mr. Handy's Blues Hall, the Dr. Feelgood Potts Band wails—a big white and red poster in the window giddily announces the show: THE DR. FEELGOOD POTTS BAND FEATURING HARMONICA is scrawled in big letters, sandwiched by two dancing red harmonicas and a handful of music notes.

Although you might not guess it now, Beale Street boasts a terrifically rich history. In the 1860s, African-Americans living in Memphis were either prohibited from visiting the white businesses downtown or allowed access exclusively via side or back entrances; once inside, they were waited on begrudgingly and only after all white customers had been properly served. Consequently, black citizens began to congregate and shop on Beale Street, where black- and Jewish-owned businesses welcomed their patronage. Slowly, the European immigrants who had previously camped out on Beale began to bail, and Beale's transformation—into a hub for African-American politics and the budding civil rights movement—was finalized between 1872 and 1878, when a yellow fever epidemic chewed up or scared off most of Memphis's white population (7,150 people were killed in all, but nearly 25,000 darted off in terror). African-Americans proved genetically less susceptible to the disease, which is spread by infected female mosquitoes, and Memphis's black population swelled. As the twentieth century pulled in, Beale became the epicenter of black southern culture, with music perpetually piping from churches and nightclubs.

Understandably, the confluence of liquor, loose music, lost cash, repression, and cultural isolation gave way to new, distinctly American laments. In 1909, the bandleader W. C. Handy was commissioned to pen a campaign theme for the Memphis mayoral candidate Boss Crump. Crump had promised voters he would shine up the city, effectively forcing Memphis police to close the houses of prostitution and dicey gambling rings that peppered Beale Street and much of downtown. Handy's original composition, dubbed "Boss Crump Blues," wasn't a wholehearted admission of citizen support: "Mr. Crump won't allow no easy-riders here / Mr. Crump won't allow no easy-riders here / I don't care what Mr. Crump won't allow / I'm gonna barrelhouse anyhow / Mr. Crump can go and catch hisself some air." The song scuttled through the streets, becoming a ferocious hit almost immediately, but Handy's howled distaste for Crump's politicking ultimately made little difference in the election: In 1909, a two-dollar poll tax effectively prevented many of Memphis's working class from voting or becoming intimately involved with local elections. White politicians routinely (and shamelessly) bought up stacks of poll tax receipts and slapped them into the hands of Memphis's black citizens, with detailed instructions on how and who they should endorse. As a reward for following orders, blacks were offered whiskey, Coca-Cola, barbecue, and watermelon. Boss Crump won the 1909 election by seventy-nine votes.

"Boss Crump Blues" may not have revolutionized Tennessee politics, but its popularity significantly altered the course of American music; the song disregards traditional pop structure (there is no verse or chorus), follows its own melodic scale (based in five—rather than seven—notes), was performed by one man, alone, and is packed with stark, honest grievances, sung with the belly-born anguish of poverty. According to Robert Palmer, Handy first heard some form of the blues in Tutwiler, Mississippi, in 1903, waiting for a train that was nine hours late. As Palmer writes, "sometime during the night a black man in ragged clothes sat down beside him and began playing a guitar, pressing a knife against the string to get a slurred, moaning, voicelike sound that closely followed his singing." Handy—who had already enjoyed considerable success leading a black dance orchestra based out of Clarksdale, Mississippi— was mesmerized.

Decades earlier, Delta-fertile Mississippi soil had played host to acres and acres of cotton fields, and the trade and abuse of West African slaves blossomed in Memphis (see the grimly unambiguous names of Memphis's four original town squares—Exchange, Market, Court, and Auction). African field songs, hollered in conjunction with the rhythm of the work, slipped into the city's musical vocabulary and could be heard years later in the birth of Memphis blues. The burgeoning cotton trade tied Memphis to northern industry, but the plantation owners harvesting the puffs were so dependent on slavery that the city obediently followed the rest of Tennessee, seceding from the Union in 1861 and entering the Civil War. Memphis was promptly declared a military depot for the Confederate Army, but after the river battle of June 6, 1862, where, according to city lore, as many as ten thousand Memphians assembled on the river bluffs to watch the Confederate Army fall, Memphis became a northern occupation. Subsequently, Memphis attracted the region's former slaves (the city's African-American population quadrupled between 1860 and 1870), who made remarkable strides in ensuring freedoms of assembly and worship, and learned to contend with enduring violence: in 1863, a three-day race riot resulted in the deaths of forty-four blacks, two whites, and the destruction of a dozen freedman's schools and hundreds of black businesses.

Like much of America, Memphis never fully worked out its biracial roots. A century later, in 1968, Memphis's sanitation workers launched a citywide strike, fighting, again, for equal rights, economic equity, and safer working conditions. Newspapers reported upward of ten thousand tons of garbage stacking up on the streets, while picketers marched somberly, clutching signs declaring I AM A MAN. Soon after, Dr. Martin Luther King, Jr., arrived to facilitate reconciliation, leading fifteen thousand people in a nonviolent march down Beale Street, from Clayborn Temple to City Hall. Seven blocks in, disgruntled youth began shattering windows and looting storefronts; almost immediately, Memphis police marched into the crowd wielding nightsticks, tear gas, mace, and guns. Two hundred eighty people were arrested, a sixteen-year-old boy was filled with bullets, and sixty protesters were injured. In response, the Tennessee state legislature demanded a 7:00 p.m. curfew and sent four thousand National Guardsmen stomping into the city. A week after the march, on April 4, 1968, while standing on the balcony of his room at the Lorraine Motel (now the site of the National Civil Rights Museum), Dr. King was assassinated.

Tonight, as I amble down Beale, a short homeless man swaddled in sweaters snatches my arm and shoves a clutch of furry red flowers into my palm. "Take care of my goddamn flowers!" he cautions. When I tense and giggle, eyes twitching instinctively toward the occupied police car idling a block ahead, he reprimands me: "I'm goddamn serious! Take care of my goddamn plants!" He has no teeth, and funnels more flowers into my limp bouquet. I nod, remembering Memphis's impious reputation for violent crime (rates here are two and a half times the national average; in 2006, Memphis racked up 147 murders—a grim ratio of almost one murder every two days—and the FBI tallied well over thirteen thousand violent crimes). His head bobs. "They're good luck. They're motherfucking beautiful. Your luck is going to change. Some people call them pussy willows; some people call them cockadoos." He pauses. "Press them in a book." I dig into my pocket and fish out a rumpled dollar bill and some quarters, but he is already gone.

Back at the Heartbreak Hotel, I brew a pot of coffee, chew pralines from a small box I bought at A. Schwab's on Beale Street (opened in 1876, A. Schwab's is the oldest store in Memphis, and sells a mix of voodoo oils, ceremonial candles, souvenir mugs, cheap clothing, and candy), and watch a rebroadcast of the PBS presentation "A Tribute to Johnny Cash," featuring performances by Dave Matthews, Kris Kristofferson, Emmylou Harris, and others. When Johnny's daughter, the singer-songwriter Rosanne Cash, strides onstage to introduce her father, photographs of a young Johnny flash on-screen. Rosanne's steady voice narrates his story. When they get to Memphis's Sun Records, Johnny Cash's first record label, Rosanne mentions proprietor Sam Phillips's decision to gently tug Johnny away from gospel songs, pushing him in a "more commercial" direction. Her voice is heavy with thinly veiled scorn. But when Johnny Cash finally strides onstage, swathed in trademark black, he's grinning largely, and the very first man he thanks is Sam Phillips.

Young and Loose and Full of Juice:

Sam Phillips, Sun Studio, and the Birth of Rock 'n' Roll

One block north of Beale Street, about a mile from the clubs at Beale and Third, Sun Studio sits, short and inconspicuous, on the corner of Union and Marshall avenues, inadvertently secluded from the tourist-riddled rib joints and blues bars downtown. Marshall Avenue, angling to the northwest, looks deserted and strange, peppered with unsightly billboards, all postindustrial detritus and anonymous retail space. Union Avenue, which darts west directly back into the center of the city, is equally spare, banked by gas stations, unsigned brick buildings, and half-empty parking lots. Sun Studio is noticeably removed from Memphis's hotel culture, but still feeds on nosy visitors, offering up T-shirts and shot glasses and a complimentary shuttle to and from Graceland. A giant, taxicab-yellow Gibson guitar rotates above the doorway; neon signs and enormous black-and-white posters of Elvis Presley adorn dirty windows. Still, Sun Studio, squat and humble, feels awfully quiet in a city best known for hoots and hollers. It hasn't always been so fixed.

In October 1949, the WREC DJ and budding entrepreneur Sam Phillips leased the middling storefront, then an abandoned radiator shop, for $150 a month. In 1950, after borrowing money from his WREC coworker Buck Turner and investing in the latest recording equipment, Phillips, now boasting a five-input mixer, amateur Crestwood and Bell tape recorders, and a portable Presto PT900 recorder (which he sensibly stored in the trunk of his car), opened the Memphis Recording Service. Although prepared to immortalize weddings, funerals, and other religious ceremonies (operating under the plucky slogan "We Record Anything, Anywhere, Anytime"), Sam Phillips began recording local musicians almost immediately, starting with a transcription (a recording on magnetic tape, made specifically for radio broadcasting) of Buck Turner's band for the Arkansas rural electrification program. The program was part of an ongoing government-led attempt to diminish the crushing divide between rich and poor, and was initiated by President Franklin D. Roosevelt in the 1930s, when nearly 90 percent of America lacked electricity; Phillips's recording was distributed to fifteen to twenty radio stations throughout the mid-South and played for rural families as they were first introduced to radio.

Phillips was not unfamiliar with rural life. Born in Florence, Alabama, in January 1923, Sam Phillips grew up on a three-hundred-acre tenant farm on the sludgy banks of the Tennessee River, dropping out of high school and taking two jobs (one in a grocery store and one in a funeral parlor) to pull his family through the Great Depression. At first aspiring to study law, Phillips settled for audio engineering after financial strains made higher education impossible. As Phillips told *Good Rockin' Tonight* authors Colin Escott and Martin Hawkins, "I was not interested in becoming a musician. But back in the 1930s, all the music of the country people—black blues, hillbilly, and spirituals—all influenced me, and in radio I saw a medium where I could do something with the music I loved." Already, Phillips was actively seeking out indigenous, regionalized performers and devising new ways to disseminate their songs. From the start, Phillips knew what he prized: "real intuitive music," hollered and strummed with uncut fervor. Most of the artists Phillips championed didn't write their own material, but for Phillips, the stamp of authenticity was earned only via passionate performance. (Plenty of contemporary rock 'n' roll purists—or rockists, as they're lovingly dubbed by pop-music defenders—would find Phillips's disregard for songwriting credits appalling.)

The building at 706 Union was eventually transformed to accommodate a modest front office, a twenty-by-thirty-five-foot recording area, and a small control room. Despite all his shiny new gear, Phillips remained understandably dubious about the functionality of tape, which, in 1950, was still an untested medium. Thus, like any decent, self-doubting archivist, Phillips faltered and opted for what he knew, recording most of his early efforts to big sixteen-inch acetate discs, cutting them at 78 rpm with a Presto 6N lathe wired to a Presto turntable. As a DJ at WREC, where he hosted *Songs of the West* and *Saturday Afternoon Tea Dance* (broadcast from the top of Memphis's Peabody Hotel and syndicated nationally via the CBS radio network), Phillips was well-acquainted with pressing acetate: in 1950, most radio programs were prerecorded onto discs and then duplicated and handed around to other stations, casting radio DJs as accidental recording engineers.

Phillips articulated his business credo to Escott and Hawkins: "My aim was to try and record the blues and other music I liked and to prove whether I was right or wrong about this music. I knew, or I felt I knew, that there was a bigger audience for the blues than just the black man of the mid-south." Soon, Phillips was entertaining a bevy of local gospel and blues musicians, culled from scrappy Memphis clubs or regional radio stations, and leasing their work to small independent labels (Meteor, Trumpet, RPM/Modern, 4-Star, and Chicago's Chess Records, in particular). The Memphis Recording Service client list included an impressive lineup of soon-to-be-famous bluesmen, including Joe Hill Louis, Bobby Bland, Little Milton, a barely-twenty-five-year-old B. B. King, and

Roscoe Gordon. Phillips was fulfilled, ecstatic. "You could look into his eyes and see whirling pools of insanity," the session player Jim Dickinson later told Escott and Hawkins.

In 1951, Phillips recorded a handful of songs by a lumbering, forty-year-old West Memphis DJ named Chester Burnett, known locally as Howlin' Wolf. Wolf is as tenderly remembered for his size-seventeen feet (he supposedly tore holes into his giant shoes to accommodate his corns) as for his earnest caterwauling. "The Wolf came to the studio and he was about six foot six, with the biggest feet I've ever seen on a human being," Phillips told Robert Palmer in an interview for *Memphis* magazine. "Big Foot Chester is one name they used to call him. He would sit there with those feet planted wide apart, playing nothing but the French harp and I tell you, the greatest sight you could see today would be Chester Burnett doing one of those sessions in my studio. God, what it would be worth to see the fervor in that man's face when he sang. His eyes would light up, you would see the veins on his neck and buddy, there was nothing on his mind but that song. He sang with his damn soul!"

Howlin' Wolf didn't stay terribly long in Memphis. By 1953 he had been contracted to Chess Records and jetted out of town, but his early work, like that of his Delta peers (the elusive Robert Johnson, especially), prophesied the next fifty years of popular music. Seizing on early blues and again mimicking the chants and work songs of West Africa, Howlin' Wolf growled loose narratives with nasty lyrics, favoring blood-and-bones emotion over technical prowess. Wolf played twelve-bar blues, a chord progression that's still the standard for most popular rock songs: twelve 4/4 bars to a verse—meaning three sets of four measures, with four beats each. Later in his life, Phillips would cite recording Howlin' Wolf as his single greatest achievement.

Earlier in 1951, Jackie Brenston, the tenor sax player in the Kings of Rhythm, a band led by the Mississippi DJ and pianist Ike Turner, howled an ode to Oldsmobile's shiny four-door sedan, the Rocket 88. Recorded by Phillips, the song was released by Chess Records almost immediately and wiggled to the tops of the rhythm and blues charts, becoming the second-biggest R&B hit of 1951. Finally, Phillips saw his artistic vision validated, telling Escott and Hawkins, " 'Rocket 88' was the record that really kicked it off for me, as far as broadening the base of music and opening up wider markets for our local music."

"Rocket 88" featured prominent backbeat and squeals of serendipitous guitar distortion that would later become fodder for a grand local legend. Supposedly, while en route from Clarksdale, Mississippi, the guitarist Willie Kizart's amp bounced off the roof of the band's car and crashed onto Highway 61, effectively ruining the speaker cone. The band hauled the broken speaker to Sun, where Phillips crammed newspaper into the cone, and in an inspired attempt at repair, overamplified the distortion rather than muffling it. Later, "Rocket 88" would become known to some as the very first rock 'n' roll song ever recorded. Bill Haley covered the track later that year, a full three years before he took on "Rock Around the Clock," another cut often considered the first rock 'n' roll song; likewise, Little Richard's "Good Golly, Miss Molly," written by Robert "Bumps" Blackwell and John Marascalco and recorded in 1955, brazenly cribbed Turner's piano introduction note for note. "Rocket 88" was a freewheeling bit of groundbreaking sound, all chunky rhythm, guitar distortion, and vaguely unhinged vocals. It was not country, not blues, and not exactly R&B.

In 1952, Phillips abandoned the Memphis Recording Service and founded Sun Studio and Sun Records, the brown and yellow burst adorning each Sun single aptly reflecting his faith in a universal power. In *Good Rockin' Tonight*, Phillips explained, "The sun to me—even as a kid back on the farm—was a universal kind of thing. A new day, a new opportunity." Bob Dylan would later howl, "The sun's not yellow it's chicken" in 1965's "Tombstone Blues," a perplexing bit of wordplay that many consider a subtle nod to the Sun logo, which featured a crowing rooster centered in its sunbeams.

On February 25, 1952, the jug band veteran Jack Kelly and the harmonica player Little Walter Horton (billed together as "Jackie Boy and Little Walter") enlisted Phillips to record "Blues in My Condition." Phillips initially offered the song to Chess Records, but Chess declined, prompting Phillips to ship the masters for processing and release the record himself. But before the single's stampers (the metal negatives from which records are developed) came back from Shaw Processing, Phillips had changed his mind, deciding that "Blues in My Condition" and its B-side, "Sellin' My Whiskey" (originally titled "Sellin' My Stuff"), weren't strong enough tracks to christen Sun. He shelved the record and decided that his first commercial release for Sun would be "Drivin' Slow," an instrumental performed by a sixteen-year-old black saxophone player named Johnny London. Trying to determine exactly why Phillips reneged on "Blues in My Condition" is futile, but the decision to suddenly trash a finished record neatly showcases Phillips's reliance on his gut. Sam Phillips abided by a detailed, unbending mental agenda obvious only to him. "Blues in My Condition" was never released.

Already, Phillips's dexterity and resourcefulness as an engineer distinguished his work in the studio—he was so intent on recreating the exact sound of a saxophone oozing out from a humid alleyway, he constructed what Escott and Hawkins describe as "something like a phone booth" over London's horn. In "Drivin' Slow," London's sax sounds thick and muted, and his wails beckon, soft and coy, from across the room, as if his only intent were to tug his listeners closer and closer to their speakers. A plodding piano backbeat teases, offering just enough structure for London's saxophone to scream free, a crayon scribbling across a blank page. Passion trumps ingenuity: "Drivin' Slow" is misty and mysterious, unrelenting in its intrigue. There is a narrative to London's longing blows, but it is different for everyone who listens, a story without explicit terms—a poem.

By the mid-1940s, the racial divide in Memphis was acute, and blues music (and, eventually, rock 'n' roll) allowed African-Americans to apply a popular voice to their woes. In June 1947, 730 AM/WDIA became Memphis's sixth radio station, broadcasting a then-characteristic mix of country, classical, and light pop music; WDIA squawked and tottered in an oversaturated marketplace, and in a desperate, last-hour stab at survival, the station owners, John Pepper and Bert Ferguson, hired Nat D. Williams, a local African-American high school teacher and columnist, to host a show called *Tan Town Jamboree*. Williams's first show, which aired on October 25, 1948, earned a handful of bomb threats from the city's white segregationists, but also found a dedicated, loving audience among Memphis's African-Americans, who comprised nearly 40 percent of the city's population. By the fall of 1949, WDIA was programmed exclusively for black audiences (though the South was still segregated enough that WDIA station managers felt obligated to meekly inform advertisers they might begin receiving black patrons after their ads ran). Staffed mostly by amateur DJs, WDIA had little concern for common radio convention, and boisterous personalities bloomed. By 1954, it was the number one radio network in Memphis and had begun calling itself "the Mother Station of Negroes." WDIA employed only African-Americans as announcers, but every executive position remained staffed by a white man or woman.

One of WDIA's first DJs, a musician and friend of Nat Williams's named Rufus Thomas, who had cohosted Beale Street's Palace Theater Amateur Night with Williams before the pair landed regular gigs at the station, commanded a two-hour evening slot called *Hoot and Holler*, where he routinely proclaimed, "I'm young and loose and full of juice / I got the goose so what's the use?" Thomas was born in Casey, Mississippi, in 1917, the son of a sharecropper, and landed in Memphis in 1940, where his verve and flamboyance promptly earned him a reputation around town. He took a job operating boilers at a textile-bleaching plant; like many early blues singers, the sound and pace of the work informed his rhythmic style.

In the early 1950s, performing an "answer" to a blues song was common practice in the clubs and on the curbs (a precursor of contemporary hip-hop, where sampling and embattled responses to "diss" tracks are prevalent), and on March 8, 1953, Thomas went to Sun to record "Bear Cat," a giddy, mischievous reaction to Big Mama Thornton's "Hound Dog," which was written by Jerry Leiber and Mike Stoller and was released just weeks earlier on Houston's Peacock Records. Per convention, Thomas howled "Bear Cat" to the exact same melody as "Hound Dog." The song opens with Thomas spitting out an alarmingly accurate string of meows and hisses before enthusiastically roaring, "You know what you said about me, don't you woman? / Well, you ain't nothin' but a bear cat, scratchin' at my door / You can purr, pretty kitty / But I ain't gonna rub you no more!"

Phillips had recorded successes for other labels, but "Bear Cat" became the first number-one hit released on the still-fledgling Sun. Shortly after the track began spilling out of radios all across the city, Don Robey, head of Peacock Records, sued Sam Phillips and Sun for copyright infringement and won a sizable settlement, somewhere around twenty thousand dollars. (Later, in 1955, Sun would sue Robey over the blues singer Junior Parker, claiming that Robey induced Parker to break his exclusive contract with Sun—the court would ultimately rule in favor of Sam Phillips and Sun Records.) It was a significant financial knock for Sun, but Phillips soldiered on.

By 1954, Phillips had opted to upgrade his equipment, first replacing the Presto with an RCA 76D radio console and then dragging in two Ampex 350 tape machines: a console model, and another to mount behind Phillips's head for tape delay echo, or slapback. His setup with those machines ultimately solidified the Sun Records sound—bouncing the signal from the console to the wall-mounted Ampex (with a split-second delay between the two) created a fullness to the voices being recorded, as if two people were singing simultaneously. In a 1998 interview with Richard Buskin, a writer for the Cambridge, England–based trade magazine *Sound on Sound*, Phillips clarified: "I was the first one to employ slapback, feeding the tape back through the board. You see, the human ear doesn't like hearing something that is aurally so different to the point of being strange. It likes something different so far as the total confluence of the sound and the song and how it's done. I knew that people had heard records on jukeboxes in live little restaurants and dives, and what I tried to do with that type of echo and the sparse instrumentation was to make the sound not too foreign to the average ear." Slapback meant deep, resonant, teeth-quaking vocals, and even now, Sun artists are typically remembered for their thick, room-filling pipes more than anything else. Already, Phillips's ever-aggrandizing mythopoeia—as the man singularly responsible for a giant chunk of twentieth- and twenty-first-century popular culture, as the most influential figure in the history of American music, the man who ostensibly created rock 'n' roll, built a popular platform for Memphis blues, and shoved microphones in front of men who would later become heroes—was beginning to develop. And by the end of the year, Sam Phillips's reputation would be indelible.

Phillips's secretary, the Memphis-born Marion Keisker, is periodically credited with the "discovery" of Elvis Presley in mid-1953, when Presley, then a clumsy appliance salesman, utilized the studio's one-off recording service—for $3.98, you could record and press your own single—while Phillips was out of town. Presley warbled two songs ("My Happiness" and "This Is Where Your Heartache Begins"), supposedly as a birthday gift for his mother, but since Gladys Presley's birthday was in April, and Elvis wandered into Sun in the middle of summer, chances are Elvis was actually more interested in hearing his voice laid to tape than surprising his mom with a tune. Elvis's unusual pipes prodded Keisker's curiosity, and she pressed an extra record to play back for Phillips, who recorded Elvis Presley's first single, a cover of Arthur "Big Boy" Crudup's "That's All Right (Mama)" almost a year later, in July 1954.

"That's All Right (Mama)" is built on a standard blues melody so

shopworn it's familiar even to folks who have never heard the song before. Scotty Moore's guitar skitters and chirps, while Bill Black's slap-bass
thumps dutifully and Presley's sharp, cartwheeling vocals lurch forward.
Elvis sounds hard, tough, and uncrackable. This is not the soft, melodramatic crooning and ballad-bellowing that marked his later work. Even
Presley sounds surprised by the looseness in his throat, the curvy, defiant
upswing on "Maaa-ma!" His voice is all energy and inertia—a scat break-
down ninety seconds in is so energetic and heartfelt you can almost see
Presley's cheeks quivering with glee.

Oddly, the B-side to "That's All Right (Mama)" is a classic hillbilly
version of Bill Monroe's "Blue Moon of Kentucky." Here, Phillips's slapback booms and echoes—imagine a small troop of men, singing together
in strange, hazy harmony—and Presley sounds less like the harbinger of
a new art form, and more like a sweet, if unremarkable, bluegrass chirper.
In his book *Lost Highway*, the Elvis biographer Peter Guralnick quotes
Keisker: "On that first record of Elvis', we sent a thousand copies to disc
jockeys, and I bet nine hundred went into the trash can, because if a
Rhythm & Blues man got it and heard 'Blue Moon Kentucky,' he tossed
it away . . . same thing if the country man heard 'That's All Right.' "

For the very first time, a white man was successfully adapting and
reflecting the sound of the black cultural experience—in Memphis, in
America—for a largely segregated public. "That's All Right (Mama)"
went on to sell thirty thousand copies, and Presley placed in *Billboard*
magazine's year-end poll, earning the title of eighth most promising new
hillbilly artist. In January 1955, six months after the release of "That's All
Right (Mama)," Elvis Presley left Sun, signing with Bob Neal and RCA
Records, who bought out Presley's Sun contract for thirty-five thousand
dollars—enough for Phillips to finally recoup funds lost over "Bear Cat."
In 1956, in what might be one of pop music's cruelest twists, Elvis's third
single for RCA became an enormous hit—a licensed cover of Thornton's
"Hound Dog," the same track that cost Phillips twenty thousand dollars
in 1953.

Elvis Presley didn't enjoy colossal success until after he'd left Sun Records: between 1956 and his death twenty-one years later, Elvis scored 146 Hot 100 hits, 112 Top 40 hits, 72 top 20 hits, and 40 top 10 hits, a string of success yet to be matched by another solo artist. What Sam Phillips ultimately commanded with Elvis in the early 1950s was a new hybrid sound, a confrontational fusion of country, blues, jazz, gospel, Appalachian folk, and R&B known as rockabilly, and, later, rock 'n' roll. The Sun signee and "Blue Suede Shoes" author Carl Perkins would eventually abbreviate rockabilly as "a country man's song with a black man's rhythm," effectively distilling the genre into its two primary components: black and white. What Ike Turner and Jackie Brenston shook up with "Rocket 88" was only later understood as the harbinger of a new movement—as Robert Gordon wrote in *It Came from Memphis*, "There was no novelty in blacks revving up R&B. White imitations of it, however, were freakish. Whites were unable to exactly mimic black music, and their failure created another hybrid. People of all colors gawked." The inherent incompatibility of country and soul, and not their synthesis, is what made early rock 'n' roll so compelling. Rock 'n' roll is a clash, quarrelsome and hotheaded, a teenager careening out of control in a school yard, arms and legs flinging everywhere, teeth gnashing, face cranberry red—it is a sound built on tension, not harmony. In a 1959 *Esquire* interview, Alan Lomax declared rock 'n' roll "the healthiest manifestation yet in native American music."

Musically, Sam Phillips purposefully engineered the foundations of early rock 'n' roll and was responsible for more than just pressing the record button and shooting a thumbs-up from behind a wall of glass. Often rigging ridiculous setups to create certain moods, Phillips pushed for passion, sloppiness, and a certain lack of sophistication; consequently, the Sun catalog is riddled with all sorts of ridiculous mistakes—slipped chords, curdled notes, off-key croons—that would be auto-corrected in any contemporary studio. Phillips favored "bottom-heavy" sounds, with the rhythm section carrying much of the melody (pre-Sun, recordings were typically mixed for balance) and picked zeal over chops, dismissing any instrumental noodling as self-indulgent and unnecessary. In an outtake of Elvis Presley's "When It Rains It Really Pours," Phillips can be heard scolding an already minimalistic Scotty Moore: "Scotty, don't get too damn complicated in the middle there!"

In many ways, Phillips's production style was more revolutionary than the artists who slurped up all the credit: even Elvis Presley's articulation of black vocal styles was preceded by a handful of lesser-knowns (see Al Jolson in 1927's *The Jazz Singer*). Still, as Guralnick declared in *Lost Highway*, "Elvis had the moment."

By 1955, Phillips had mostly ditched the blues to pursue rockabilly—as Nick Tosches wrote in *Hellfire*, his 1982 biography of Jerry Lee Lewis, "Along came Elvis, and Sun was soon no longer a blues label, but instead the premier label of whitefolk rock 'n' roll." By the mid-1950s, Phillips commanded a glowing roster. Carl Perkins joined Sun in 1954, and a young gospel singer named Johnny Cash began strumming for Phillips in June 1955 (recording "Hey Porter" / "Cry Cry Cry" almost immediately, and releasing his hit "I Walk the Line" in 1956). The bespectacled Texan Roy Orbison signed on in 1956, and later that year, a raucous, twenty-one-year-old piano pounder named Jerry Lee Lewis read an article about Elvis in *Country Song Roundup*, sold thirteen dozen eggs for traveling cash, ditched Ferriday, Louisiana, for Memphis, and pestered Jack Clement, a producer and engineer Phillips had hired, into letting him record a demo at Sun. Phillips later told Robert Palmer, "I had been wanting to get off this guitar scene and show that it could be done with other instruments. They put that tape on, and I said, 'Where in hell did this man come from?' " Phillips released Jerry Lee Lewis's first single, "Crazy Arms," on December 1, 1956.

Lewis was the archetypal American sinner, captivated and puffed up by staunch religious fanaticism, but ultimately destroyed by debauchery that honked in the face of his faith. Tucked at the very end of the Sun compilation *Sun Spots Volume 2: Oddities and Obscurities* is a cut titled "Religious Discussion—Sam Phillips/Jerry Lee Lewis." The track is full of hollers of "Jeee-sus!" and cries of "Brother!" while Sam Phillips tries his rational best to talk Lewis down from a riff: "Now look, Jerry, religious conviction doesn't mean anything resembling extremism," he counsels, speaking in firm, gentle tones. Lewis sounds undeterred.

When the raucous, squawking "Great Balls of Fire" was released in December 1957, Elvis Presley was yanking at the laces on his army-issue combat boots, preparing to fulfill his draft duties, meaning Jerry Lee Lewis was left to command the number one spot on nearly every national chart. "Great Balls of Fire" is doused with slapback, echoing and uncomfortably full, all rollicking piano licks and shrill vocal hiccups. Lewis was so unhinged and unpredictable at his piano bench, half-standing and hurling his hands at the keys, wavy blond hair whipping in all directions, that he was breathtaking to observe. Unfortunately, Lewis opted to marry his thirteen-year-old cousin, Myra Gale Brown, in January 1958 (Brown was Lewis's third wife, and their wedding took place before Lewis had actually divorced his second), and Americans screwed up their faces in collective, untempered disgust.

The notion of the early rock 'n' roll singer as periodically repentant sexual deviant is far from unfounded. In her 1985 memoir, *Elvis and Me*, Elvis's ex-wife, Priscilla Presley, describes his preoccupation with her premarital virginity (the upshot of a childhood packed with fire-and-brimstone Pentecostal threats) but also admits to his numerous extra-marital affairs, including a relatively high-profile relationship with the Swedish-born actress and singer Ann-Margret, who also recorded for RCA. Even after his 1973 divorce, Presley continued to pursue multiple women at once (Presley eventually invited Linda Thompson, a twenty-one-year-old pageant queen, to join him at Graceland, but continued sleeping with his backup singer Kathy Westmoreland, actress Cybill Shepherd, and most likely a few others). It's hard to find an Elvis book that doesn't pause to contemplate Presley's seemingly insatiable lust for women. In *Elvis: Unknown Stories Behind the Legend*, the author, Jim Curtin, quips that Presley's "list of one-night stands would fill volumes."

The idea of the Christian and the sinner battling in the same body is inherent to early rock 'n' roll. It's a classic American paradox—sinners obsessed with salvation, puritans engrossed by *Playboy*, gluttons obsessed with healthy eating—that pops up again and again, from early secular music (see the *Goodbye, Babylon* box set) through Elvis and Jerry Lee Lewis and even Johnny Cash. (The idea of the rock star as sinner persists today, though mostly without the Christian bits.) That remarkable tension—between right and wrong, carnal and spiritual—is essentially what fuels rock 'n' roll music, and it accounts for much of what made Memphis's early rock stars such mesmerizing (and recognizably American) figures.

The following morning, stumbling through Sun's glass front door, I face a modest café, where a woman is frying peanut-butter-and-banana sandwiches (Elvis's favorite), pouring Cokes, and selling $9.50 tickets to the studio tour. The café bar is edged by spinning chrome stools with red vinyl tops, and framed posters of studio alumni hang haphazardly from the walls. A small gift shop offers buttons and shirts and posters and refrigerator magnets; the back room has a selection of CDs and a wall of original Sun singles, which range in price from $25 to more than $100. I buy a ticket and a bottle of root beer, and wait.

Rock 'n' roll is probably the most well-known, financially viable, and critically celebrated embellishment of traditional Americana music, and anyone who visits Sun Studio is promptly rewarded with a walloping sense of the gravity of the genre, in terms of both its artistic and its cultural implications. Today's tour is led by a sweet-faced twentysomething in jeans and a button-down blouse, and when she announces its start, nine ticket holders gallop to the back of the café, gathering around her before being led upstairs to a memorabilia-stuffed room (all the keepsakes are safely sequestered behind big glass cases). The tour is informative and features audio samples of relevant songs and glimpses of Sun's material history (including guitars, records, and high school programs), but it doesn't reach transcendental levels until we descend a narrow, unsteady wooden staircase and shuffle into the actual studio's front room (the café and upstairs gallery are part of an adjacent building).

Here, Marion Keisker once perched at a humble desk (its tiny wooden top is still beset with a small black fan, a telephone, a typewriter, and a brown plaque with her name inscribed in white block letters), the first line of defense between would-be crooners and Sam Phillips. Keisker's desk is small, but for many it was the world's single largest roadblock.

After inching through Keisker's office, my tour group shuffles slowly into the studio. Whereas Sun's upper gallery is professionally detached, an airtight capsule crammed full of rockabilly remains, museum-distant and emotionally unobtrusive, its downstairs is messy, guttural, and real. Occasionally, Sun still functions as an active studio: in November 1987, the Irish rock heroes U2 recorded the bulk of their sixth studio album, *Rattle and Hum*, at Sun while simultaneously shooting footage for a (notoriously pretentious) band documentary of the same name. White soundproofing tiles (now crumbling and streaked with gray) line the walls, and a grubby linoleum floor is littered with instruments and standard recording debris: a bright-blue drum set, a mess of electric and acoustic guitars, a student-model pedal steel, swirls of cables, amplifiers, cases, stacks of black box speakers, microphones perched on stands, pedal boards, and a table fan. The light fixtures haven't been updated since 1951; a stripe of hospital green paint accents the bottoms of the walls. A black-and-white photograph of the Million Dollar Quartet—the unplanned, contractually dubious, and initially unreleased Sun recording session with Johnny Cash, Jerry Lee Lewis, Carl Perkins, and an RCA-bound Elvis—has been transferred onto the wall tiles above a small piano, centered and petrified in the exact same spot it was taken fifty years before. Carl Perkins has an acoustic guitar slung low around his neck; Elvis is seated at a piano, his lippy mouth curled into a tiny *o*. Jerry Lee Lewis looks slightly perplexed; Johnny Cash is still wearing his jacket. Around them, tourists now mill and sniff, and our guide drags out the clunky microphone used for the original Sun sessions. Before she sets it down, she warns, in a dusty southern drawl: "Please don't lick, bite, or kiss this."

It's clichéd, and possibly more the convoluted product of nostalgia and tourism than any real, profound enchantment, but the room feels haunted, thick and heavy with ghosts: I stare at Sun's big, awkward microphone, gleaming inches from my face, and feel strange. The cult of literature surrounding Sun Studio and Memphis and the birth of rock music is overwhelming, and I can understand the desire to pinpoint the details of what happened here a half century ago, to parse the history, to define the moments, to capture the impetus behind each guitar wail and vocal glitch. Everything feels big, connected to the rest of the universe by millions of little invisible strings, stretching through the open bedroom windows of gangly teenagers sewing patches on their backpacks, glaring at their parents, and playing air guitar.

Cowering in Sun's rehearsal space, it's easy to be seduced by the mythos of the studio, to solemnly anoint Sam Phillips the savior of modern music. But his legacy is not beyond dispute. Phillips is long credited with bridging race barriers in a pre–civil rights southern city, but even his seemingly supportive efforts are often held suspect—like John and Alan Lomax decades before, or WDIA's owners and executives, Phillips was a white man commanding and profiting from the sale of black music. In Guralnick's *Lost Highway*, Rufus Thomas (who died in Memphis in 2001, at the age of eighty-four) derides what he understood as Phillips's imperialist tendencies: "You know how if blacks had something and didn't have no way to exploit it, and white dudes would pick it up and do something about it, they'd just beat him out of all of it, that's all. Well, that was him, that was Sam Phillips. Oh man." Later, in an interview with the U.K. paper *The Independent*, Thomas proclaims, "I couldn't see Elvis's potential at first—he was a white boy trying to sing black and it didn't reach me at all."

Phillips defended himself to Buskin: "I have been accused of having had my attention diverted from making blues records by working with Elvis, and to an extent it's true, but it was not for the reason people might think. I had a very small operation, and by that time I knew that there was an awful lot of excitement over rhythm and blues records—or, as they were mainly called then, 'race records'—being produced by so many different labels. I had felt all along that as long as the artists were black, you were going to get a limited amount of play on the air . . . I did not want anybody who did not have a natural feel, but I said to myself— and this is true—'Man, if I can find a white person who can give the feel and true essence of a blues-type song, black blues especially, then I've got a chance to broaden the base and get plays that otherwise we couldn't.' "

The notion of the white man pilfering and profiting from black music is so commonplace in twenty-first-century pop culture that it's often assumed to be an essential element of modern art-making, from Led Zeppelin's uncredited riff-lifting to Eminem's whiny diatribes ("Without Me," the 2002 lead single from Eminem's self-aware LP *The Eminem Show*, boasts, "I am the worst thing since Elvis Presley / To do black music so selfishly / And use it to get myself wealthy"). Still, Phillips never made very much money off his records: in the early 1950s, recording nationally untested blues singers was hardly a lucrative prospect, and for years, Sun Records was barely sustainable (in *Good Rockin' Tonight*, Marion Keisker recalls sneaking her own dollars into the company's petty cash box, surreptitiously disguising Sun's financial instability from her boss). Phillips consistently posited that his decisions were born exclusively from a longstanding infatuation with blues music; regardless, the weight of Phillips's influence and the sanctity of his decisions are still fodder for hot debates, and whether those gripes are reasonable attacks or just bitter laments is often hard to discern. In 1979, the rockabilly legend and vaguely disgruntled Sun alumni Charlie Feathers even questioned Phillips's producing talents, prodding Guralnick in 1979's *Lost Highway*: "You tell me what happened to the Sun sound when the people responsible for that sound—Elvis and Jerry Lee and Carl Perkins and Johnny Cash—all left him. I'll tell you, buddy. Sam Phillips just about got out of business. Because to be honest, I don't think Sam Phillips knew how to get the sound himself."

Standing on the floor of the studio, huffing in dust and splinters and the dull musk of decades-old cigarette smoke, I am less concerned with what Sam Phillips did or didn't do, exactly, and more entranced by the mysterious sequence of events that led to the conception of rock 'n' roll music. Our tour group has disbanded, with most of its members meandering back into the café next door. A young Irish couple engages in outrageous poses with the microphone. I sit on the piano bench with my hands folded in my lap and try my best not to be too melodramatic, thinking hard about all the music birthed in this room.

Sun Records began its anticlimactic decline in the early 1960s; the texture and scope of American music was shifting fast, and rock 'n' roll continued to trample traditional genre distinctions. In 1958, 90 percent of the records on the national R&B charts could also be spotted on the pop charts. According to the historian Charles Hamm, "At no other point in the two-hundred-year history of popular song in America had there been such a drastic and dramatic change in such a brief period of time." Phillips felt steady pressure to diversify; the classic Sun sound, with its stripped-down, bare-bones aesthetic, was suddenly unfashionable, its popularity usurped by grander wall-of-sound productions (think Phil Spector and the Beatles' "The Long and Winding Road.") In 1969, Phillips, thoroughly disgruntled with the move toward long-playing albums and the widespread desertion of the single, sold Sun Records to the Mercury Records executive Shelby Singleton for one million dollars. Singleton renamed the imprint Sun International and began extensively reissuing the Sun catalog. You can tell a reissue by the difference in the record's logo—the Sun rays still shoot out from the center hole to the top half of the yellow label, but now the string of music notes only follows the top perimeter, and not the entire circle.

"It changed the world, what we did at that little studio," Phillips told Buskin. "I'm taking nothing away from all of the other great independent labels, but what we did managed to cut through the segregation to such an extent that it was way beyond what I had even hoped we could do. That not only affected this nation, it affected people around the world, and it absolutely had a lot to do with encouraging communication between people of different races." Sam Phillips died in Memphis on July 30, 2003, of respiratory failure—he was eighty years old. His legacy is complicated, but the Sun discography is not: Phillips was the first producer to redefine traditional Americana music, threading together disparate bits harvested from dark southern landscapes. Rock 'n' roll may have been the most explicitly revolutionary synthesis of Americana tradition, but it certainly wasn't the last.

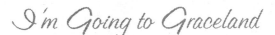

4

I'm Going to Graceland

The complimentary breakfast buffet at the Heartbreak Hotel consists of cereal, doughnuts, a bowl of peeled, skinned grapefruit slices, toast, English muffins, bagels, and a basket of overripe bananas. A thermos of coffee-flavored water sits to the side. Most of the buffet's patrons are wearing Elvis-themed outfits—Elvis boxers worn as shorts, Elvis T-shirts, Elvis pajama pants. "Suspicious Minds" blares out of stereo speakers. Many of us, I determine, have been up late watching Elvis movies on the Hotel's all-Elvis television channel. I dump some cornflakes into a plastic bowl, dispense milk from the spout of a large rubber container, and sit down. I am the youngest person here, by at least fifteen years. I chomp my cereal and read brochures.

After breakfast, I stroll through the Heartbreak Hotel's parking lot, wander under a maroon awning with "Graceland" scrawled in white cursive, trot over a small wooden bridge, meander past the *Lisa Marie*, Elvis Presley's personal jet, and enter a large tourist complex. Graceland is grounded by Graceland Plaza, an extensive staging area located directly across the street from the mansion. Here, visitors trot back and forth, purchasing tickets, perusing overstocked gift shops, and lining up for shuttle service to Graceland's front door. Bewildered but giddy, I stand midstream, gawk at Elvis-themed trinkets, snicker at the trash cans (three, arranged in a row, read THANK YOU, THANK YOU, and VERY MUCH), and fret over what sorts of souvenirs I should buy. I count four distinct shopping areas, each teeming with stuffed Pink Cadillacs, rotating racks of postcards, T-shirts, decorated purses, gold jewelry shaped like lightning bolts, Elvis-style sunglasses, an assortment of coffee mugs and drinking glasses, magnets, coasters, hats, figurines, CDs, videos, and key chains. The stores all boast pithy names: Elvis Threads, Gallery Elvis, Good Rockin' Tonight. There are also two restaurants (not counting Shake, Split & Dip, an "old-fashioned" ice cream parlor) serving standard, cafeteria-style regional fare—cheeseburgers, barbecue, and fried peanut-butter-and-banana sandwiches. I buy postcards and a chunky dancing Elvis magnet, curl into a pink-and-aqua-swathed restaurant booth at Rockabilly's Diner—which I choose over Chrome Grill, although I sense they are essentially the same establishment—chew fries, sip a Coke, and scribble home. When I am finished, I dump my postcards into the mail slot (there is a fully functioning post office at Graceland Plaza, punching a tourist-coveted Graceland postmark), and pass my ticket to the woman handing out audio tour headsets. She ushers me onto a short bus, and we roll across Elvis Presley Boulevard, disembarking at Graceland's front steps.

Staring up at the mansion's four Clorox-white Corinthian columns and impeccably maintained Tennessee limestone exterior, I find Graceland polite and agreeable, not entirely dissimilar to the kind of house you'd find in an affluent suburb, or featured as the primary headquarters of a fictionalized sitcom family. It feels soothing, unpretentious, and sweet; I half-expect a golden retriever to leap out from behind a bush, stalking a drool-covered tennis ball. There are green shutters and square windows and a familiar brass plaque—erected by the Department of the Interior to designate Graceland's spot on the National Register of Historic Places—and shrubs and flowers and benches and two large ceramic lions flanking a short staircase. But Graceland feels, in its own strange way, incredibly real and livable, detached from the box-built mansions that pepper the Hollywood hills, or the colossal compounds favored by contemporary pop sensations. The mansion was built in 1939 by Dr. and Mrs. Thomas D. Moore; Elvis arrived in 1957, but Graceland's exterior remained more "affluent doctor" than "King of Rock 'n' Roll."

Tourists of varying ages and nationalities circle the grounds in pairs, sniffing and snapping photos, smiling blankly, posing with their arms wrapped around one another before ambling inside. I had been warned by friends that it's easy to be underwhelmed by Graceland, distracted by its weird domesticity, miffed by its modest scale and tasteless (but ironically appreciated) decorations. In her book *Graceland*, Karal Ann Marling writes, "The house is full of things that we all have or used to have, or used to want, or hate." She's right: Graceland is a bewildering mix of *Pee-wee's Playhouse* and glitzy American standards, the kind of thing an overgrown teenager tottering on the verge of adulthood might think up (Elvis was twenty-two when he moved in). There are television sets everywhere, and monkey figurines, and loads of records; ostentatious crystal goblets gleam inside china cabinets, purchased, perhaps, out of an obligation to wealth, to marriage, to celebrity. An uninhabitable living room is disarmingly symmetrical, all blue and gold and cream, with peacock-themed stained glass windows. The infamous Jungle Room, Elvis's primary living space and the room adjacent to his kitchen, is noise-proofed with a carpeted ceiling and flanked by a rock wall decorated with fake greenery and a small waterfall. His armchairs are large and ornate, their bases carved into faux ferocious beasts. The carpet is a moldy green. Three separate air conditioners sit low to the ground.

Graceland's quirks, including the startling disconnect between its inside and its outside, are more endearing than befuddling, and as I stand in Graceland's foyer, fiddling with the zipper on my sweatshirt, it is the very first time that Elvis Presley has felt comprehensible to me. He liked monkeys and watching television in the kitchen.

Visitors are allowed to mull as long as they wish but are only granted access to seven of the mansion's "rooms"—the living room, dining room, spare bedroom (where Elvis's parents lived), kitchen, Jungle Room, TV room, and billiard room. The upstairs is roped off and scheduled to remain so indefinitely. On August 16, 1977, sporting a blue top and yellow pajama bottoms, Elvis was found dead, facedown on the floor of the upstairs bathroom, just after 2:00 p.m. Graceland's staff take the notion of the mansion's upstairs as sanctuary quite seriously (supposedly, the actor Nicolas Cage, who was married to Lisa Marie for three months in 2002, is the only non–family member to have ventured upstairs since Elvis's death; if one believes rumors, even President Clinton was denied a visit). No photographs of the top floor have been released to the media, although anyone with a computer and an Internet connection can find hundreds of supposedly authentic photos of the barricaded rooms, meticulously arranged under bombastic but enchanting headlines like "The Last Magnificent Enigma of Americana."

Still, limiting Graceland to seven kitsch-infested spaces allows the mansion to exist on a scale that makes a certain amount of sense to middle-class Americans (according to U.S. census figures from 2000, the average owner-occupied American home has 6.1 rooms), and its relative smallness is exactly what makes Graceland so haunting. There's a toaster sitting on Elvis's kitchen counter that reminds me of the one in my own childhood kitchen, all orange levers and fake wood paneling. I see glasses in a style my mother used to own, recognize colors and shapes and uncomfortable, boxy designs. There are flower-patterned tin canisters for flour and sugar and tea bags. Everything is perfectly, impeccably frozen, from green, push-button desk telephones to oversize blenders to Lisa Marie's giant teddy bear. The dining room table is set for a formal dinner, napkins rolled, flowers arranged, forks selected—and despite the tourists and Plexiglas and digital cameras and security staff, I can't escape a creepy suspicion that the Presleys are about to return home, settle into their favorite seats at the dinner table, and pass a basket of rolls. I feel stupid in my headset and sneakers, peering at their ridiculous knick-knacks and trying to imagine what Priscilla looked like, legs crossed, hair up, lounging on a couch.

My shamefulness is ultimately unfounded. In the largest sense, Graceland belongs to its pilgrims. The second-most-visited home in the nation, after the White House, it accepts seven hundred thousand visitors each year and requires five hundred thousand dollars for annual upkeep. Priscilla and Lisa Marie will never wander casually back inside, reclaim the objects of their respective childhoods, pop popcorn, or snuggle into armchairs. Graceland is inanimate: the teddy bear is always slouching casually in the Jungle Room, the racked triangle of balls on the pool table will never clink and break. The house is a commodity, a photo op, a rite of passage, a funny place to buy T-shirts, a haven for travelers chasing the trail of kitsch. Still, there is more to Graceland than snickers: the mansion, however inadvertently, promises to answer big American questions about talent, wealth, fame, decline, failure, death. If we can see, firsthand, what kind of books Elvis read, the strange furniture he favored, the colors of the tiles that lined his kitchen, will we be better equipped to understand the biggest of all American myths? Will we know what happened to the ones-who-died-too-young?

Presley's spectacular stardom and equally extraordinary tumble are the stuff of classic tragedy—the sweet, rural-born genius who enjoys sudden, tremendous success, succumbs to its excesses, and collapses. It's Kurt Cobain pressing a gun to his skull in the room above the garage, Janis Joplin shooting too much heroin in a Los Angeles motel, Jim Morrison slumping over in a Paris bathtub, Marilyn Monroe slamming barbiturates in her Brentwood bedroom. It is undignified and tragic.

Shortly before Elvis Presley left Sun Records in 1955, he signed with

Hank Snow Attractions, a management company run by the Canadian country singer Hank Snow and the Dutch-born manager and promoter Colonel Tom Parker (Parker's birth name was Andreas Cornelius van Kuijk; the "Colonel" was purely ornamental, and, depending on whom you ask, was doled out by either the Tennessee governor Frank G. Clement, in 1953, or the Louisiana governor Jimmie Davis, in 1948). Parker, who aggressively marketed Presley's likeness, slapping it onto lunch boxes and turkey platters, unapologetically cashed in on Presley's big, swooning fanbase, scooting Presley out of the army and into Hollywood in 1960, resulting in a seven-year musical silence. Like most celebrity moneymakers, Parker is constantly vilified by irate fans (Alanna Nash's compelling *The Colonel: The Extraordinary Story of Colonel Tom Parker and Elvis Presley* even suggests that Parker may have fled Holland after committing murder) and is typically blamed for Presley's gradual decline and occasionally for his death—by feeding Elvis too many movies, too many sandwiches, too many handfuls of prescription pills. It is far easier to blame Parker than to consider that Presley's fulfillment of the American dream—his accumulation of wealth, his philandering, his television habit, and his love of fried food and painkillers—was actually what ruined him.

Elvis Presley is buried at Graceland, alongside his mother, father, grandmother, and stillborn twin brother, in a small green area called the Meditation Garden. The Garden features a twelve-foot circular fountain, complete with wrought iron fence, six jets of water, and a kaleidoscope of colored floodlights, and is surrounded by a short, curved wall, crafted from Mexican brick and festooned with four stained-glass windows. Fresh bouquets of flowers (mostly roses, some in vases) and stuffed animals surround the headstones. There is color everywhere. Homemade memorials litter the grass or sit proud on easels—some look like elementary school projects (glitter and magazine photos glue-sticked onto poster board, with hardware store stickers spelling things like ELVIS

LIVES), while others are eerily professional, accessorized with elaborate floral arrangements, American flags, and bits of heartfelt text. According to my headset, all arrangements deemed appropriate are placed in the garden until the flowers begin to wilt, at which time they are replaced by fresher offerings. Dedications from determined fans in France, Japan, the U.K., and Germany mingle with more regional goodbyes.

Presley's body was originally placed in Memphis's Forest Hill Cemetery, alongside his mother's grave, but after an attempted theft, the coffins were shifted to Graceland. Presley's grave is the last stop on the Graceland audio tour, after visitors are steered through a hermetically sealed gallery of Elvis memorabilia, including framed canceled checks (which make an unsubtle point about Presley's impressive philanthropy), spectacular costumes, the Hall of Gold (a collection of Elvis's gold and platinum records), and any and all mountable remnants of Presley's career. The Garden is quiet, and visitors pause matter-of-factly before Presley's grave, stare for a few seconds, and begin to look uncomfortable. I remember U2's drummer, Larry Mullen, talking in *Rattle and Hum*: "Seeing the graves and the eternal flame . . . I wish he hadn't been buried in the backyard. I wish he was buried somewhere I couldn't have gone. I would have felt better. I don't know why," he admits, voice flat.

A squat blond woman wearing nurses' scrubs blows her nose. I keep my head down and stumble back toward the shuttle bus. The next day, I will leave Memphis for Clarksdale, Mississippi. It will be an uncomfortably long time before I can shake the city's ghosts.

Trail of the Hellhounds:

Clarksdale's Deep Mississippi Blues

The blues go but it don't stop.
—*John Lee Hooker*

* ✹ *

The Mississippi River is 2,357 miles of impossible curves, slithering south from Minnesota's Lake Itasca and dumping hard into the Gulf of Mexico. On maps, the river looks menacing and serpentine, bucking reason and straight lines as if it were scribbled into place by an irate child.

The Mississippi is feral, nastier and more indecent than other American rivers, responsible for countless drownings and two of the most devastating floods in United States history: In 1927, after a period of heavy rain in the southeast, the Mississippi erupted, crashing through its levees in 145 different places and flooding twenty-seven thousand square miles of farmland, carpeting the region with more than thirty feet of water. Two hundred forty-six people died; seven hundred thousand were displaced. Fourteen percent of Arkansas was underwater. In 1993, the river staged another catastrophic outbreak, cracking 1,000 of its 1,300 levees and hitting St. Louis with crests of 49.6 feet.

The first time I see the Mississippi in person, scuttling down a grassy hill and perching by its mucky banks, I realize there is something daunting about the river's indecorum, its flat, dim, dirty water, its ominous curls. Each twist hits like a challenge. As *Old Glory: A Voyage Down the Mississippi* author Jonathan Raban writes, "People do see [the river's] muddy turmoil as a bodying-forth of their own turbulent inner selves. When they boast to strangers about their river's wantonness, its appetite for trouble and destruction, its floods and drownings, there's a note in their voices that says, 'I have it in me to do that . . . I know how it feels.' "

The river's retention time—the gap between origin and end—clocks in at ninety days. The Mississippi is about twenty miles shorter than the Missouri River, the country's longest, but carries the heaviest volume of water, making it the most powerful. The river meets the Gulf in New Orleans, where, over the last five thousand years, alluvial deposits have extended the Louisiana coastline southward nearly fifty miles. Now the river hits the Gulf at the edge of the continental shelf, meaning its sediment plunges into deep water, where it sinks and dissipates without consequence. Scientists are already plotting new ways to divert its flow, harnessing its precious, nutrient-rich runoff to feed Louisiana's fading wetlands rather than the bottom of the ocean. This is the river's delta, although it's the almond-shaped area nearly four hundred miles north—stretching, as people say, from the lobby of the Peabody Hotel in Memphis to Catfish Row in Vicksburg, Mississippi—that most people know as the Mississippi Delta.

There's a certain logic to the misnomer. Every American social studies student eventually reads an illustrated textbook chapter about ancient Mesopotamia, the lush tract of delta land between the Tigris and Euphrates rivers, also known as the Cradle of Civilization—the spot where complex, literate societies first developed in the fourth millennium B.C. This is my very first memory of the word *delta*, and it's all tied up with notions of original life, of creation and realization and nascency. And the Mississippi Delta, with its colossal cotton plantations, hard-working soil, and legacy of prosperity and hardship, is arguably the world's most bountiful sonic ground—not just the land where the blues began, but where it all began, where many of America's most important musicians were reared and set free.

As far as I can tell, the story of Mississippi Delta blues is as much a story about the river—and what it did to the soil, and what that soil does to cotton—as anything else. In 1820, after Choctaw territory was offered up to early settlers, determined pioneers hauled West African slaves into the area, gobbling up tracts of land, clearing, draining, and planting cotton in thick black soil. Spectacularly flat and enriched by thousands of years of flooding, Delta dirt was obscenely fertile, and agriculture thrived. By 1930, Mississippi boasted 4,136,000 acres of cotton; in 1937, 2,692,000 bales were harvested. The United States became—and remains—the world's largest cotton exporter. Before long, southern politicians began to refer to the plant as King Cotton.

Meanwhile, black laborers were sucked into sharecropping, working farmland typically owned by white businessmen in exchange for room, board, and a cut of the harvest. The system was inherently biased and a little too close to indentured servitude. Plenty of workers were cheated out of money, or paid with "plantation coins" redeemable only at local businesses, which helped landowners tether their workers to a specific region. Still, it was on cotton plantations—deep in fields that, during peak season, turned so white that the ground and the horizon seemed to melt into one big, blinding mess—that Delta blues was born. As the Ole Miss professor Adam Gussow writes in the 2006 music issue of *Southern Cultures* magazine, "Mississippi was indeed the home of the blues: it was the wellspring not just of blues *music* but of blues *feeling*, a whole complex of emotions and attitudes engendered in its African-American residents—a swirling mixture of fear, despair, fury, heartache, extreme restlessness, freely ranging sexual desire, and a stubborn determination to persist against all odds and sing the bittersweet song of that persistence."

Even for the most versed scholars, defining the sound of the Delta blues is still an awkward, thankless endeavor, hampered by qualifiers and relativity and spats with one's peers. Loosely, Delta blues is a strand of regional American folk music performed on guitar, with the occasional help of a knife or bottleneck slide; conceived by and for (mostly) southern blacks; influenced heavily by African slave songs; and with a "tendency," as Robert Palmer writes, toward twelve-bar, A-B-A verses, or pentatonic melodies with a flattened third. Culturally, the Delta blues is understood as black dance music, pounded out in response to, or as an elixir for, generally desperate situations of romantic, social, and economic designs. (Speaking in generalities, it is in this way that the blues most closely resembles contemporary hip-hop—black music born of hardship; unconcerned with already established forms; occasionally vulgar; often marked by religious, violent, and highly sexual themes; riddled with slang, euphemisms, and double entendres; and eventually fetishized and commodified by affluent whites.) Unlike the offshoot Chicago blues, Delta blues is more acoustic than electric; Delta blues is also more firmly rooted in slave songs and spirituals than neighboring Mississippi Hill Country blues, which itself is generally electric and more indebted to early fife and drum music.

People like to talk about the Delta blues' rawness and ferocity, its sexuality and danger, its realness and simplicity—usually at the expense of the music's sophistication. Delta blues is complex and elusive, making it incredibly difficult for non-Delta-born musicians to ever master its nuances. As Palmer writes, "Delta blues is a refined, extremely subtle, and ingeniously systematic musical language. Playing it and especially singing it right involve some exceptionally fine points that only a few white guitarists, virtually no white singers, and not too many black musicians who learned to play and sing anywhere other than the Delta have been able to grasp."

That hasn't stopped hundreds of musicians—including, most notably, a handful of famed 1960s British rock bands—from doing their best slide-and-growl, howling into a microphone, trying hard to channel Delta technique despite colossal geographic, social, and economic disparities. The influence of Delta blues on contemporary rock 'n' roll is so obvious and profound that it can't be overstated; the Western world's most beloved rock musicians (Led Zeppelin, the Rolling Stones, Eric Clapton) have all snatched liberally from Delta song- and stylebooks. But Delta blues, maybe more than any other strain of American music, is specific to its time and place, and most of the genre's true players were born on Delta soil.

The Delta blues guru Charley Patton "wasn't what you'd call a real colored fellow," according to Hayes McMullen, who saw Patton playing blues on Mississippi's Dockery Plantation in the 1920s. Only one known photograph of Patton exists: it's black-and-white and well-worn, and in it, Patton's wearing a crooked bow tie, white shirt, and jacket. His hair is cropped short, and his creamy skin—plenty in the Delta claimed that Patton was not his father's child and was either part Mexican or, as Howlin' Wolf reportedly declared, full Cherokee—and too-prominent ears make him look vaguely goofy, out of step with his grim, narrowed eyes. Charley's father, Bill Patton, was a strict Christian who considered music immoral and indecent. Charley was punished—physically and mercilessly—for his penchant for song, and for following around and performing with the Chatmons, a musical family best known for playing syncopated dance music, spirituals, ballads, jump-ups, and ragtime at local parties and events.

Charley Patton grew up south of the Delta proper, in Hinds County, Mississippi, but in 1900, when he was a teenager, his family moved more than a hundred miles north to the Will Dockery Cotton

Farm and Saw Mill Plantation near Ruleville, on the swampy, alligator- and mosquito-infested shores of the Sunflower River. At Dockery, Patton continued to play and perform despite his father's disapproval, taking up with a musician named Henry Sloan, who played rough, rhythmic guitar. Patton developed a reputation around the Delta and was as beloved for his antics—tossing his guitar, cradling it behind his knees, stretching it around his neck and playing hard—as for his gutsy, rambling blues. He was one of the very first Delta players to perfect what we now understand as blues music; he would ultimately influence scads of subsequent bluesmen, including Howlin' Wolf. But Patton's greatest protégé was a local teenager named Robert Johnson.

In May 1911 (the exact date is still unconfirmed, but most people agree it was probably the eighth of the month), somewhere around Hazlehurst, Mississippi, Julia Major Dodds, who had already birthed ten children by her husband, Charles Dodds Spencer, gave birth to an illegitimate son following an affair with a plantation worker named Noah Johnson. Robert Johnson—then known as something like Robert Leroy Dodds Spencer—spent his first three years shifting through southern plantations until his mother's estranged husband, now living in Memphis (Spencer had fought with a member of an esteemed white family and was forced to flee the subsequent lynch mob), finally agreed to take him in. At some point between 1918 and 1920, Johnson returned to his mother and the Delta, and came of age in Robinsonville, Mississippi. As a teenager, Johnson started hanging around Willie Brown, a friend of Charley Patton's, and watched as Brown and Patton began playing with Son House, a chillingly intense bluesman who eventually recorded for Paramount Records (and for the Library of Congress, via Alan Lomax). Johnson was awed by Patton; he would later tell interviewer Jeff Titon, "I would listen to Charley's [records] way before I ever started to play or think about trying to play."

Johnson, then still an amateur player, ditched Robinsonville abruptly in 1930, presumably retreating to Hazlehurst. When he returned a few months later, Johnson was suddenly and mysteriously capable of playing with, as Palmer writes, "dazzling technique and almost supernatural electricity." According to the scholar Mack McCormick, Johnson's family promptly started whispering about Johnson's deal with the Devil, claiming they could even locate the exact country crossroads where the deal went down. Son House and Willie Brown were understandably flabbergasted watching Johnson make his little guitar moan and shuffle like a five-man band; as Palmer explains, "Fellow guitarists would watch him with unabashed, open-mouthed wonder." Johnson's voice is high, strong, and rippled with grimaces and grunts; it bounces and jiggles, alternately playful and desperate, soothing and scary. But it's his guitar work that really staggers: Johnson manages to make so many different sounds simultaneously, it's impossible to comprehend, intellectually or emotionally, how they're all coming from the same set of hands. It is the sound of one man using his entire being to create a noise so deep it's unfathomable.

Robert Johnson is one of the Delta's most celebrated and influential performers not only because of his talent, but also because his arc is so easy to romanticize. Johnson embodied—maybe even invented—the archetype of the wandering, lonesome bluesman, a perpetually troubled troubadour requiring only a guitar and a bottle. He spent much of his short life roaming across northwestern Mississippi, slipping through tiny Delta towns, taking up with various women in various bars, establishing no peers and few friends, and leaving little evidence behind. Accordingly, there are only a few dates and places to which Johnson can be definitively linked. From November 23 to 27, 1936, Johnson recorded a handful of songs in a hotel room in San Antonio, Texas, brought there by Ernie Oertle, an agent for the American Record Company, following a recommendation from Patton's former mentor, H. C. Speir. Likewise, on June 19, 1937, Johnson recorded a few tracks in an abandoned warehouse in

Dallas. And on August 16, 1938, after playing a house party in Green-wood, Mississippi, flirting with someone's wife, and (allegedly) taking a slug of poisoned whiskey, Johnson died. He was twenty-seven years old. Johnson's mythology was complete.

No matter how closely you examine the sparsely detailed lives of its early practitioners, exactly how and where the blues began in Missis-sippi is still almost impossible to discern. But a disproportionate number of its primary players (including W. C. Handy, John Lee Hooker, Son House, Muddy Waters, Charley Patton, and, incidentally, the playwright Tennessee Williams and the soul singers Ike Turner and Sam Cooke) seem to be connected to the area surrounding Clarksdale, Mississippi, a town of about twenty thousand people in the northwest corner of the state. (In 1998, Led Zeppelin's Jimmy Page and Robert Plant re-corded a truly terrible reunion album called, appropriately, *Walking into Clarksdale*).

By the mid-twentieth century, the blues existed elsewhere in Amer-ica—in Texas in the 1930s and '40s, Ma Rainey, Lightnin' Hopkins, and Blind Lemon Jefferson played variations on Texas blues, a swing-influenced sound reliant on guitar solos and jazz-style improvisation. Perhaps more famously, Chicago blues developed in response to mass plantation layoffs in the South. By 1930, Chicago had the most Missis-sippi-born residents outside Mississippi, and a 1944 *Time* magazine arti-cle estimated that, since the start of the decade, fifty thousand blacks had left Mississippi for the North. Chicago blues, being an urban form from the start, required bigger, louder sounds—full bands, with amplified gui-tar, drums, piano, and bass. In May 1943, Muddy Waters, a Clarksdale native who grew up on the nearby Stovall Plantation, ditched the Delta, catching the four o'clock Illinois Central train to Chicago. Muddy Wa-ters eventually became synonymous with Chicago blues, taking the songs of the Delta and making them louder and more rollicking. Likewise, Hill Country blues, based primarily in the north*eastern* corner of Mississippi (a chunk of land better known as the location of Faulkner's fictional Yok-napatawpha County), was dirtier and more electric than the blues being played directly to its west.

Tonight, driving south into Clarksdale from Memphis, on Highway 61, I watch as Memphis's bulletproof liquor shops and gas stations gradually give way to cotton fields and catfish ponds. Colossal billboards for "riverboat" casinos stack up; Tunica, Mississippi, is the third largest gambling haven in the United States, and tall, overstretched casinos leer creepily over the cotton fields, a juxtaposition that, while slightly absurd, is not particularly remarkable in twenty-first-century America. Giant signs promise ten-thousand-dollar limits, one-dollar buffets, Wheel of Fortune, a Rod Stewart tribute band, Kenny G. Without the kitsch and twinkle of Las Vegas or even Atlantic City, however, the casinos, with their plastic dragons and faux-castle accents, look foreboding, cold, and unpleasant, surrounded by cotton, highway, and anonymous apartment complexes.

I stop for supper at the Blue & White Restaurant, where the Sunday buffet is still intact: I heap a plate with fried chicken, roast beef, sweet potatoes, green beans, chicken and dressing, and okra. There is a half-hearted salad bar adjacent to the buffet, with a big bowl of iceberg lettuce, a vat of ranch dressing, and a few canisters filled with tomatoes and shredded cheese. After I finish eating, my waitress brings over a plate of homemade peach cobbler and whipped cream.

I get back into my car and pull onto Highway 61, tuning the radio to WROX, Clarksdale's renowned blues station.

Rolling into town, it's impossible not to notice the famed "Crossroads," the intersection of Highways 61 and 49, where, according to Delta legend, Robert Johnson traded his soul to the Devil in exchange for guitar virtuosity. Blues historians tend to snicker at the story, which has deeper ties to ancient voodoo folklore, and while Johnson's "Cross Road Blues" does contain a verse about asking God for salvation, it makes no explicit mention of Satan or guitars or Faustian bargains. It also seems likely that the story, however ridiculous, may have originated with another Johnson: according to researcher David Evans, in the late 1920s, the bluesman Tommy Johnson of Crystal Springs, Mississippi, told his brother LeDell that he "Sold hisself to the Devil. I asked him how. He said 'If you want to learn how to play anything you want to play and learn how to make songs yourself, you take your guitar and you go to where a road crosses that way, where a crossroad is. Get there, be sure to get there just a little 'fore twelve o'clock that night so you know you'll be there. You have your guitar and be sitting there playing a piece. A big black man will walk up there and take your guitar, and he'll tune it. And then he'll play a piece and hand it back to you. That's the way I learned how to play anything I want.' " As Palmer notes, the Devil-Crossroads legend is "at least as old as the blues."

So even though the "Crossroads" in Clarksdale is spurious on many levels (61 and 49 don't cross here—they merge—and highway realignments mean that this particular crossroads hasn't always been in this exact spot), the city has still hoisted three giant blue electric guitars onto a pole, crisscrossed their necks with route markers for 61 and 49, put up signs that say THE CROSSROADS, and lit the entire mess with floodlights. The otherwise unremarkable intersection features a Church's Chicken, a gas station, Delta Donuts, Crossroads Furniture, and a mural advertising Abe's Bar-B-Q.

My first three nights in Clarksdale, I stay in the Commissary at the Big Pink Guesthouse. Adjacent to the main property, the Commissary is a sizable pink barn with two bedrooms, a bathroom designed to look like an outhouse with a sloping tin roof and weathered barn-wood door, and a room stuffed with blues memorabilia, random old LPs, two refrigerators (one surprisingly well stocked with cans of V8), and decorated exclusively with Hawaiian shirts, a ukulele, a saxophone, beach umbrellas, a velvet Elvis, a packet of multicolored pipe cleaners, a giant checkerboard, a big-screen television, two credit card machines, a *Hot Chick Hot Rod Stoner BBQ* DVD, a Heineken windmill, two Schlitz chandeliers, a Frank Sinatra CD box set, unopened mail, a desktop computer, a three-foot-tall stuffed Bugs Bunny, a George Foreman grill, toothpicks, a jar of peanut butter, one wine glass, Bake Easy baking spray, a portable phone and answering machine with fourteen messages, a jukebox, a stove, a stack of plastic lawn chairs, five different kinds of bug repellant, a full mug of cold black coffee, Mardi Gras beads, and a whole mess of other weird shit. After switching the latch on the glass front door, I pull the barn doors shut and pick up the piece of lumber leaning against the wall, sliding it through the doors' metal handles, effectively establishing a barricade. This is the first time I have ever locked a door this way. The barn's backdoor, I notice, has been duct-taped shut.

Before I go to sleep, I sit in a rocking chair in front of the television, half-watching sitcom reruns and reading the Big Pink's guest book. Someone has written, "I will be back but I will deny it." Someone else has written, "Go Steelers!!! Scout. Pittsburgh Steelers XLSB champs!" In the morning, I realize that the windows lining the ceiling of the main room have been tinted blue; as the sun rises, the barn fills with soft, cerulean light. It's like being inside a spaceship, or a lava lamp.

I get dressed, tug the lumber out from the door handles, and wander down Third Street to the Bluesberry Bakery, where I buy a Styrofoam cup full of coffee, sit on a stool at the counter, and dump in two packets of powdered creamer and a scoop of sugar. Three motorcyclists from Omaha are crowded around a tiny plastic table, sharing a breakfast pizza. I chat with Art, the bakery's proprietor and chef, who moved here from Florida and concurrently manages a heavy metal band named In Code. Another local—someone Art calls the Mayor—shuffles in and sits down. He asks about the sales tax and price of gas in New York City and tells me that Clarksdale attracts loads of European visitors. "You have to be a millionaire to live in Europe." He nods. "Gas is eight dollars a gallon and cigarettes are six dollars a pack."

I ask the Mayor about Clarksdale's best juke joints, and he tells me to check out Ground Zero and Red's. "Make sure you bring an umbrella to Red's," he snickers, "because it rains inside! And he hasn't cleaned that place since it opened."

I finish my coffee, thank Art, and circle the block to Cat Head, a local record and folk art shop. In Code's bassist and backing vocalist, Cade Moore, is working behind the counter, wearing a black hat and studded leather wrist cuffs. Cade is not so into the blues, although he says he occasionally plays it in town "for money." I buy a double album by Clarksdale's own Mr. Tater (sealed in a DVD case with a poorly photocopied black-and-white cover, with one picture of Mr. Tater dancing, and one of him in the studio, playing guitar), titled *That Bullshit's Got to Go!*

Cat Head is a few doors up from the Delta Amusement Cafe, a no-frills luncheonette decorated with framed photographs (including a blurry shot of the World Trade Center towers, circa 1978, which retails for $175) and newspaper clippings. I sit at an empty table and ask for a biscuit and some hash browns. A few minutes later, my order (which the Cafe has interpreted as a plate of heavily buttered toast and a mound of mangled Tater Tots) is plopped down by an affable man wearing blue sweatpants who—based on bits of conversation overheard at the nearby cash register—I begin to think is maybe also the town bookie.

Although the Cafe's rich, unpretentious fare feels pretty standard for the region, Clarksdale does boast one fine-dining restaurant, Madidi, which is partially owned by the actor and Mississippi native Morgan Freeman. Unlike the Delta Amusement Cafe, Madidi offers diners sauce-drizzled plates of beef carpaccio, foie gras, crème brûlée, and "hydroponic bibb lettuce." I appreciate Freeman's mission to pull more tourist-cash into Clarksdale, but plopping a preposterously gourmet dining room into the middle of an otherwise impoverished community still seems awkward at best—even though the long-term ramifications of Madidi are positive for Clarksdale (development yields development), I don't see how I—or anyone—could stomach cramming down a twenty-six-dollar plate of "Roasted Breast of Duck served over Red Pepper Corn Cakes with Black Eyed Peas and a Truffle-Cranberry Reduction" just blocks from rows of dilapidated homes.

Besides Madidi, there is nothing else in downtown Clarksdale—save a cell phone store—to suggest that it is 2006. Nor is there much to indicate that anyone actually lives here. Downtown is uniformly desolate, several shops are shut down and boarded up, and precious few cars are parked on the streets. The town feels stuck in time, like an abandoned movie set. There are tire shops, some barbers, auto parts stores, the Chicken Market (where a hastily hand-painted sign advertises frog legs, rabbits, and crawfish), liquor stores, and lots of gas stations, but I can't seem to discern where one would go to buy a bottle of shampoo.

Blues tourism is prevalent here, but not entirely self-evident. Most sites are unmarked and difficult to locate; Steve Cheseborough's exhaustive *Blues Traveling*, with its regional breakdowns, is essential reading. There is a long, ambivalent history of white people trawling the Delta for information on blues singers. As Palmer writes, even in the 1940s, black men huddling and chatting at crossroads gas stations responded to folklorists' "questions about Robert Johnson and other blues singers with oblique, noncommittal mumbles and, if pressed, drifted away in sullen twos and threes." As Gussow points out, Mississippi has managed to transform the blues into "a so-called cultural resource, rather than a disreputable subculture . . . The nascent blues-tourism business may of course turn out to be one more way in which white capital extracts profit from black artistry without truly sharing the wealth."

The Delta Blues Museum in Clarksdale is set up in a squat brick building in the center of downtown Clarksdale, adjacent to the Big Pink, and formerly the site of the Yazoo and Mississippi River Valley Railroad depot (later the Illinois Central Railroad freight depot). After lunch, I walk over and buy a ticket. For seven dollars, I get a traveling photography exhibit about the disparity between weekend wilding and church-day repenting, appropriately titled *Saturday Night / Sunday Morning*, organized by the Leica Gallery in New York, curated by an NYU professor, and only tangentially related to Mississippi blues, given that it includes, for instance, a shot of Sean "P. Diddy" Combs and several pictures of Harlem. There are also some stage outfits in glass cases, handmade instruments, Stella guitars, and, the museum's centerpiece, Muddy Waters's Stovall Plantation sharecropper shack. The shack is complete with a life-size wax statue of Waters and the famed Muddywood guitar, commissioned by ZZ Top's Billy Gibbons in 1989 and carved out of a slab of cypress wood salvaged from the original cabin. The guitar itself is white with brass-colored fixtures and a big, brown squiggly stripe, edged in green, to represent the Mississippi River. The museum is empty while I browse, and eventually I decide that maybe there are more exciting things to see outside of town.

South of Clarksdale, the two-lane Highway 49 is mostly empty, flanked by cotton fields, abandoned farm equipment, Baptist churches, and the occasional swamp. Delta landscapes are notoriously flat, and after the clouds clear, water gathers everywhere in big, still puddles, reflecting sun, catching wayward cotton puffs. It is one of the wettest places I've ever seen.

I veer right onto 49 West in Tutwiler and chug past more cotton fields until I spot the Mississippi State Penitentiary (better known as Parchman Farm). It looms on the side of the road, stretching out for nearly eighteen thousand acres. Cars are discouraged from slowing down out front, and armed guards pace protectively beneath a white gate with the words MISSISSIPPI STATE PENITENTIARY written in silver block letters. All male prisoners on death row in the state of Mississippi are housed at Parchman; as of July 2006, there are sixty-six inmates awaiting execution. Convicts were hanged in Mississippi until 1940, when the gallows were replaced by the electric chair; in 1955, the gas chamber replaced the chair; in 2002, lethal injection became Mississippi's weapon of choice. At Parchman, all executions occur at 6:00 p.m.

The Mississippi State Penitentiary has a rich musical history. Bluesmen Bukka White and Son House were both incarcerated at Parchman (White's "Parchman Farm Blues" is now a blues classic), and in 1939, John Lomax recorded Parchman inmates for the Library of Congress. The prison also has a sordid history of abuse. In *The Land Where the Blues Began*, Alan Lomax describes the "Southern penologists" at Parchman as gruesome despots who "joyously and self-righteously humiliated, bullied, beat, often tortured, and sometimes murdered their charges." In 1972, the civil rights lawyer Roy Haber, along with four Parchman inmates, pieced together a case against the prison superintendent, claiming that prisoners were subject to cruel and unusual corporal punishment. Federal judge William C. Keady sided with the prisoners, declaring that behavior at Parchman Farm violated modern standards of decency. All unconstitutional practices were ordered to end and Parchman's "trustee system," wherein certain inmates were granted control over others, was immediately abolished.

Prisoners at Parchman work the land surrounding the prison, logging, in 2006, a total of 716,160 hours in the prison's agricultural program. In the summer, drivers on Highway 49 can watch inmates, outfitted in stripes, toiling on the land surrounding the jail, hunched over cotton or yanking up vegetables. Today, I slow my car down just enough to snap a photograph, and imagine John Lomax dragging his big recording machine through the prison gates, looking for songs.

If you double back from Parchman, veer left instead of right in

Tutwiler, and follow 49 East to Greenwood, the Cotton Capital of the World, you can hunt down the most credible of Robert Johnson's three supposed gravesites. The famed Johnson researcher Steve LaVere validated the spot after interviewing Rosie Eskridge, whose husband, Tom, supposedly dug Johnson's grave. Following the interview, LaVere purchased a proper gravestone for Johnson, which has since been placed near the identified spot.

After exiting 49 East, I follow Grand Boulevard north, crossing a tiny bridge out of downtown, and another arching over the Tallahatchie River. A little more than two miles from the riverbanks, the Little Zion Missionary Baptist Church is set back from the road, on my left. A big white sign advertises CHOIR PRACTICE EVERY 2ND/3RD SATURDAY and SERVICE EVERY THIRD SUNDAY, 11 A.M. The church is led by Pastor McArthur McKinley.

Little Zion sits directly across the street from a colossal cotton field and feels displaced from civilization. I drive by twice before I even realize it's there. The tiny, one-room white church has the number 63530 pasted on the front with hardware-store stickers, a short front porch with a green awning, a small white cross on top, and a hole in the front façade just over the porch roof. There are rectangular white posts jammed in the ground in front of the church. Pine needles and broken plastic stems from silk flower arrangements litter the ground. It is completely silent the entire hour I am here, save one pickup truck rattling north on Grand Boulevard. Robert Johnson's grave is near the back, a few feet to the left of a towering pecan tree. All you can see, in either direction, is highway and cotton. It's hard not to hear Johnson bellowing, "You may bury my body, down by the highway side / So my old evil spirit can catch a Greyhound bus and ride," the grim concluding lines to his staggering "Me and the Devil Blues."

A few feet to the right of the church an old green mailbox sits on the ground, flag up. Someone has painted "Please contribute to the Little

Zion M.B. Church and the upkeep of the Robert Johnson burial site" in neat white letters. Along the front lip of Johnson's gravestone, well-wishers have lined up a telling assortment of objects: a cork from a bottle of red wine, a purple silk rose, three guitar picks, a brass slide, and some coins. Coins have also been spaced out along the top of the stone. Along the back edge, a handful of clear crystals gleam, painstakingly arranged. The stone reads: ROBERT L. JOHNSON, MAY 8, 1911– AUGUST 16, 1938; MUSICIAN & COMPOSER; HE INFLUENCED MIL-LIONS BEYOND HIS TIME. Below the main inscription is an offset, un-even triangle, filled with Robert's own near-illegible script, which is translated in an engraving directly below it: JESUS OF NAZARETH, KING OF JERUSALEM. I KNOW THAT MY REDEEMER LIVETH, AND HE WILL CALL ME FROM THE GRAVE.

Johnson's grave sits just a few minutes' drive from an affluent residential neighborhood, and after leaving Little Zion and driving back and forth through Greenwood's two halves, watching the trappings of upper-middle-class wealth—expensive patio sets, over-tended lawns, painted wooden shutters—give way to considerably less manicured lots, I am disheartened by the town's blatant economic segregation, even though it is really no different from anywhere else, including Brooklyn. This is the way we live in America: rich and poor, and never the twain shall meet.

My last night in Clarksdale, a Thursday, I show up at Red's juke joint per the Mayor's advice. Red's is in an old brick building with LAVENE MUSIC CENTER painted above the awning and an assortment of barbecues littering its front sidewalk. A refrigerator, pieces of awning, and big blue trash cans are lined up along the front entrance; someone has written "NO DRUGS" in black marker near the door. Red's is just a few houses down from the Riverside Hotel (formerly the G. T. Thomas Afro-American Hospital), which has hosted Ike Turner and his band, Sonny Boy Williamson II, Robert Nighthawk, and, curiously, John F. Kennedy, Jr. (plus date, in 1991). Unfortunately for me, Red's, which has no telephone or clear, advertised set of operating hours, is closed.

Dejected, I wander down Sunflower Avenue, cross the train tracks, and approach the Ground Zero Blues Club, a juke joint that, like Madidi, is co-owned by Morgan Freeman (this time, Freeman partnered with Howard Stovall of the nearby Stovall Plantation where, incidentally, Muddy Waters worked as a sharecropper in the 1930s and early '40s). Ground Zero is considerably less disheveled than Red's, although the club's management has encouraged a certain amount of organized disarray: the walls are covered in Sharpie graffiti, with "I ♥s" and "Class ofs" scribbled haphazardly. Overstuffed couches—also plastered with smeared messages—litter the club's front porch. Postcards are taped to the windows. Inside, strands of Christmas lights drip from the ceiling, and old concert posters, bits of memorabilia, and beer sponsorship banners hang on the walls, vying for attention amidst nonsensical inscriptions.

I sit at the bar, order a barbecue sandwich and a side of fried green tomatoes (the menu is blues-cute, with a list of salad dressings that includes "blues cheese," "blind lemon-garlic," and "honeyboy mustard") and wait for the local blues hero Super Chikan (performing tonight with his band, the Fighting Cocks) to walk onstage. A man wearing all white is poised near the microphone, itching to dance. Super Chikan's guitars, most of which he crafts himself out of oil cans and bits of debris (he even has an axe made out of an old toilet seat, appropriately dubbed the Shittar), are lined up onstage, giving audience members ample time to admire Chikan's skill with a paintbrush: using a mostly psychedelic palette of purples, blues, greens, and golds, Super Chikan embellishes his instruments, lovingly brushing on all sorts of creatures and designs. When Super Chikan and his band finally take the stage, half of Ground Zero gets up to dance. Chikan plays modern blues-rock, riff heavy and pop palatable. After each song, he shouts at no one in particular, "Shoot that thang!" He hollers the phrase at least twelve times before I finish eating and head outside to my car.

Later, Daddy Rich, Super Chikan's twenty-five-year-old bass player, tells me about Clarksdale's innate connection to the blues. "You can't help it. If you're from here, you've got the blues in your veins as soon as you're popped out in the hospital. The economy is terrible here—it's hard not to have the blues. I've been here all my life; I was born here. I still keep a smile most of the time, though," he explains. "That's how you make it day to day." Rich is well aware of the challenge of maintaining a sound that's so specific to a certain region and a certain time. "Things have changed," he admits. "The blues gets watered down a bunch. I strive to keep as much of the 'old' in my music as possible but at the same time not limit myself. I do sometimes think the genre gets stretched too far, but hey, good music is good music. Might not be good blues though. I've been at blues fests before, just thinking to myself, This is *not* the blues, nowhere close, and has no soul at all . . . Lots of folks that move to Clarksdale think they know everything about the blues and will attack you if you aren't playing their idea of the blues. But I believe that being born here overrides their opinion. Blues is just a feeling. Blues music is blues music."

After I leave Ground Zero, I drive back out of town, passing the Deco-restored Greyhound bus station where Muddy Waters caught his ride to Chicago, and head back toward the Crossroads. Tonight I've secured a shack at the Shack Up Inn Bed and Beer, which is located on Clarksdale's old Hopson Plantation. Hopson was established in 1852 and is the birthplace of the mechanized cotton picker, which was tested and implemented there in 1944—no small event, considering the picker essentially rendered the sharecropping system obsolete, helping to send loads of black laborers north to Memphis and Chicago.

The Shack Up Inn consists of a "six-pack" of individually named shotgun sharecroppers' shacks that, modern conveniences aside, haven't changed all that much since their plantation days. Plenty about the Inn's premise is offensive (sharecroppers weren't exactly treated fairly or with respect in the segregated South, and the notion of paying to sleep in a shack once "rented" to a black plantation worker is both absurd and exploitative), but the spirit in which it's run seems innocent enough—the shacks were conceived as a sort of creative retreat for writers and musicians, and co-owner Bill Talbot contends that the Inn is actually instrumental in preserving an essential bit of Delta culture. Hopson is the former home of Muddy Waters's legendary piano player, Mississippi's own Pinetop Perkins (who drove a tractor and picked cotton at Hopson, and has since been back to stay in his namesake shack), and in a 2001 interview with NPR Talbot insists, "From a historical standpoint, [sharecropper shacks] were disappearing here in the Mississippi Delta. We decided we should probably get a couple before they disappeared, just from a preservation standpoint." Although the Shack Up Inn may seem, on paper, like another instance of white people profiting financially from the despair of black workers, I am inclined to buy Talbot's conservationist defense—steamrolling or museum sealing the shacks doesn't seem like an especially responsible approach either, and I can't see how anyone remotely interested in or compelled by Delta history would pass up a chance to camp out at Hopson.

Earlier in the day, a man named Guy with a syrupy southern accent left a voice mail on my cell phone saying that he'd changed my reservation to a different shack because last night someone spilled beer all over the mattress in mine, the Fullilove. Late that night, when I finally pull up to the Inn's lobby (which doubles as Talbot's living room), there's a map and a key clipped to the screen door: "Amanda—here is the key to Robert Clay. Thanks. Bill."

Using a key chain flashlight and Delta moonlight, I follow the highlighted map to the Robert Clay, sidestepping vintage farm equipment and assorted pieces of furniture. As far as I can tell, I am the only patron of the Shack Up Inn. A few minutes later, I locate the Robert Clay; the lights are on and the screen door is already open. Three sizable rooms are arranged railroad-style: a living room, a full kitchen, and a bedroom with a double bed. The Robert Clay is considerably larger than my Brooklyn apartment, and, at sixty dollars a night, almost less expensive, too. I drop my duffel bag and flip on more lights.

Someone has left a mini Moon Pie on my pillow. An old television, balanced on a wood-burning stove, plays something called "The Blues Channel," exclusively. There are two doors to the Robert Clay, and a sealed sandwich baggie of clear liquid is tacked to the top of each frame, for reasons I will never discover. Threadbare Oriental carpets cover the plank floors. Like at Big Pink, objects abound: a piano, a guitar stand and tiny amp (no guitar), sheet music, a white porcelain statue of a unicorn, dozens of empty wine bottles, a bowling pin, a stuffed duck, a dried wedding corsage, an old issue of *Marie Claire*, a Faulkner quote scrawled in marker on a Domino's Pizza box and tacked to the wall by the stove, a bowl of bottle caps, a reel of audio tape, a lamp made out of driftwood, random business cards, and a church pew. On top of the television, there is a VCR and a stack of VHS tapes: *Cape Fear*, *Nothing but Trouble*, *Blame It on Rio*, *Titanic*, *The Night of the Hunter*, *Flashdance*. There is no telephone.

I take a bottle of Budweiser out of the fridge, wrap myself in a quilt, and head for the shack's breezy front porch, sinking into an ancient plaid couch that's likely infested with all sorts of spindly Delta creatures, and watch headlights and taillights roll up and down Highway 49. The porch is lined with blue Christmas lights, and inside, Muddy Waters plays on the Blues Channel, wisps of slide guitar drifting through the screen door.

The Robert Clay isn't exactly the cleanest place I've ever stayed, but I get the general impression that its décor is fluid, changing with each guest. As Guy said to my voice mail, "This is a loose place." Indeed, the

Inn's website recommends you "don't dick around" with an incomplete reservation, refers to PBS as "Pure Bull Shit," and suggests that the owners cannot afford the psychiatric help they require because they lack health insurance.

That night, I'm woken up by a chorus of frantic chirping, which I can only presume is a colony of vampire bats hanging from the porch roof, or maybe a pack of irate plantation rats. Lying in bed, waiting for the squeals to subside, it occurs to me that I'm uncharacteristically calm, breathing evenly and deeply: given its isolation and its history, I wasn't expecting the Shack Up Inn to feel so comforting. But now, curled up in an over-slept-in bed, thumbing through crinkled, outdated magazines, and eating my Moon Pie, I feel a curious communion with everyone who has been here before me, staring at the alarm clock, waiting out a summit of critters. Despite initial misgivings, I know I will be sad to check out at daybreak—I know I will wonder if a longer stay might have revealed bigger Delta secrets.

The next morning, as I'm paying for my room, I learn from Bill Talbot that Robert Clay was a tractor driver on a nearby plantation (if his rate was anything like Muddy Waters's, he was earning about twenty-two and a half cents an hour) who raised seven sons in his cypress wood shack, without running water or electricity. Many years later, when his family tried to rouse him from his shack, Clay refused to leave; after his death, a moonshine still was discovered in the attic, which, Talbot muses, might have had something to do with Clay's steadfast desire to stay. Clay's photo, ironing board, and dresser are still inside. In 1998, Talbot bought the shack for six hundred dollars, moved it to Hopson, power-washed the entire interior, and added indoor plumbing and power.

I say goodbye to Bill and leave Hopson, skirting past a Styrofoam cooler of Miller Lite (free for guests) and pulling my car around an abandoned police cruiser. I stop at Hick's for homemade corn-shucked hot tamales and a can of Coke—a variation of the meal Robert Johnson twitters about in "They're Red Hot"—and follow Highway 6 east to Oxford, Mississippi, passing more cotton fields, rolling through Quitman County, Panola County, Barksdale, Batesville, Sledge, Lambert, Crowder. I pass Enon Baptist Church, tractor dealerships, and gas stations with ancient-looking pumps. Tarps stretched over soggy cubes of cotton give staid religious council: FOR GOD TO BLESS AMERICA, AMERICA MUST HONOR GOD. EVIL PREVAILS WHEN GOOD PEOPLE DO NOTHING. FREEDOM REQUIRES SACRIFICE.

The Ole Miss campus is sprawling and bucolic in the manner of all old, southern universities: impeccably maintained lawns, stately brick buildings, men in shorts, and pretty blond coeds walking in pairs. Tomorrow, Ole Miss and Alabama's Auburn University will scrap on the football field, and Oxford is already swarming with dads in sweatshirts and students lugging cases of Bud back to their dormitories. Local restaurants have started taping game day menus to their front doors; cars are painted and wrapped in banners. Still, this is markedly subdued chicanery compared to standard pregame celebrations. Less than a week ago, a twenty-year-old sophomore named Daniel Cummings was pulled over by a university police officer while speeding down Fraternity Row. While the officer, Robert Langley, was walking toward his car, Cummings, presumably inebriated, shot off unexpectedly, striking and dragging Langley a lethal two hundred yards. Cummings has been charged with capital murder, and, if found guilty, will face possible execution. The mood in Oxford has since dulled accordingly.

The Ole Miss blues archive—my destination—is on the third floor of the J. D. Williams Library, in the middle of campus, directly behind the Lyceum. I arrive to find that the archivist Greg Johnson's office is, like all archivist's offices, littered with phenomenal objects, arranged casually: a thirteen-thousand-dollar Japanese laser record player that won't damage precious vinyl, an Edison phonograph from 1902 (its horn adorned with big red flowers), original wax cylinders, a homemade three-string guitar, a six-string banjo-guitar hybrid, a 13th Floor Elevators LP, a color-coded map of Mississippi's musicians' hometowns, a state-of-the-art digital recorder. At the Ole Miss blues archive, the largest of its kind in the world, Johnson commands a collection of thousands of priceless blues LPs, 45s, 78s, wax cylinders, CDs, MP3s, and DVDs—fifty thousand recordings in all, plus a slew of photographs, papers, flyers, posters, and other artifacts. The archives opened to the public in September 1984, under the watchful eye of Bill Ferris, former Ole Miss professor and founder of the Center for the Study of Southern Culture, after a series of priceless donations, including B. B. King's personal record collection. As its keeper, Johnson—a smart, affable scholar with glasses and a long, dirty-blond ponytail—welcomes all types of probing visitors.

"It's a mix of blues fans, blues scholars, people doing general southern history or culture pieces, students," Johnson explains. "And German fans. It seems to me that the Germans, the French, the Scottish, the Irish, the South Koreans, and the Japanese are the biggest blues fans, according to the traffic we get through here. There was a Japanese man who came through and couldn't speak any English. The only thing he could say was 'Professor Longhair.' He was looking for photos of the New Orleans pianist; he didn't even want articles."

The archive houses both Chicago and Delta blues, although Johnson is hesitant to define the two formats as binary oppositions. "When Chicago blues was really taking off as a genre in the 1940s, it was more electrified than the Delta blues. Initially, Delta blues—I guess you could say all blues—was acoustic. But Chicago blues basically took the Delta blues sound and amplified it. Muddy Waters is often given credit for doing that, but other people were playing electric guitars at least four years before [Waters] was. Robert Lockwood, around 1939, in Kansas City, he was playing electric guitar, and it was 1943 when Muddy Waters first went up to Chicago and started playing electric," Johnson explains. "But that's the big difference. Part of that is that [Chicago] is a bigger city, so you have to compete with more noise. Plus with Chicago blues, you have the development of the modern rock band setup, with a drummer and an electric bass player. That started around 1951, when Fender was mass-manufacturing jazz basses, and people were using them because they were portable and a lot more convenient than an upright. So you have an electric bass player, a drummer, a guitarist, a vocalist who might double on harmonica. The band element was the most important element to Chicago blues, rather than the [Delta's] solo acoustic guitar player who also sings. Of course, you have that in Chicago, too. A lot of these divisions are there for a reason, but it's too easy to overgeneralize."

The archive also contains plenty of recordings from the Hill Country, another branch of Mississippi blues. "North Mississippi Hill Country is the region around Holly Springs," Johnson explains, pulling over his color-coded map. "There are pockets all over, but the last vestiges of fife and drum music are in [the Hill Country]. Othar Turner passed away two years ago, but he was the patriarch of the Turner family, who hosted the Turner family picnic with a goat roast and a drum line and a home-made cane fife. The sound of the drums could be heard from five miles away sometimes. All the neighbors would know to go to the picnic. And they would spend all night roasting goat. Now his granddaughter is carrying on the tradition. He taught her how to make fifes. I think she's twelve? She's a natural-born performer." Johnson smiles. "This tradition—a lot of people look back to its African roots, because there are a lot of drum and dance ensembles in West Africa, especially in Ghana. So there's sort of a parallel there, but people don't give any credit to the military fife and drum bands that existed in the United States, but that could also be a precursor to it. It's probably both.

"You always hear [Hill Country blues] described as raw. And that's sort of true, on some level," Johnson continues. "There's a big difference harmonically between most Hill Country blues and Delta blues. There are many, many exceptions to this, but with Delta blues—and this is a generalization—there's a three-chord harmonic structure, twelve-bar blues. One-four-five chords, sometimes extensions of that. A lot of Hill Country blues use only one chord or one tonality. And you never really vary or stray from that. Of course, you can have Hill Country musicians playing Delta blues style. But you set up almost a trance, a repetitive rhythm, a riff that goes over and over, but you don't change chords. It's intended as dance music. A lot of blues was intended as dance music. We don't necessarily think of it that way now." He shrugs.

Johnson is always updating the archive with new recordings, ordering out-of-print LPs and 78s from eBay, and stocking fresh CDs before they become difficult to track down. "I'm constantly ordering new releases, or getting complimentary copies from record labels. I keep up. What's new today is going to be archival quality in the future, and it's good to order them now while they're available," he points out. I ask Johnson about his favorite labels. "If you're looking for blues-rock, there's Alligator [Records] and Blind Pig [Records]. And there are a lot of archival-type labels, like Smithsonian Folkways or Document Records, which is a label that started in Austria and is now in Scotland," Johnson offers. "Their goal is to put out everything that's been released prior to 1950. They get away with it because European copyright laws are different, and you can get the complete recorded works of almost any blues artist from the 1930s and 1940s. There's a more commercial label called JSP that's doing the same thing. The quality isn't always the best; sometimes it's a pretty crappy transfer from an old 78. But at least it's out there."

Up until recently, Oxford was also home to Fat Possum Records, a mostly blues-based label established in 1991 and operating under the humble (if accurate) motto: "We're trying our best." Fat Possum is the brainchild of Matthew Johnson, a fervent, if eccentric, blues fan who was lovingly described by the author Jay McInerney, in a 2002 *New Yorker* profile, as primarily interested in "barmaids, firearms, trucks, no-name vodka, and the kind of drugs that keep you up for three days. I couldn't quite determine whether he was an erudite redneck or a degenerate preppie." Johnson, an Ole Miss alumnus, used a four-thousand-dollar student loan to kick off Fat Possum and began trawling trailers and tractor shops for crude, defiantly unrefined blues performers almost immediately. (He told McInerney, "I wish I had a dollar for every time I heard some kid shout, 'White man at the door' "). Johnson's signings—Junior Kimbrough, T-Model Ford, R. L. Burnside—didn't sell crates and crates of records, but the label attracted a handful of famous fans, from Richard Gere and Uma Thurman to Iggy Pop and Bono. Still, most of Fat Possum's original artists are old, ailing, or dead (Junior Kimbrough died in 1998, R. L. Burnside in 2005), and Johnson has had to tinker with his mission in order to keep working. As he told McInerney, "The last thing I want to be is a folklorist . . . You have to change or it's dead . . . The young black kids in Mississippi are listening to rap and smoking crack."

Accordingly, Johnson started signing new bands, some of whom are only tangentially blues-related (Fat Possum put out the fifth LP from Chicago's Fiery Furnaces, who play stompy, epic rock songs), and some of whom, like Akron, Ohio's the Black Keys, play sloppy, modern blues. These records are targeted at the artists' (and Johnson's) peers, a group I know well—white twentysomethings boasting iPods, ironic T-shirt messages, and disposable income—rather than Japanese tourists or the drooling fetishists he archly refers to as "blues geeks." As Johnson is certainly aware, the fact that almost all of his new blues artists are middle-class white people, or backed by bands of middle-class white people, marks a compelling—if not entirely comforting—cultural shift.

At the start of the decade, the blues enjoyed a certain renaissance within young, white urban culture. The Black Keys' debut album, *The Big Come Up*, was released by Alive Records in May 2002, about ten months after the Detroit blues-punk duo the White Stripes gained national attention for their shrill, electrifying blend of punk rock posturing and raucous blues guitar. Although the White Stripes enjoyed considerably more commercial success than the Black Keys, the two bands were instantly compared. Both featured only two members (a singing guitarist and a drummer)—a curious lineup in a sea of five-man rock bands—and both played vaguely unhinged songs, featuring feral slide guitar, twelve-bar blues, and double entendre–riddled lyrics. The White Stripes managed to bring blues licks back to pop radio, now further freed from the constraints of revivalism, while the Black Keys embedded Hill Country roughness into fey indie culture. The Black Keys' follow-up, *Thickfreakness* (reportedly recorded in a fourteen-hour stint in the drummer Patrick Carney's basement, on a vintage eight-track recorder) was released on Fat Possum in 2003, and their third LP, *Rubber Factory*, appeared on the label in 2004. In 2006, the band released their last recording for Fat Possum, a tribute to the bluesman and late labelmate Junior Kimbrough, titled *Chulahoma: The Songs of Junior Kimbrough*. They would eventually sign with Nonesuch Records, a subsidiary of the industry monolith Warner Bros.

Labelmates and fellow Ohioans Heartless Bastards came to Fat Possum through the recommendation of Patrick Carney of the Black Keys, although the frontwoman and songwriter Erika Wennerstrom is hesitant to call the band's heavy, soulful garage-blues blues proper. "I do really like certain blues, and I can say that it probably has been an influence, but I like a lot of soul music, which I think goes along with the blues," she explains. "I love Ray Charles and Aretha Franklin, stuff like that. For a while, I thought about blues as Chicago blues, which I can't get that into. But I've rediscovered [Delta] blues in the last ten years."

Although the label tends to exist in financial limbo, Fat Possum is at least partially responsible for attempting to reintroduce blues music as a viable contemporary genre, thus insuring that Greg Johnson still has a few new records to buy for his archive. I appreciate Matthew Johnson's dedication to preserving the functionality of blues music, and his refusal to let the genre become the exclusive terrain of record nerds. Even if the blues never manages to reappear on its own terms, his is still vital, important work.

After thanking Greg and watching some archival footage of the Turner family picnic, I leave the archives, open a map, and figure out that Tupelo, Mississippi—where Elvis Presley was born in a two-room shack in 1935—is only about a forty-five-minute drive straight east from Oxford, on Highway 6. I remember, again, why Elvis Presley is so important to any story about the blues: he tugged the blues out of the Delta and into suburbia, via rockabilly stylings and white-boy good looks. Tupelo, I decide, is worth seeing. I curl one hand tightly around the steering wheel as Memphis Minnie moans from my car stereo.

The Presley house still sits downtown, in the freshly landmarked Elvis Presley Park, a strange little haven for tourists and fans. When I pull up a few minutes past five o'clock, the tiny museum has already closed for the day, but I'm still free to walk the perimeter of the house. Small and white, the shack is on raised pilings, and has gray steps, a front porch, and a porch swing that faces to the right. There is a screen door, framed in black, and one lone window facing front. The house has been so meticulously restored, its white paint so blindingly clean and proper, that it's difficult to imagine Vernon Presley, Elvis's truck-driving father, hunched over in the unforgiving Mississippi sun, dirt smeared across his face, sweat dripping into the earth, nailing boards together, forging shelter for his family.

I've heard that there is an Elvis-themed McDonald's just a few miles from Presley's birthplace, but I opt instead for the Tupelo Hardware Company, the general store where Gladys Presley bought her son his first guitar. I meet the company president, George Booth II, whose family has owned and operated Tupelo Hardware for decades, and he lets me stand behind the counter where the guitar was sold, snapping a photo and smiling kindly at my dumb excitement. Even though the store is about to close, George digs out a letter from Forrest L. Bobo, a former Tupelo Hardware employee who handled the famed transaction. Bobo writes: "[Elvis] wanted a 22 cal. rifle and his mother wanted him to buy a guitar. I showed him the rifle first and then I got the guitar for him to look at. I put a wood box behind the showcase and let him play with the guitar for some time. Then he said that he did not have that much money, which was only $7.75 plus 2 percent sales tax. His mother told him that if he would buy the guitar instead of the rifle, she would pay the difference for him."

Beyond Elvis and rock 'n' roll, the blues still exists, ostensibly— Muddy Waters toured through the late 1970s (he died of heart failure, in Westmont, Illinois, in 1983), and contemporary players like Keb' Mo' and Corey Harris and Super Chikan still churn out their own brand of modern blues, while newer, more rock-influenced acts like the White Stripes and the Black Keys and Heartless Bastards fill dingy punk clubs with blues guitar—but, much like jazz, blues has become a niche market. It's not played on commercial radio very much, and it takes up only a tiny little section of most record stores, typically lumped in with blue-grass and folk and world music. Every year, dozens of small-town blues festivals (including Clarksdale's own Sunflower River Blues and Gospel Festival, which is held, regrettably, in brain-smoldering August) invite re-vivalists and fans to shuffle like it's 1935, but weekend throwdowns can only do so much to transform the blues into a contemporary, living form. It sometimes seems like the Delta's legacy is most present in mod-ern hip-hop, where its basic tenets are still being perpetuated, even if the form has altered dramatically.

Back in my car, I follow Highway 78 northwest to Memphis, where I eat barbecue at Charlie Vergos' Rendezvous and take another shuffle through the Civil Rights Museum. Mississippi takes time to understand, although there are some things in the Delta that never change: The Mis-sissippi River still snakes and snickers, supporting uncouth enterprises (then plantations, now casinos). Clarksdale is still home to disadvantaged, segregated black families. The Mississippi State Penitentiary inmates still stab trash and plant seeds on the side of the road, decked out in full-body stripes. Cotton still grows, eating up acres and acres of magic Delta soil. But the blues, for the most part, has moved on.

Music City, USA:

Building the Nashville Sound

The cops all carry capos
In case you wanna change your key
In Nashville, Tennessee

—Bobby Bare, Jr.

* ✷ *

I leave Memphis just before sunrise, rubbing my eyes and listening to my favorite predawn LP, Wilco's 2001 opus, *Yankee Hotel Foxtrot*. Gripping the wheel, I groan along with Jeff Tweedy, blearily navigating the two-hundred-mile stretch of Interstate 40 between Memphis and Nashville, known, unfortunately, as the Music Highway. I count small, rectangular white signs nailed to tree trunks, each with JESUS printed neatly in red paint; by the time I ease into a truck stop for gas, ninety minutes later, I've tallied six, noted in long dashes in the dust on my dashboard. Pumping petrol, I watch bits of cotton swirl into tiny tornadoes, fueled by highway wind and blasts of exhaust. Cotton gathers everywhere, collecting into speckled white puddles on the sides of the road. I pick up a ball and squeeze it between my fingers. The cotton feels soft and stringy, punctuated by seeds and dirt and bits of dried leaves. I shove the ball deep into my sweatshirt pocket and walk toward the store.

Leaning hard on the drinks counter, I dump powdered creamer into a cup of watery coffee, stirring vigorously with a red plastic straw. Individually wrapped slabs of traffic-cone-orange cheese are arranged neatly on the counter. Truckers shuffle toward the register, some fingering the stacks of truck parts for sale, others tugging their hats low over their faces. On the counter, packets of mysterious powders, remedies with unfamiliar names (Horniest Goat Weed and Truckers Luv It!) hang from a rotating display, flapping slightly each time the front door swings open. The woman at the register tosses a heavy perm and slaps the counter once she's handed me back my change. "Have a grahht day," she slurs.

Driving faster, I pass exit 56, passageway to the West Tennessee Delta Heritage Center, which houses three separate museums: the Cotton Museum, the Scenic Hatchie River Museum (which accommodates and preserves native river fish in more than four hundred gallons of water), and the West Tennessee Music Museum (featuring one of Tina Turner's early dresses and the instantly recognizable black jacket Elvis Presley wore during his post-army press conferences). Brownsville, where the Heritage Center is located, also claims the oldest practicing synagogue in Tennessee, Temple Adas Israel, and is the home of the late blues legend Sleepy John Estes. In my favorite Estes song, "Married Woman Blues," Estes growls, voice rich and trembling, about the woes of matrimony, rumbling over freewheeling harmonica and steady guitar strums. "She will get all your money," he seethes. Unsurprisingly, Estes sounds impossibly tired. It is an excellent song to play at rehearsal dinners.

Estes moved to Brownsville from nearby Ripley in 1915. Half-blinded by a baseball accident at age six, he supposedly suffered from bouts of narcolepsy, earning him his nickname. Rigging rudimentary guitars from cigar boxes, Estes began playing Beale Street in the late 1920s, as part of the Three J's Jug Band, with the mandolin player James "Yank" Rachell and the jug player Jab Jones. A 1930 session for RCA yielded "Milk Cow Blues," a song that would eventually become a part of Robert Johnson's twenty-nine-song discography. Estes recorded in Chicago and New York, returned to Brownsville in 1941, went completely blind a year later, and died on June 5, 1977. His cabin has been preserved and partially reconstructed, and is now open to the public, stuffed with photographs and mementos of Estes and his fellow Tennessee bluesmen Rachell and Hammie Nixon.

About thirty miles east of Brownsville, I roll through Jackson, the former home of Carl Perkins. Appropriately, Jackson boasts the Rockabilly Hall of Fame and the Carl Perkins Center for the Prevention of Child Abuse (supposedly, after seeing a photograph of an abuse victim who resembled his own son, Perkins organized a benefit concert and funded the center). I play Dolly Parton's version of "Silver and Gold," my favorite Perkins original, think about one of the last publicity photos Perkins posed for before his death in January 1998, currently taped above my desk in New York—white shirt splayed open, multiple chains, tan chest, giant, gold-framed aviator-style glasses, curly grayish blue hair—and beam.

A few miles east of Nashville proper, I see exit 198, the famed passageway to the Loveless Cafe, which sits just out of reach of I-40, at the northern terminus of the Natchez Trace Parkway. Over the last half century, the Loveless has hosted countless tour buses full of Grand Ole Opry patrons (and television cameras from the Food Network), slathering dinner plates with their famous red-eye gravy, country ham, fried chicken, and homemade preserves, always topping off the table with a steaming basket of Carol Fay's renowned secret-recipe biscuits. Ignoring my rumbling belly, I plow forward to Nashville.

The Loveless is one of the last vestiges of "country charm" before Nashville's shiny sprawl starts etching into the countryside, all layered highways and big gray buildings. Nashville's squeaky-clean industry bent is evident from the moment I speed into town: there's something palpably corporate about the city's genial, shirt-tucked-in atmosphere, about its clean streets and efficient layout. Exiting I-40 at Broadway and puttering through the city's tidy downtown, I understand that there is nothing ambiguous about Nashville, no confusion about its role as the central processing plant for most contemporary country music. The city makes an intense first impression, even from the inside of a car.

The city's tourist-focused downtown is a functional and completely coherent tribute to country—instantly distinct from Beale Street's failed, plastic homage to the blues. Tidy, amiable, and easily browsed, "the District," as Second Avenue, Broadway, and Printer's Alley are more casually known, is a stretch of restaurants, cowboy boot retailers, and music-themed saloons, most of which double as music venues; many of Nashville's bars play host to some form of live music almost twenty-four hours a day, making its "scene" unusually consistent and readily available. The District was incorporated in the 1980s and is governed by a nonprofit organization of the same name, formally dedicated to "fostering economic revitalization and preservation of historically and architecturally significant sections of downtown." The area is bordered to the east by the Cumberland River, which shaped the area's development as a mercantile district in the nineteenth century. Now known as Riverfront Park, Nashville's wharf once sucked in shipments of dry goods, groceries, and hardware, most of which were shot into neighboring stores and sold on Second Avenue (then known as Market Street). The riverfront is also where the city was founded, on Christmas Day 1779. Nashville, then known as Nashborough, was considered North Carolina territory until Tennessee was named the sixteenth state in 1796, with Nashville becoming its permanent capital in 1843.

I park and shuffle nervously into the ornate, gold-plated lobby of the downtown Sheraton, half looking for a room, half curious about the mobs of men and women costumed in freshly pressed business casual, separating into blues and grays and khakis. I tuck my hair behind my ears, tug at my Pixies T-shirt and ripped jeans, and feel ridiculous. Today, the Sheraton's "474 spacious guest rooms" and "25,000 square feet of flexible meeting space" are stuffed, and after hearing a smiling "No vacancies, sorry!" from the desk clerk, I stop to talk to the concierge, who nods apologetically, telling me, "Nashville is, like, the convention capital of the world. Everyone has conferences here. We're always full. Pretty much everywhere is always full. Maybe you could try out by the airport?"

I move toward the Sheraton's big glass doors, pushing past a clump of men in their early thirties, all soaked in the same cologne. "Yeah, we had to drive over to Memphis," one intones darkly, shaking his head. I pause. "That place is . . . you know . . ." he drops his chin, lowering his voice, all conspiracy and secrets. "It's dirty or whatever. It's poor." He shakes his head. I tumble outside, huffing in air. Just two blocks away from the Sheraton, the Nashville Convention Center looms, 175,000 feet of convention-ready real estate, complete with a staff of audio-visual technicians and its own catering company. I move toward it, stop, and roam the perimeter of the building, running my fingers along its concrete edges, gawking at its modern, purposeful exterior, wondering what kinds of things are accomplished at conventions, why Nashville is the perfect host, and how long it would take me to drive back to Memphis.

"There's a fervency and a grassroots thing in Memphis that Nashville's never had," Edd Hurt, Tennessee native and music writer for local alt-weekly the *Nashville Scene*, explains. "Memphis is a crazy, isolated city, one of the very few places in the United States that isn't just like every other place. But any opposition of cities like Nashville and Memphis is just an exercise, and you can't really knock Nashville for doing what it does, because it does it well."

"Nashville exists because geographically it's in the right spot," Nashville-born Bobby Bare, Jr.—solo artist, former frontman for the country-infused punk rock band Bare Jr., and son of country superstar Bobby Bare, Sr.—will later agree. "And Nashville music is great because all great music comes from the South. All American music comes from the South, or is derivative of the South. Or it's out of Chicago, by people who moved from Mississippi to Chicago. If you're a great musician in Knoxville, you go to Nashville. If you're a great musician in northern Kentucky, you go to Nashville. Elvis went there to record. All his buddies, all his musicians—they all lived and worked in Nashville." Even today, Nashville remains the default destination for eager-eyed country music hopefuls, singers and songwriters desperate for a platform: like Hollywood and headshots, every chipper waitress and dimpled bartender seems to have an acoustic guitar and a tambourine stowed in the trunk of her or his Honda.

To the rest of the world, Nashville is best known for churning out perfectly press-ready pop-country superstars, red-faced men and red-lipped ladies who blaze up and down the Billboard charts, hocking a smarmy, undeniable mix of rock-inspired theatrics and aw-shucks southern charm. The city boasts an unyielding grip on the entire industry, from start to finish—Nashville is not only the de facto destination for aspiring country songwriters and performers, it's also the premiere location for producers, recording engineers, and studio musicians, the functional work center for the entire industry, including the country music divisions of nearly every major record label, the Country Music Hall of Fame, the headquarters of Country Music Television (CMT), the Country Music Association, and the *Grand Ole Opry*, a country music radio show broadcast live from Nashville every week since 1925. Hopefuls are crowd-tested in Nashville bars, seduced by Nashville executives, ushered into Nashville studios, and marketed on Nashville-based networks and radio stations. Consequently, nearly every successful pop-country singer of the last two decades has shacked up in Nashville (see Faith Hill, Tim McGraw, Shania Twain, Martina McBride, Kenny Chesney, Trisha Yearwood, and just about anyone else you can think of—even the notably non-Nashville-born successes Clint Black and LeAnn Rimes eventually settled in the city).

In 1980, *Urban Cowboy*, a semiridiculous John Travolta–Debra Winger film about honky-tonk bars, mechanical bulls, ten-gallon hats, and jilted lovers cast country-chic as the new black, and sales of country music (the only obvious accessory to boots and bolos) momentarily soared—but when the economy crashed, so did Nashville's high, prompting *The New York Times* to glibly declare country music "dead." Nashville's reemergence as an imperative industry center ultimately came a few years later, courtesy of a doughy, black-jean-loving, Nashville-by-way-of-Oklahoma yelper named Garth Brooks.

Climbing back into the driver's seat, I unfold a street map and, holding the top corners in my teeth, locate the city's famed Music Row, the nucleus of Nashville industry. I point my car accordingly and drive as slowly as I can. Composed of two parallel streets—Sixteenth Avenue South and Seventeenth Avenue South, known respectively as Music Square East and Music Square West—the short stretch is lined with small cottages and bigger glass-and-granite office buildings. I park and start walking. Music Row accommodates mostly music publishers (the executives in charge of licensing songs for films, recordings, and other forms of media and performance, then doling out half the accumulated royalties to the artist), with space left over for a handful of record labels, recording studios, video production houses, and radio networks. The local headquarters of ASCAP (the American Society of Composers, Authors and Publishers) and the publishing branches of a whole mess of major labels (RCA, Sony, MCA, Mercury, EMI, and more) glower here, their exteriors well-maintained and mostly colorless, save the manicured ivy curling neatly over their granite walls.

The *Grand Ole Opry* has been broadcasting from Nashville since 1925, but it wasn't until the 1950s—when the *Opry* announcer David Cobb casually declared Nashville "Music City, U.S.A."—that Nashville's reputation became internationally known (that reputation was only bolstered in 1955 when, as Bare, Jr., pointed out, Elvis signed with RCA and headed east from Memphis to record). Today, Music Row is full of picket fences and eerily well-maintained shrubbery, and walking the sidewalks I feel like I'm roaming any one of America's countless residential subdivisions—only with more office buildings and less litter. The streets are silent; even though there isn't a practice space or garage or studio in sight, I still strain for wisps of pedal steel or warbles or backbeats, for some sign of musicians at work. All I hear are bird chirps and distant horn honks.

My disappointment is confirmed by Hurt. "In general, Nashville is a fairly average American city with some guitar pickers and lots of music-biz apparatus, but I've always thought that the essential impulse toward making music is actually somehow lacking in Nashville," Hurt admits. "Which is why a formalist art like modern country music can flourish here. And certainly, Music Row speaks to Middle America today in a way that is unique, and which challenges notions of 'rock 'n' roll' and 'pop' and 'manufactured' and 'populist.' "

Still a polarizing force among country music fans, Nashville's Music Row is responsible for more than just packaging up and shipping out superstars. Over the last fifty years, the city has spawned its own take on traditional country, slathering it with gloss and completely rearranging both its parameters and its priorities.

In 1946, the Tennessee-born guitar nerd Chet Atkins made his *Grand Ole Opry* debut as a member of the country-gospel star Red Foley's band (five years later, in 1951, Foley's *Peace in the Valley* would become the first gospel record ever to sell more than a million copies). As a guitarist, Atkins was alarmingly proficient, emulating the country singer

Merle Travis's syncopated thumb-and-fingers roll, fighting to shove the electric guitar (and the electric guitar solo) to the forefront of the country sound. Eventually, Atkins ditched Nashville and began bouncing around the nation, trying desperately to score a viable record deal. Steve Sholes, head of RCA's Nashville office, was impressed by Atkins's chops, and invited him back to Nashville to record. But Atkins's songs lacked the spark necessary for a commercial hit, and rather than continuing to churn out unsellable records, Sholes instead crowned Atkins RCA's Nashville studio guitarist in 1949—meaning his flamboyant axe-stylings can be heard on nearly every RCA record pumped out of Nashville that year.

Studio musicians like Atkins flourished in Nashville. The concentration of industry drew a steady influx of musicians and songwriters who managed to squeeze fairly consistent work out of Music Row. Nashville's studio players were renowned for their skill and efficiency—according to Bill Malone's *Country Music, U.S.A.*, Nashville's session players devised a numerical system of annotating music, still in use today, that allowed them to adapt quickly to new artists and styles.

Still, having the same eight musicians play on every record meant that, no matter how ambitious the vocalist or clever the songwriting, everything eventually started to sound the same.

In 1950, Atkins accepted a job backing Maybelle and the Carter Sisters (an incarnation of the Carter Family consisting of Mother Maybelle and her daughters, Helen, Anita, and June) and re-landed on the *Opry* stage later that year. Continuing to work for RCA (now in an administrative capacity), Atkins helped organize and manage recording sessions for RCA artists working in Nashville.

Meanwhile, as rock 'n' roll burrowed deeper into the cultural lexicon, a cohesive youth culture was beginning to emerge in America. Postwar prosperity meant teens had more cash to toss around, and they opted to spend their newfound funds on rock records, pissing off their parents and raising the eyebrows of cash-hungry music executives. Rock 'n' roll had obvious roots in country music as well as blues, and in the 1950s and early '60s, the two genres shared a mess of "crossover" stars, including all three members of Sun Records' holy triumvirate—Johnny Cash, Elvis Presley, and Jerry Lee Lewis. As rock rumbled forward, country stars and their label heads wanted a bigger taste of rock's profits and popularity. As Bare, Jr., says, "[Memphis] was the first place where white people were sincerely influenced by black people. I'll be in music festivals in, like, Holland, and see all their musicians, and it's the whitest people. And genetically, we're probably just as European as they are. Jerry Lee Lewis is just as European as they are, but the one big difference is that he grew up loving black music."

Without historical precedent or a thriving blues scene, Nashville couldn't emulate Memphis's sloppy, blues-based rhythms. Instead, Nashville's players borrowed just enough from rock 'n' roll to slide country songs into the mainstream. "Memphis music [was] about something else entirely. Not giving a shit [was] a big part of it, while everyone in Nashville cares, or acts like they do," Hurt says. Nashville couldn't harness rock's spirit, but it could learn from its commerciality. Country music was beginning to change.

In 1957, after Sholes's success with Elvis earned him control of RCA's pop division in New York City, Atkins was awarded sole custody of the company's Nashville interests. Working with the pianist and studio owner Owen Bradley, Atkins figured that the only way to plump up country music's national sales was to homogenize the sound, pushing country toward pop-palatability by slipping in rhythm sections, relying heavily on postproduction tweaks, eliminating or scaling back steel guitars and fiddles, smoothing and softening song structure, and insisting on tight choruses. Urban audiences had no empathy for (or interest in) the dusty trials of rural, front-porch life, and country's hard, twangy sound didn't translate well. Likewise, plenty of country singers were seduced by the possibility of "crossing over," understandably excited by the artistic and financial perks mass popularity could introduce.

The country-pop hybrid that Atkins and Bradley ultimately engineered would resuscitate country music commercially and became nationally known as the Chet Atkins Compromise, or, later, as the Nashville Sound. Borrowing as much from early rock 'n' roll as big band jazz and swing, the Nashville Sound combined the commercial finesse of other genres with the detailed storytelling so inherent to early country, immortalizing crooners like Patsy Cline, Jim Reeves, and Eddy Arnold. As legend goes, when Atkins was asked what, specifically, the Nashville Sound comprised, he reached into his pocket, jangled some loose change, and glibly proclaimed: "That's what it is. It's the sound of money."

Naturally, response to the Nashville Sound was divisive—the records sold well, but country purists were agitated by the commercial appropriation of honky-tonk, and the calculated watering-down of an adored (and widely respected) tradition. Hundreds of miles away, migrant workers from the South and Midwest (Oklahoma, Texas, and Arkansas, especially) were landing in California's central valley, retooling their favorite country styles to incorporate the scruffier aspects of rock 'n' roll (backbeat, electric guitar), and establishing the murkier Bakersfield Sound—named after the default destination in California for dust bowl migrants, and anchored by the Oklahoma-born songwriter Merle Haggard.

By the late 1960s, the Nashville Sound had further divorced itself from its country origins and transformed into countrypolitan—a cleaner pop-country fusion marked by shiny, melodramatic production, with loads of gloppy keyboards, swooning strings, and tightly harmonized vocals. Prefabricated and carefully controlled, Nashville country was derided for its standardized, predictable, and uninspired temperament. Performers squeezed into ridiculous rhinestone suits (the invention of Hollywood-by-way-of-Kiev tailor Nudie Cohn, whose ensembles were appropriately dubbed Nudie Suits), hired armies of backing vocalists and studio diddlers, and rolled out gushy, sentimental pop songs.

Meanwhile, folk music was undergoing a parallel conversion, with urban pop-folk singers like Peter, Paul and Mary and the Kingston Trio birthing another hybrid sound, now less leftist and more family friendly. The Ironton, Ohio–born country singer Bobby Bare, Sr., whom Atkins signed to RCA in 1962, began to incorporate urban folk into his country sound, composing and performing long, narrative tracks, including loads of giggly novelty pieces, cowritten by the children's author Shel Silverstein. Despite his goofy lyrics—including a Grammy-nominated hit in 1976 with "Dropkick Me Jesus (Through the Goalposts of Life)"—Bare was a maverick, vital to the evolution of country music: he became the first RCA artist to produce his own records and is widely credited as the inventor of the concept album, beginning with 1967's *A Bird Named Yesterday* and continuing with 1973's renowned *Lullabys, Legends, and Lies*, also cowritten with Silverstein.

The urban-folk-and-country fusion and the Bakersfield Sound were only the first indications of mass dissent in Nashville. By the 1960s, a loose, unorganized group of anti-Nashville pluckers cribbed the grimace-and-horse-dust iconography of the American cowboy, resurrected traditional country songs, and attempted to lasso country back to its basic, uncomplicated roots. These so-called Outlaws (a name supposedly derived from the Lee Clayton song "Ladies Love Outlaws," growled by Waylon Jennings on his 1972 record of the same name), sniffing at Nashville's clean-cut sound and image, squeezed into leather pants, grew their hair long, and embraced western-hippie fashion, matching cowboy hats with bandanas and beards and calling for a bold return to form.

Born June 15, 1937, the premiere Outlaw Waylon Jennings grew up in Littlefield, a small, poverty-stricken town just south of the Texas panhandle, and wiggled his way into the rockabilly circuit as a young man, singing and playing guitar alongside Buddy Holly and Roy Orbison, and eventually snagging a spot playing bass in Holly's touring band—an impressive coup, considering Jennings had never actually learned how to play the bass. While out on tour in February 1959, Jennings relinquished an airplane seat to a cold-suffering J. P. Richardson, also known as the Big Bopper, who, along with Holly and Ritchie Valens, was killed when their plane crashed in Mason City, Iowa (an event that later inspired Don McLean's "American Pie"). Jennings, along with the rest of Holly's band, stayed behind to shiver on their unheated, perpetually stalling tour bus.

Following Holly's death, Jennings scored a regular, six-nights-a-week gig at a Phoenix, Arizona, country music club called JD's, before signing with Chet Atkins and RCA and moving to Nashville in 1965. Jennings, who was accustomed to performing and recording with his own band, felt stifled by the studio constraints of the Nashville Sound. In his auto-biography, the aptly titled *Waylon*, Jennings writes, "I always wanted a live sound in the studio . . . I liked things that weren't perfect. It was OK if the microphones leaked into each other, like a stage performance . . . I could never play with a band that moves on the beat, or under the beat. I couldn't get into it. It has to be on the edge. My music is built on edge; that's the rock and roller in me. [The backing band] The Waylors may not have been great musicians, but neither was I. Neither was all that slick shit I was hearing. That wore me out. I couldn't even find a place to come in." But regardless of Jennings's distaste for Nashville tradition, his gut respect for Atkins remained intact: "Chet and I respected each other's intelligence," Jennings writes. "He stayed with me, because he knew when to let things take their natural course and when to let me find my way."

Addicted to amphetamines, struck with hepatitis, and now divorced three times, Jennings was on the verge of retirement and dissolution when he agreed to allow the New York business manager Neil Reshen to renegotiate his contract with RCA. In January 1973, Reshen, attempting to expand Jennings's platform, arranged for a performance at the infamous New York hotspot Max's Kansas City, where, Jennings writes, he had "never seen such spangles, guys in earrings, girls with hair teased in four different directions."

New York City in 1973 was pre-disco and post-rock. Like the rest of the country, things were in a state of flux: the Supreme Court had recently ruled in favor of Jane Roe, Elvis Presley's "Aloha from Hawaii" concert special had played to a billion people worldwide, and Richard Nixon had declared peace in Vietnam. Max's Kansas City, like its brother club CBGB, was better known for hosting punk rock visionaries and avant-garde artists than country singers, attracting Andy Warhol, the New York Dolls, the Velvet Underground, and Patti Smith. When Jennings tripped onstage, he announced to the crowd: "My name is Waylon Jennings. We're all from Nashville, Tennessee, and we play country music. We hope you like it. If you do, I want you to tell everybody you know how much you like it. If you don't like it, don't say anything mean about it, because if you ever come to Nashville, we'll kick your ass." Jennings stayed at Max's for the next six days, eventually declaring the run "a triumph." Apparently, Outlaw—as an ideology, a look, an attitude— translated nationwide.

Reshen ended up also representing Jennings's old pal and fellow Texan Willie Nelson, after Jennings introduced the pair at a Nashville airport. Nelson, recently dropped by RCA, was now enjoying a successful career with Atlantic Records and gaining popularity with mainstream rock audiences. Atlantic was interested in re-creating Nelson's crossover sales with Jennings; Reshen leveraged Atlantic's interest and persuaded RCA to dole out a healthy advance (seventy-five thousand dollars) and cede creative control to Jennings.

Like Willie Nelson in Austin, Jennings embraced his antiestablishment tendencies, assumed the Outlaw stance, and cashed in, releasing a string of commercially successful records: *Lonesome, On'ry and Mean* and *Honky Tonk Heroes* in 1973, *The Ramblin' Man* and *This Time* in 1974, and *Dreaming My Dreams* in 1975.

In retrospect, it's awfully easy to embrace Jennings's macho postur-ing and scrappy, rollicking sound, while simultaneously disparaging the ridiculous confines of the Nashville Sound (personally, I've always found Jennings's bluster infinitely preferable to Atkins's smarm, and far more conducive to house parties and late-night car trips—which is to say, it's more fun), but both schools still center around a meticulously calculated image. Much of the Outlaw movement was conjured independently of the artists involved, cooked up by a story-hungry press, and reiterated by record labels' promotional departments, which were anxious to latch on to a marketable scene. Jennings's first beard was a result of hospitaliza-tion—after he was released, Reshen suggested that he should keep it, per Outlaw archetype. Ultimately, the most genuinely renegade component of the entire movement was less a decision to dress in black and grow a scraggly ponytail than the mostly unprecedented assertion of musical in-dependence, of shunning studio musicians and label interference and outside producers. In 1976, Jennings and Nelson collaborated for *Wanted! The Outlaws*, which, perhaps ironically, went on to become the very first platinum record ever produced in Nashville.

A decade before the Outlaws started wiggling into leather vests and stopped combing their ponytails, Sun Records' alumnus Johnny Cash successfully straddled both sides of the Nashville split, wrapping himself in black clothing and adopting the dark, bloodied-knuckles persona of the outlaw-convict (see 1968's number one country single "Folsom Prison Blues") without alienating traditionalists or fans of the new Nashville Sound. Cash's thick, emotionally absent vocals were so deep, artless, and sluggish (I don't think Cash could have sung any faster if he were being chased by a garbage truck), so removed from Elvis's seductive croons and Jerry Lee's godless yelps that his colorless "Man in Black" façade both alienated and hypnotized his audiences. And while Cash may not have actually served a murder sentence in Folsom, his vices (drug addiction, adultery) and his tragedies (losing his older brother,

Jack, to a table saw) were so aptly reflected in his stern songs that it didn't much matter. Cash would later tour with Kris Kristofferson, Jennings, and Nelson as the Highwaymen, and in 1994, he forged an unlikely coupling with rap and hard rock producer Rick Rubin, releasing *American Recordings*, a collection of covers and original compositions that introduced Cash to a new generation of fans—kids who donned black T-shirts with the word CASH and a picture of Johnny throwing up his middle finger, buying in, once again, to the notion of a "true" American rebel.

Post-Outlaw, traditional country music continued to undergo a number of comparable revolutions, almost all of which were launched in response to the supposed homogeneity of the Nashville Sound. Likewise, plenty of noncountry artists began appropriating bits and pieces of country history, splicing country affectations into folk and rock songs. Bob Dylan (whose 1969 *Nashville Skyline* was recorded in Nashville, with Nashville studio players), Gram Parsons and the Byrds, John Fogerty and Creedence Clearwater Revival, the Nitty Gritty Dirt Band, and plenty of others approached country music from a decidedly utilitarian standpoint, taking what they needed and ditching what they didn't like.

Music Row may have spawned various schools of rebels, but the Nashville Sound certainly found its global following, and most contemporary pop-country acts proudly follow in its mold, mining the hybrid precedent Atkins set decades ago. In 1989, Garth Brooks's eponymous debut—a neo-traditionalist blend of hard country and rockier ballads—was an immediate critical and commercial triumph, landing at number thirteen on the Billboard pop chart, and birthing two number-one country singles, "If Tomorrow Never Comes" and "The Dance." In 1990, Brooks's ambitious follow-up, the significantly less traditional, pop-country hybrid *No Fences*, sat at the top of Billboard's country chart for twenty-three consecutive weeks, peaked at number three on the pop chart, and racked up global sales of more than sixteen million. *No Fences* spawned four number-one country singles, including "The Thunder Rolls," a bombastic story about a cheating husband, wherein *actual rolls of thunder* periodically interrupt Brooks's strums. Brooks plastered on a scowl for the video, playing an ornery, abusive husband, a role so controversial the clip was ultimately banned from CMT. Still, what's most compelling about the track is its uncanny, unblinking universality—it's reminiscent of nothing, and sounds like it could have been conceived and executed by a computer program. Brooks's pipes may be flooded with country twang, curling up at the ends and belying his southern roots, but the overall tone of "The Thunder Rolls" is wholly generic. However, Brooks continued selling out stadiums, strapping on a headset mic and galloping across the stage, entrancing country audiences who had never seen one of their own appropriate bawdy rock high jinks. Brooks also offered up an ornate light show, complete with pyrotechnics, and occasionally squeezed into a harness, swinging out over a fawning crowd.

Brooks's third record, *Ropin' the Wind*, was released in September 1991. Four million preordered copies shipped immediately, helping the album debut at number one on the pop chart, a first for a country singer. Almost immediately, Garth Brooks became one of the most successful artists of all time. *Ropin'* reignited commercial interest in Brooks's previous records; consequently, Brooks occasionally found himself in the odd (but enviable) position of occupying the top two spots on the pop chart—with records released in different years. Brooks would produce one more full-length album (1992's *The Chase*) before delighting pop pundits with one of America's most ill-conceived novelty records, 1999's *In the Life of Chris Gaines*, an alt-rock concept album written and performed by Brooks's titular alter ego, the scrappy, slimmer, and soul-patched Chris Gaines. Brooks retired in 2001, and shortly thereafter, his final studio album, *The Scarecrow*, hit number one on both the country and pop charts. To date, he has sold more than 100 million records worldwide. Polite, pioneering, and intuitively tapped into the needs and desires of a greater pop consciousness, Garth Brooks is an apt personification of Nashville proper.

Despite—or maybe because of—Brooks's astounding commercial success, folks still bicker about the proper definition of country music. As Bill Malone writes, "A traditionalist-modernist dialectic has animated country music since at least the late fifties in the wake of Elvis Presley's emergence and the country-pop revolution made by Nashville producers. It has only grown stronger in our own time." Unsurprisingly, the persistent watering down of the genre still isn't especially appreciated by purists, particularly given the Country Music Association's tendency to, as Malone notes, recognize country as "any artist or form of music marketed as such by the recording companies," regardless of content or form. Malone cites the popular 2000 song "Murder on Music Row," performed by the quasi-militant traditionalists George Strait and Alan Jackson, for its telling (and, OK, sort of funny) laments: "They never found the fingerprints / Or the weapon that was used / But someone killed country music / Cut out its heart and soul / They got away with murder / Down on music row / The almighty dollar / And the lust for worldwide fame / Slowly killed tradition / And for that, someone should hang."

Ironically, Strait is often cited as the chief impetus for the wave of "hat acts" (a term of derision supposedly coined by the Outlaw-emulating singer Travis Tritt) that flooded Nashville in the 1990s, post–Garth Brooks. Born in Poteet, Texas, in 1952, Strait was intent on revitalizing and retooling the traditional country he was weaned on (Merle Haggard, Hank Williams) while avoiding the pitfalls of forced commercialization. Mimicking the sounds and styles of his hard country forefathers, with a cowboy hat plastered to his head, Strait inadvertently influenced the attitudes and appearances of a then-forthcoming batch of neo-traditionalist singers, including Clint Black, Dwight Yoakam, and, of course, Garth Brooks. (Yoakam and Black stayed the course; Brooks eventually ditched his hard country pretenses.) These hat acts co-opted and repackaged historical iconography, finally settling, like their Outlaw predecessors, on the stubborn, pioneering symbols of the American cowboy: boots, hats, pearl-button shirts, jeans.

In *Creating Country Music: Fabricating Authenticity*, the author and scholar Richard A. Peterson examines the machinery behind "the sense of authenticity that allows something new to be plausibly represented as something unchanging," which permitted the neo-traditionalists to fulfill, as Malone notes, "symbolic expectations about cowboys" while also "being encouraged to perform contemporary styles that would appeal to a large audience that had little to no experience with country music." Country music is riddled with these kinds of awkward oppositions—new playing old, country playing pop, conformist playing Outlaw—and, consequently, is struck with all sorts of problematic presumptions about legitimacy.

Unsurprisingly, then, the tension between the traditional and the commercial (or, as it tends to be understood, the "authentic" and the "popular") is just as palpable in contemporary Nashville as it was when word first got out about the new Nashville Sound. That dichotomy is the central, inevitable argument of nearly every critical and casual dialogue on country music. Critics tend to be partial to the easily intellectualized and historically relevant elements of traditional country and horrified by its commercial cousin—meaning most pop-country criticism is soaked in a specific kind of thinly veiled, upper-crust contempt. "I honestly think it's a class thing. In the same way critics have traditionally not liked heavy metal much," offers Chuck Eddy, former music editor of *The Village Voice* (where he co-coordinated Pazz & Jop, the *Voice*'s annual music critics' poll) and author of 1997's *The Accidental Evolution of Rock 'n' Roll: A Misguided Tour Through Popular Music*. "It's sort of a red state vs. blue state thing. [Critics] jump to the conclusion that somehow people who listen to country are lowbrow—which is [an] absurd [idea]," Eddy finishes.

Having wandered up and down Music Row three successive times (and having spotted only one other pedestrian, who immediately unlocked an SUV and drove off), I slump back into my car, pull onto the highway, and drive with my shoulders hunched to my ears, heading out of the city and toward the airport, skirting endless construction following the advice of the Sheraton's concierge. I am too tired to track down a Nashville phone book and start calling bed-and-breakfasts. Eventually, I score a room at a giant Holiday Inn Express after spotting a sign from the road and squealing onto the next exit. Even here, the lobby plays host to clumps of convention-goers, all wearing requisite dress (flats on ladies, polo shirts on men). As I'll later learn, Nashville's convention crush demands a governing body: the Downtown Nashville Convention Collection describes itself as "a cooperative alliance of hospitality professionals working in conjunction with the Nashville Convention and Visitors Bureau to research and develop opportunities for conventions, conferences, meetings, exhibitions and tradeshows for the Downtown Nashville Convention Destination." Its mission statement makes me tired, and I silently contemplate a numbing avalanche of plastic name tags, blazers, tubes of lipstick, file folders, over-air-conditioned auditoriums, PowerPoint presentations, and spreads of stale bagels and little plastic tubs of cream cheese.

When I ask the Holiday Inn desk clerk about Nashville's convention opportunities, she explains that the city contains three other convention centers: the Nashville Municipal Auditorium, the Gaylord Entertainment Center, and the Gaylord Opryland Resort and Convention Center. The Opryland Resort is so patently absurd that, after spending days irrationally preoccupied with convention culture, I will eventually succumb to its draw, drive fifteen miles out of town, park illegally, and tiptoe inside: climate controlled at seventy-two degrees, Opryland's colossal resort houses twenty different restaurants; four glass atriums; nine acres of gardens, pathways, and waterfalls; a full-service spa; laser-light and fountain shows; a "Delta River" indoor canal occupied by Danny, an eighty-pound catfish, and a fleet of tour-ready, Mississippi-style flatboats; a mess of gift shops; 2,881 rooms; and six hundred thousand square feet of meeting and exhibit space. Later, hunting online, I come up with a photo of the resort's notoriously enthusiastic Christmas decorations, including a giant, saxophone-playing stuffed panda, dressed in a Santa Claus suit, suspended from the ceiling by wires.

My room at the Holiday Inn Express is generically appointed but comfortable enough; it is a marked departure from the Shack Up Inn. I take a quick shower, check my e-mail, and try to figure out the best place to see a local band or two. The desk clerk recommends a place called Legends Corner, and when I pull up their website on my laptop, I am instantly impressed by their claim to be "world famous." I locate my car in the Inn's colossal parking lot and careen back into the center of the city.

Legends Corner is located, appropriately, on the corner of Broadway and Fourth Avenue, in the booze-soaked heart of the District. When I ask the doorman if there's a cover, he grins, cocks his head, and proclaims: "No, just some good ol' country music!" I smile, half-expecting him to tip his hat, and step inside. Legends is crowded, loud, and pub-dark. Aged wood walls are slathered with country music memorabilia, including yellowing record sleeves layered from floor to ceiling and random honky-tonk signifiers (an oil painting of Johnny Cash, a backpacker guitar, an Autoharp). Legends' scrambled décor seems the likely precedent for what's now become the de facto "Americana" design scheme, on display in T.G.I. Friday's nationwide: tons of noncohesive crap tacked haphazardly to the walls, with the hope of evoking some sense of hometown timelessness. Weirdly, at Legends, it works—this stuff is genuinely aged, splattered with spit and whiskey, and entirely unique to Nashville.

The dance floor up front is teeming with bolo-sporting patrons and bearded barflies, and I push boldly to the back, finally settling at an empty bar stool and ordering a beer. By the door to the bathroom, a giant, mullet-ed cardboard cutout of "Achy, Breaky Heart" architect Billy Ray Cyrus stands proud. Onstage, a nondescript-but-skillful country band plays Johnny Paycheck covers, their hat-wearing frontman occasionally gulping his drink and spewing, "Is anybody out there drunk tonight?"

Declaring authenticity is a dicey proposition for country music in general, but there's something charmingly functional about Legends and nearly all of the bars along this particular stretch of Broadway: it feels real, like a genuine honky-tonk, with actual music fans enjoying actual aspiring bands, in a city that thrives on processing and distributing actual music. Unlike blues or rockabilly or even, to an extent, traditional country, which are performed, almost exclusively, by revivalists and enjoyed by a limited few, Nashville country is still very much alive.

I slurp my pint of beer and lean against the bar. I'll spend the next day pacing through the hundred-year-old lobby of the Ryman Auditorium, the most celebrated former home of the *Grand Ole Opry*, nodding at its deep red bricks and white window frames, staring at gleaming bronze statues of Roy Acuff and Minnie Pearl. I'll stomp into Ernest Tubb's Record Shop (which Tubb opened in 1947), thumb through racks of obscure country records, and buy *You Ain't Talkin' to Me: Charlie Poole and the Roots of Country Music* from a tall, skinny clerk who wisely shoos me off to Jack's Bar-B-Que across the street. Eventually, I will drive out to the *Opry*'s current home, a few miles east of downtown Nashville, just off Briley Parkway, on a former farm plot deep in the Pennington Bend of the Cumberland River. I will slump in my car and stare at the new *Opry* auditorium, sitting, unfazed, across the parking lot from a Bass Pro fishing tackle superstore and in the shadow of Old Navy. I will read about how the *Opry* moved in 1974 to accommodate television broadcasts and currently shares its painstakingly paved land with a sprawling Grand Ole Mall called Opry Mills. I will learn that since 2004, its broadcasts are introduced as "The *Grand Ole Opry* presented by Cracker Barrel." I will realize that this is how the *Opry* has adapted, endured, survived.

It is as American as anything.

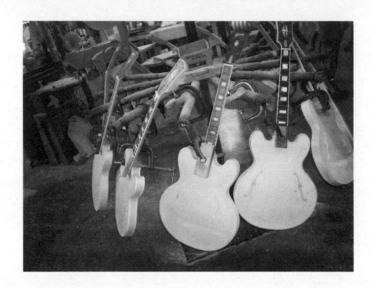

I'm Going Where There's No Depression:

Alternative Country

This is gettin' funny

But there ain't nobody laughin'

—Waylon Jennings

✦ ✦ ✦

I'm fairly certain that Nashville hosts pockets of public dissent—pissed-off kids with mohawks and switchblades, people who spit out their gum on the street—but during my stay, I have difficulty finding anyone who isn't enthusiastic, forthcoming, and exceptionally polite. In terms of country music's present trajectory, this makes a certain amount of sense. The rebels are deeper underground. And they're not all that rebellious.

As the Outlaws and Bakersfield players began to shuffle into retirement or semiobscurity, the country kingdom seemed stuck for action. Years before Atkins landed in Nashville, country music was malleable and open-ended, inspired by a variety of styles, sounds, and traditions. In the early 1930s, a Rosine, Kentucky–born mandolin player named Bill Monroe began playing string music with his brothers, Birch and Charlie. Birch left the band in 1934, but Charlie and Bill continued performing throughout the southeast as the Monroe Brothers before finally disbanding in 1938. Later that year, Bill joined up with the guitarist Cleo Davis, the fiddler Art Wooten, and, eventually, the bassist Amos Garen, and, paying homage to his home state, he declared his new outfit the "Blue Grass Boys," took up singing, and snagged a coveted slot on the *Opry*. Monroe's virtuosity as a vocalist and a mandolin player attracted loads of attention. In 1945, a twenty-year-old North Carolina–born banjoist named Earl Scruggs joined the Blue Grass Boys, bringing along a syncopated three-finger picking style. Between 1945 and 1948, bluegrass music was born and, many argue, reached its artistic zenith; the Blue Grass Boys played hard and fast and remarkably well, defining the bluegrass sound—high, yipping guitar, choppy mandolin, three-finger banjo, walking bass, fiddle, and no percussion.

Besides bluegrass, honky-tonk—a genre name originally reserved for songs based around a Ragtime-influenced piano boogie, and later hopelessly conflated with the brand of country music played *in* honky-tonks, or Texas saloons—emerged as a distinct new style in country music. Honky-tonk country had to be particularly cacophonous in order to be heard above the standard barroom buzz, overpowering foot-stomping and rowdy beer-hollers by folding in closed chords, more bass, piano, and, occasionally, electric guitar and drums. The Texan Ernest Tubb is probably the most notable alumni of the honky-tonk circuit, joining the *Opry* in February 1943 and enjoying a long career recording electric riffs for Decca Records.

Meanwhile, Hank Williams, a guitarist and singer from Alabama who supposedly learned his trade from a street-bound blues singer named Tee-Tot (also known as Rufus Payne), joined the *Opry* in November 1949, after a triumphant stint on Shreveport, Louisiana's brand new radio show, *Louisiana Hayride*. Williams was playing a bizarre blend of honky-tonk and traditional gospel and became one of country music's very first superstars, beloved for his grim, melancholy laments. Later, western swing, another country hybrid born from southwestern honky-tonks, slapped together disparate bits of country, folk, polka, New Orleans jazz, blues, and swing, folding in drums, horns (saxophones, mostly), piano, and pedal steel to form the traditional country sound. In 1953, Williams, long addicted to alcohol and morphine, was found dead in the backseat of a baby blue Cadillac, wearing cowboy boots and accompanied only by a few empty cans of Falstaff beer and the lyrics to an unrecorded (if creepily prescient) song titled "Then Came That Fateful Day." Williams was twenty-nine years old.

But by the end of the 1960s, country music felt stagnant. Various insurgents began grasping for a grand return to form, questing for purity, scouring studios for more "realness," trying their best to wiggle away from the strict Nashville formula. Around the same time the Outlaws lost their razors and Johnny Cash began complaining about the water at Folsom Prison, Gram Parsons, the Florida-born grandson of a spectacularly wealthy citrus baron, joined the folk-pop supergroup the Byrds, replacing a recently departed David Crosby. Parsons, a lanky Harvard dropout who began his recording career as the frontman for the International Submarine Band and later played with the Flying Burrito Brothers, claimed he wanted to create "cosmic American music," and did so by fusing classic country with psychedelic rock, helping form the Byrds' landmark LP, *Sweetheart of the Rodeo*, after dragging the California band east to record in Nashville.

Not long after *Sweetheart* was released to middling success, Parsons ditched the band, either in a bold statement against apartheid (Parsons refused to play a scheduled show in South Africa), or, as his former bandmates suggest in Gandulf Hennig's 2006 documentary *Fallen Angel: Gram Parsons*, because he wanted more time to pal around London with the Rolling Stones. Parsons would go on to release two solo records, *GP* and *Grievous Angel*, both with the then unknown singer Emmylou Harris, before overdosing on drugs in 1974. What happened to his body is still the stuff of legend: desperate to fulfill what they contend were Parsons's final wishes, two of his buddies, road manager Phil Kaufman and friend Michael Martin, drunk and righteous, snatched the body from the Los Angeles airport, where it was being readied for transport back to Parson's family, drove it deep into the California desert, dumped a gallon of gasoline in the coffin, and left Parsons, half-cremated, by the side of the road. In the decades since his death, Parsons has become a hero to a new nation of country insurgents eager to fuse traditional country with new, youthful noises.

In 1990, the Belleville, Illinois–based Uncle Tupelo released their debut LP, a collection of eleven original tracks and two traditional folk songs titled *No Depression* (the title nods to the Carter Family staple of the same name, which Uncle Tupelo covers here) on the independent label Rockville. *No Depression* is, however arbitrarily, typically touted as the harbinger of an entirely new offshoot of country music, also known originally as No Depression, and eventually as alternative (or alt. or alt-) country. Defined as either the fusion of underground rock and traditional country, or as the contemporary meeting place of scrappy country rock (see Gram Parsons) and earnest Midwestern folk (see Woody Guthrie), alt-country, as it's understood today, originated sometime in the late 1980s or early 1990s, and, at least on paper, functions under the same antiestablishment, anti–Music Row auspices as Outlaw country: it is a rallied, youth-oriented response to Nashville (and, to an extent, pop) hegemony.

In 2003, *No Depression* was reissued by Legacy Recordings. Its new liner notes, written by the band's drummer, Mike Heidorn, fail to mention anything about alt-country, instead citing influences typical of any late-eighties garage rock band: "The records we were listening to a couple of years ago (i.e. '60s garage stuff) had morphed into the other side of the sixties: bands like the Byrds, Flying Burrito Brothers, Texas Tornadoes, The Band, Neil Young. Jeff [Tweedy, later of the Chicago country rockers Wilco] always had Dylan tapes around and Jay [Farrar, later of Son Volt] always had a Johnny Cash song on hand." *No Depression* opens with "Graveyard Shift," a raucous, grizzled rock song, rolled out with the kind of exuberant energy inherent only to teenagers and people clutching electric guitars—Farrar crows bravely, Tweedy yelps in the background, and everyone pounds their instruments like the studio's on fire. There's a certain manic twang to the way Farrar hollers "Graveyard Shift!" and it quickly becomes clear that *No Depression*, however great and convincing, is a mash-up of pinched affects: punk boisterousness and country crooning, slapped together haphazardly, performed with unbridled rock 'n' roll flair.

Around the same time Uncle Tupelo was traversing the Midwest in a green Dodge van, two Louisville, Kentucky–based punks—Catherine Irwin and Janet Beveridge Bean—began performing country covers together. Irwin and Bean recorded a handful of demos—a mix of covers and Irwin's originals—in the basement of Bean's parents' home, and continued performing in local clubs, opening for their friends' garage bands and billing themselves as Penny and Jean or Mojo Wishbean and Trippy Squashblossom (recording as the former, Bean and Irwin contributed a cover of Woody Guthrie's "Little Black Train" to a 1987 WNUR compilation called *Hog Butcher for the World*, named after the first line of Carl Sandburg's poem "Chicago.")

Eventually Bean and her boyfriend (later her husband), the singer and guitarist Rick Rizzo, moved to Chicago, where they formed Eleventh Dream Day, joining with the bassist Douglas McCombs and the guitarist Baird Figi, with Bean playing drums and sharing vocal duties with Rizzo.

In 1987, Eleventh Dream Day released an eponymous debut EP on Amoeba Records, and, in 1988, EDD cranked out the full-length *Prairie School Freakout*, infamously recorded in a six-hour guitar binge with a squealing, half-dead amp. *Prairie School Freakout* is dissonant and spectacularly weird, an underappreciated alt-rock landmark as essential as the (not so dissimilar) 1983 debut from the celebrated noisemongers Sonic Youth.

Prairie School Freakout invited major label interest, and the band signed a contract with Atlantic Records, releasing *Beet* in 1989, *Lived to Tell* in 1991, and *El Moodio* in 1993; all three records were commercially innocuous and Atlantic unceremoniously dropped the band soon after. EDD returned to recording for independent labels, finally landing on the renowned Chicago independent Thrill Jockey, founded by Bettina Richardson, who had originally signed Eleventh Dream Day to Atlantic before breaking with the corporation to start her own, more experimental, label.

Meanwhile, Bean continued recording with Irwin, now as Freakwater. Despite their geographic separation, the pair released a self-titled debut in 1989 (also on Amoeba Records) and followed it up with five additional full-lengths, all on Thrill Jockey. In 2005, they released their sixth long-player, *Thinking of You*, a collection of perverse, imperfectly sung murder ballads. Freakwater appears to understand alt-country as another facet of scrappy Louisville punk, and *Thinking of You* is appropriately squawking and defiant: Bean's and Irwin's loose caterwauls blend together into a perfect howl, and their women-wronged laments are so darkly comic (but so sincerely caustic) that it's hard to know whether to giggle or check the locks on your windows.

As an umbrella genre term, *alt-country* can be tricky to pin down, mostly because alt-country (unlike Outlaw country) lacks a functional set of willing participants: for whatever reasons, nobody wants to admit to having anything to do with it. Maybe because of its self-alienation, alt-country can be oddly endearing in its awkwardness, routinely (if inadvertently) cast as the unfashionable, slightly embarrassing stepchild of indie-rock and "credible" (i.e., not-from-Music-Row, nonmainstream, noncommercial) country music. Alt-country's supposed founders disavow the movement, hipsters decreed it lame sometime around 2000, and country music scholars continue to retroactively induct everyone from Johnny Cash to Gene Clark to Willie Nelson, muddling things up even more.

The definition of alt-country might seem preposterously broad, but does that mean it doesn't exist? And is that vagueness really unique to alt-country? Do any musical genres exist in perfectly distinct terms? Weeks later, when I'm back in New York, Freakwater books a show at the 250-capacity Mercury Lounge on New York's Lower East Side, playing in support of *Thinking of You*, and I persuade them to let me follow them into their basement dressing room to talk about country music. We curl through a tiny hallway and dip into a dim, concrete space. Exposed pipes, autographed in black marker by local bands and anxious visitors, snake across a low ceiling, while white paint chips fall to the floor. Amenities are scarce: a few ripped-up rolling vinyl desk chairs congregate in the front corner, a plastic Poland Spring water bottle stands proud near the back, big plastic cups are stacked on a folding table, and a rickety wooden bench lines the far wall. It is the end of October, and the East Village is brisk, cold, delicious—the dressing room at the Mercury Lounge, however, is approximately ninety-five degrees, and everyone's face is red. Freakwater squeezes onto the bench; I wheel over a chair, pull my hair back, and throw my sweater on the floor.

"I've been defining alt-country lately as country music done by people who don't make very much money," Irwin declares. "It's country music that's not as popular as normal country music." She pauses. "The alternative aspect of it," she says, sighing, "is that not a lot of people like it. It's not exactly a badge to be worn proudly."

"A lot of triple-A radio stations that are supposed to play adult Americana stuff, those are just filled with pop anyway," Bean shrugs. "People will take on any kind of term that lets them sell records, even if it means nothing." She's right: triple-A stations, which focus primarily on Album Adult Alternative, are considered the primary heirs to the free-form album-oriented rock (or AOR) stations that emerged in the late 1960s and early '70s, mostly in response to singles-focused format impositions. But this week, the top fifteen spots on the triple-A charts include Coldplay, U2, Jack Johnson, Santana, Train, and the Dave Matthews Band—big, male, mainstream bands.

"People like Garth Brooks really are without shame," Irwin announces. "You'd think a person would feel . . . I mean, he cites James Taylor as an influence."

"That's not fair," Bean counters.

"But when people ask him, in an interview, who he considers an influence, he says James Taylor!"

"Right, and Alison Krauss's favorite band is Bad Company. I mean, influences can be removed from country music," Bean insists.

"Right. I mean, nothing bad against James Taylor. James Taylor was one of the first concerts I went to. I got drunk out of my mind. But it was really good." She pauses, glancing at my tape recorder. "Only say nice things about James Taylor."

"So how did you two come into country music, then?" I venture.

"Through James Taylor," Irwin deadpans. "It was 'Rockabye Sweet Baby James.' That was the album that first made me turn my head." Bean laughs. "No, it was just through liking to sing. And for me, having been exposed to a lot of Pete Seeger records and Clancy Brothers and terrible 1950s folk music, when I was kid. You know, Kingston Trio, stuff like that. And lots of Irish records. And Woody Guthrie. Those are just such fun songs to sing."

"I grew up in Florida, and then Alabama, and then a little bit in

Kentucky," Bean explains. "So country music, for me, was always bigger than life. I didn't really think about it, and my family—we didn't really listen to it. But the costumes were always very over the top, and really, that's the same in punk rock music. For me, it was just this crazy dress-up idea that I went along with, punk and country, being able to pretend you're someone else."

"Right." I nod. "And the idea of being working-class, being a nihilist, whatever . . ."

"They're politically based in the same thing, the idea of struggle. I mean, the Republican aspect [of country music] is strange. But early country music, Hank Williams and stuff—I don't know what his personal political agenda was, but the messages in his music certainly aren't that different from a lot of punk rock music."

It turns out that Freakwater wasn't the first band to redefine country music in terms of its punk rock roots. After spending forty-five super-hot minutes in the basement of the Mercury Lounge with Irwin and Bean, I dart home to Brooklyn and strike up an e-mail correspondence with Grant Alden, the coeditor and copublisher of *No Depression*, a bimonthly music magazine once dedicated to the exploration of "alt-country (whatever that is . . .)" and, as of its tenth anniversary in 2005, committed to "surveying the past, present, and future of American music." (The print edition of *No Depression* folded in early 2008).

"We started a magazine about music we were interested in," Alden writes. "It tied into country music somehow but had nothing much to do with the mainstream country boom headlined by Garth and Shania and that crowd, hence our embrace of the 'alt' tag. That it is now perceived a movement (or as a commercially failed movement) is only so much silliness. It is, as either Eric Ambel or Steve Earle or both have said, just the latest in a roots-rock credibility scare which occurs episodically in American music history."

Alden has been aware of alt-country almost since the inception of the term. "I first heard [the term] from an old friend, Bev Chin, who I met when she was part of the A&M team promoting Soundgarden. Bev has an unerring instinct for what's about to be hip. I thought then and think now that the phrase is absurd, and embraced its absurdity," Alden explains. "But, as [the Mudhoney frontman] Mark Arm long ago said, irony doesn't translate. We thought it an interesting counterpoint to the fact that we had started a magazine focusing on country music's tangents [Uncle Tupelo, Freakwater] in the citadel of grunge [Pearl Jam, Nirvana], but, y'know, nobody really got that after a while."

For every other month of its thirteen-year print run, the cover of *No Depression* offered up a grim, artful photograph of an earnest and/or troubled-looking man or woman, sometimes holding an instrument, often shot in black-and-white. The men tended to have beards; the women clutched violins and looked serious. Most of the magazine's cover stars were semiforgotten Americana heroes (see: John Prine, Kris Kristofferson, Joe Henry) or lucky up-and-comers (my favorite *No Depression* cover is a blurry, half-recognizable snapshot of the southern rockers Drive-By Truckers, with the guitarist Patterson Hood frozen in fuzzy axe-euphoria, gripping his guitar, eyes squeezed shut, hair wet, mouth half-open, his entire face twisted into a classic display of ecstatic pain).

Unsurprisingly, *No Depression* got a lot of shit for being boring and earnest and overly concerned with authenticity, despite the fact that Alden has frequently spoken out about how "authenticity," at least as it relates to art, is mostly bullshit. On his *No Depression*–linked blog, Grant's Rants, Alden muses, "My current hunch is that [the dragon chase for authenticity is] one of those things one becomes concerned with at certain phases of investigating roots music, but that, ultimately (to borrow, again, from [Mesoamerican shaman] Castaneda), it is a path without heart. Either the music draws you in, or it doesn't, and there is artifice involved as soon as a second person steps into the room where the sound is being made."

Alden is right: determining how "authentic" a song or an artist is isn't a particularly useful way of thinking about music. Still, much of contemporary alt-country is marked by a certain adherence to "authentic" principles and traditions. Hank Williams, Johnny Cash, and Gram Parsons are typically touted as the genre's grandfathers, but there is no particularly resonant poster child for the current movement, although the North Carolina–born singer-songwriter Ryan Adams, the Chicago band Wilco (fronted by Uncle Tupelo's Jeff Tweedy), Louisiana's beloved Lucinda Williams, and Texas-by-way-of-Virginia's Steve Earle are probably its most recognizable faces. All four play country-infused rock music that occasionally borrows from folk, punk, and other forms of (mostly white) American roots music. Meanwhile, there are boatloads of eerily benign, Starbucks-approved singer-songwriters who lug around acoustic guitars and notebooks full of lyrics, cooing anonymous, inoffensive folk songs, drinking tea from old thermoses, sometimes singing with a bit of a drawl, often wearing cowboy boots or jackets with fringe. For some reason, these folks get called alt-country, too: since alt-country can appear to lack any discernable parameters, it also functions, for critics, as a vague, watered-down catchall applied to almost all forms of new Americana-inspired music.

In a feeble attempt at further clarification, music writers, marketers, and musicians are constantly dismantling the alt-country nation into a mess of willfully distinct subgenres, all with ridiculous names—see twang-core, country-punk, insurgent country, lo-fi, roots rock, desert rock, gothic country, and, a personal favorite, y'allternative. Some fold in indigenous elements: desert rock incorporates southwestern marimba, horns, and heavy drums; gothic country focuses on death, sorrow, and longing; and lo-fi stays slow, scrappy, and menacing. Still, the description is almost always the same: alt-country is dark and "authentic," performed by singer-songwriters whose voices are regularly described as "lilting" or "twangy," self-separated from mainstream pop, rock, and country, and, for the most part, commercially unviable. Musicians, particularly independently operating ones, tend to instinctually lambaste the notion of a coherent "scene," insisting that a group of bands performing similar styles of music at the very same time does not necessarily add up to anything culturally or artistically significant. Consequently, it is difficult to find anyone willing to defend alt-country's existence.

"It just seems really stodgy, like coffeehouse music," says Chuck Eddy, sighing. "Really, what alt-country is good at, if it's good at anything, is songwriting. So when I listen to a lot of those records, even ones I like, they still sound like demo records. It's like, OK, this sounds like a good song—now all it needs is an actual singer and a band."

Jonathan Marx, horn player and multi-instrumentalist for Lambchop, a Nashville band frequently cited as another forefather of alt-country, is no more enthusiastic, telling *Rockpile* magazine in 2001 that "Pigeonholing bands is a matter of convenience. I just don't think alt-country is accurate. There are so many particular associations with that term, and none of them are things that we deliberately try to associate ourselves with."

Considering its lack of working characterizations, alt-country is most frequently defined by what it isn't: in 2003's *South by Southwest: A Road Map to Alternative Country*, the British author Brian Hinton categorizes his book's subject as "a series of concentric circles, all united by one thing, an antipathy to what has become the dead hand of the Nashville country-music industry."

Or, alternately, it is not defined at all: "Pointing toward a first alt-country record presumes there is such a thing, and I don't make that presumption," Alden says. "To the extent that *No Depression* reflects a re-fusion of rock and country, arguably the Byrds' *Sweetheart of the Rodeo* is the first alt-country album, though it existed firmly in the mainstream. Or Johnny Cash's Sun singles. Or Charlie Rich's prefame career. Rick Nelson's *Garden Party* is sometimes cited. Or you can move forward a generation into the Blasters–X orbit, or skip another generation into Uncle Tupelo and Bottle Rockets."

Like pop-country, alt-country isn't always warmly received by traditionalists who deride the cold, self-conscious distance they believe inherent to the genre. In an interview with "real country" magazine *Take Country Back*, the author of *Country Music, U.S.A.*, Bill Malone, claims: "Most of the alternative acts, even those that like to sing in honky-tonks, are simply reluctant to go the whole way and be emotional about all the basic things that country music does. They can sing about getting drunk, and about cheating and not having a good time, but it's hard for them to sing sentimental songs about Mama or the family, which is just as much a part of country as these other things are. Hank Williams certainly wasn't reluctant to tell people what he was really feeling . . . You are just not going to find that kind of sentiment expressed by any of these 'alt' people. I can't imagine them doing a song like George Jones's 'Flowers for Mama,' or 'He Stopped Loving Her Today,' for example. I think it's because it's hard for them to feel those emotions or maybe they think that their audience, which in many cases are recent converts from rock music, will laugh at that stuff. It's probably a product of rock culture . . . they all have to keep the music as 'ironic' and as 'kick ass' as possible."

A few weeks later, I'm back at the Mercury Lounge, huddled at a table near the front bar, sipping Diet Coke with the alt-country performer Bobby Bare, Jr., while his opening act shuffles around onstage, plugging in guitars and adjusting microphone stands. "When I do interviews in Europe, they really think that me, and, say, Wynonna Judd hang out and stuff. But [that part of] Nashville might as well be in Portugal. I never liked that Music Row music." Bare shrugs, smiling. "I don't see myself going out and opening up for Kenny Chesney. When I was in college, I saw the Replacements on the *Let It Be* tour; I saw Black Flag. What I try to do is sincerely embrace Nashville with one hand, and then mock and molest and pervert and twist it with the other."

Bare released his first record, the playful, solo-riddled *Boo-Tay*, in 1998, as the frontman for a new alt-rock band called Bare Jr. *Brainwasher* landed in 2001, and in 2002, Bare went solo, releasing *Bobby Bare Jr.'s Young Criminals Starvation League*, and following it up with *From the End of Your Leash.* Bare's voice is all wobbles and yelps, and his solid, poppy, bar-band rock songs are country-infused only insomuch as he makes no attempt to conceal his natural Tennessee drawl, and howls frequently (and candidly) about the dark, tambourine-shaking secrets of his hometown. He is as charming and affable in person as he is on record, all grins and nods.

"I'm from Nashville," Bare continues. "I open up my mouth and I sound like I'm from Nashville. I'm not gonna fight it. I mean, the guys from Big and Rich, they were all friends of ours. And now they're millionaires, making really, really bad music. And I have to go across the rest of the world to defend Nashville. I promise that there *is* good music that comes out of Nashville, it's not just Kenny Chesney and Rascal Flatts, I swear to God. And that's difficult. That sucks. There was a band called Jason and the Scorchers in Nashville, who were just unbelievable—and we still have bands that good in Nashville. The amount of talented people per capita is double anywhere I've been. In my neighborhood, David Berman [of the indie-rock band the Silver Jews] lives about two hundred yards from my back door, the drummer from Pavement lives within a mile, the lead guitarist from My Morning Jacket lives a mile away, the lead guitarist for the Black Crowes lives there[, too]," he explains. "And these are just the guys that hang out at the bars and drink. There's a band called Th' Legendary Shack-Shakers who are un-fucking-believable. They're *the* most aggressive punk rock hillbilly thing I've ever seen. I put my goofy-ass friends up against anyone in any city, anytime, they're just so creative and unbelievable. Go see Th' Shack-Shakers, and tell me it's not the most Oh-My-God thing you've ever seen."

So it's on Bare's effusive recommendation that I first encounter Th'

Legendary Shack-Shakers' scrawny frontman, the disarmingly intelligent, Kentucky-born J. D. Wilkes. The Dead Kennedys' vocalist and seminal politico-punk Jello Biafra reportedly dubbed Wilkes the "last great rock 'n' roll frontman," and Th' Shack-Shakers' riotous live act is a notorious blend of spit and elbows and wickedly flailing feet, perfectly anchored by Wilkes's convulsive harmonica playing. A few hours before Wilkes is due onstage at the Mercury Lounge, I squeeze (again) into the Lounge's busted dressing room to talk about country music.

"I really hate [alt-country]," Wilkes spits. "I don't like dreary, forlorn, mundane music that wears a cowboy hat but really has more in common with, like, the bleak dirges of art-damaged folkies. It's not fun at all. And I love it when they put out, like, a Hank Williams tribute record with all the latest alt-country heroes and they take the life and pulse and spunk out of the songs. It's joyous music with painful lyrics, but they strip the joy out of it and just give you the pain, and it's maudlin and melodramatic and mundane as hell, and I want nothing to do with that style of music, and I'm sorry if we're involved in that whole thing," Wilkes hollers, his thin voice peaking, clearly agitated. "I write country music—there's no need to alter it, the real stuff is good on its own. How can you improve on Carl Smith, or Ernest Tubb, or Bob Wills, or Hank Williams? These guys are awesome—you should try and be the next one of those, in your own style, which doesn't include wistful, teary-eyed, mealy-mouthed mewling. I just can't stand it! [Old country] is ornery, it's cantankerous, it's lively, it's got pain at its heart, but it's laughing to keep from crying. It's for dancing. But the Hank Williams tribute record is all postmodern, whiny-baby crap with an acoustic guitar. It's more about the fucking hairdo than about getting people up and rocking."

Th' Shack-Shakers fearlessly marry foot-stomping old-time country jams with gypsy-punk exuberance, crafting a sound that's almost indecipherable, all sweaty foreheads and bleeding knuckles and broken guitar strings, removed from Music Row and, interestingly, from most alt-country acts. "Sometimes it just seems like [our audience] isn't actually listening to the songs that we're playing." Wilkes shrugs. "They're moshing to hoedowns and polkas. We *are* playing them really loud and fast. But that's essentially what rock 'n' roll is, hoedowns and polkas, two-beat music, played loud and hard. That's nothing new," Wilkes says. "They were playing loud and hard back in the day—maybe not *as* loud and hard, but what you hear on those old 78s, that's how they were playing them in honky-tonks and juke joints. So I don't think it's anything new to subvert or pervert roots music, because [roots music] has always been music for the vulgar masses.

"[The press] tries to put us in that whole 'fuck Nashville' camp, but I think Nashville's a really neat town," Wilkes admits. "[Music Row] has stripped anything even remotely reminiscent of hillbilly music out of country music. That whole Music Row thing, that's something in and of itself—that could take place anywhere. It doesn't seem to me to be the entire culture of Nashville—there's a seedy underbelly that rebels against that, and that takes place in the honky-tonks and the rock 'n' roll clubs. That's more a part of the culture of the town. There's a kind of aristocratic, old money, L.A. yuppie contingency, but there's also a blue-collar Nashville vibe that's more at home with punk rock and real country music. That's the stuff that I'm into."

Wilkes, unlike plenty of alt-country artists, also steadfastly avoids the trappings of the folk revival of the 1960s, claiming, "It all turned inward during the sixties—the folk singer and the rock singer became the new high priests, the new clergy. We all gathered around, sitting at their feet, as the pearls of wisdom fell from their mouths. And it became less about community and dancing with girls and getting to know one another and having a good time and leaving the place exhausted and sweaty and grinning from ear to ear."

Wilkes's fierce, uncompromising admiration for old-school country jams (pre-Atkins, pre-Outlaw) doesn't necessarily bleed through Th' Shack-Shakers sound—which skews a bit more modern—but fires up whenever he speaks about country music, alt- or otherwise. "Old-timers get out and square dance, they'll have a cake walk, and there's a hillbilly band playing George Jones's music, and they'll start it all off with a prayer. It's just this vestige of a bygone era that I really like, little jamborees in small towns, where old-timers and youngsters gather and square dance and two-step. To me, that's counterculture. All these people that shave their hair into mohawks and talk about hardcore country! We're gonna fuck it all up! They think they're the real counterculture. Punk rock has kinda gone the way of Green Day, and gone the way of Wal-Mart—you can go get a faux-hawk or a mall-hawk, there are Hot Topics in every mall. So that's not counterculture anymore, that's *part* of our culture. You can have uncensored cursing on cable TV—there's nothing taboo anymore. So the real counterculture to me is the square dancers, the people playing acoustic music, the devout, the homeschoolers, the Amish. They're the ones who are really fucking the system."

Like Wilkes (and unlike Bill Malone), many critics and musicians chide contemporary alt-country for its mushy, indistinct flavor, declaring it precious and boring, exclusively and tediously practiced by longhaired, oversentimental singer-songwriters—less country-punk, more faux-country-lite. But there's also the perennially sticky question of the genre's continuing whiteness, which comes up again and again. Wilkes insists—and his songs concur—that Th' Shack-Shakers are swallowing up all kinds of American sounds, figuring out the most comfortable ways to synthesize the past. "When we moved to Nashville, I was playing in some blues bands, and then I realized I can't be a minstrel act, I can't be a skinny white guy from Kentucky playing blues with a fake black accent . . . So I started delving more into rockabilly, because that seemed to be the white interpretation of the blues, with country music tied in, which is a part of white heritage. I love bluegrass, and I love country music, and Th' Shack-Shakers began as an experimental crash course in roots music, in rockabilly and blues and country, and has since gone on to incorporate anything and everything else that strikes our fancy— punk, gypsy music, Latin music, polka. We're a nation of immigrants, of different styles and traditions," Wilkes insists.

Th' Shack-Shakers embrace of immigrant tradition—marked by a decision to incorporate, as Wilkes says, snippets of punk, gypsy, Latin, and polka music—is compelling, and a handful of other bands identi- fied, wrongly or not, as alt-country have taken similar steps (see the Spanish-influenced country of southwestern American bands like Calex- ico). Still, the touchstones of alt-country—indie-rock, traditional coun- try and bluegrass, punk—aren't especially ethnically or racially diverse.

It's possible to draw a parallel between the rise of grunge in the mid- 1990s—which sucked the silliness and the showmanship from rock mu- sic, infusing it, instead, with earnestness, scowls, and flannel shirts—and the emergence of alt-country, which (with a few very notable exceptions) stripped away the Nudie Suit, boots-and-beard extravagance of country music and replaced it with something more "authentic." Just as grunge acts like Pearl Jam shunned the rhinestones, groupies, and sculpted hair- dos of their hard-rock predecessors, alt-country artists are (unfortu- nately) best known for eschewing country excess and replacing it with a specific brand of glumness. Both genres are aggressively unglamorous and self-consciously rebellious, but alt-country, unlike grunge, never managed to reach critical mass—alt-country hardly ever gets played on pop radio, and even its presumed constituency refuses to stand up and howl its praises. The genre's supposed proponents are almost apologetic about the term's continued existence, and since it no longer works as a signifier, alt-country is perhaps best remembered as an object lesson on the dangers of trend spotting. When a movement is named (and, thus, legitimized and given limits), it stops working in the same ways. Never mind that alt-country began as an offshoot of punk rock, complete with costumes and ecstatic yelping, and has since birthed a litany of sub-genres, each with distinct and compelling characteristics—all anyone can think about now is self-serious mewling and bad haircuts. Still, the creation (and disavowal) of alt-country did ultimately signify the beginning of a new branch of Americana music: a youth-oriented, punk-influenced, experimental sound that draws heavily upon ancient traditions—and works just as hard to pervert them.

I-64 West:

Charlottesville, Lexington, Charleston

Slurping cider and chewing hot apple donuts from a grease-stained paper bag, I flick clumps of sugar off my fingers; between bites, I exhale sweet Virginia air. I left Nashville three days ago and have temporarily camped out in Charlottesville, my home, catching up with old friends and revisiting cherished haunts. Today, I am visiting Charlottesville's Carter Mountain Orchard, which could double as the set for a tourism commercial, all toothy grins and people holding hands and cute babies gurgling in strollers. Americana clichés are coming to life all around me: Sticky toddlers trot between pumpkins, hurling their short, stubby arms at overgrown squash. Couples giggle and lace their arms around each other. Everyone is holding a bag of apples.

Later today, the University of Virginia's football team will play an undefeated Florida State—and win—but for now, the apple barn's back porch is twittering with pregame giggles, families draped in orange and blue, lugging plastic sacks of handpicked apples back to Subaru wagons, and pointing out the stadium in the landscape, around the corner from the hospital and already swathed in light. On the grass below the porch, a six-piece string band plays bluegrass and old-time classics. There are two electric guitar players, and the vocalist—a spectacularly rotund, fully gray man in a baseball cap and plaid shirt—stands offstage, holding a microphone (no stand) and howling at the orchards.

Carter Mountain is home to an impressive spectrum of apple trees. I savor their names: Pink Lady, Gala, Braeburn, Winesap, Crispin, Rome, York, Stayman, Ginger Gold. I am filling up on apples and donuts before driving four hundred miles west to Lexington, Kentucky. Licking the last bits of sugar from my hands, I climb into my car and meander down the orchard's pothole-addled driveway, kicking up dust and bits of gravel. I will coast back through town one last time before leaving Charlottesville via Interstate 64, chugging west into Appalachia via the eastern edge of the Blue Ridge Mountains, and landing in Lexington, where I have scheduled a meeting with the scholar Angela Hammond. A Ph.D. candidate at the University of Kentucky, she is currently shoulders-deep in a dissertation exploring how whiteness in country music began mostly as a marketing ploy—driven, in part, by nativism and Jim Crow laws, which restricted and segregated African-Americans right up through 1964. Hammond has promised to tell me her stories.

Even though I deliberately opt to follow a meandering route to the interstate, thus indulging in one final glimpse of downtown Charlottesville, I am giddy and anxious the entire time, blind to landmarks and scenery: my whole body is craving the highway, and I am reminded, again, of my weird, unshakable affinity for Interstate 64. It is a large and important road, and, at least in central and western Virginia, not particularly crammed with cars (although drivers based in the eastern half of Virginia—where a constantly clogged 64 connects Williamsburg to Norfolk—will probably offer up a different impression). Construction on Interstate 64 began in 1961, and, at present, the road runs 961 miles from St. Louis, Missouri, to the eastern seaboard of Virginia. The highway is still officially unfinished—the Missouri Department of Transportation plans to stretch I-64 to I-70 in Wentzville, eventually accommodating a tie-in with Missouri State Highway 364—but even incomplete, I-64 provides primary interstate access to a mess of big mid-southern cities, including Richmond and Williamsburg, Virginia; Charleston, West Virginia; Louisville, Kentucky; and St. Louis. In Virginia, I-64 crosses a wide spectrum of terrain, from the flat, coastal plains of Hampton Roads to the central plateaus of Piedmont, to the Allegheny and Blue Ridge mountains in the west, and, for me, Interstate 64—with its generous speed limits and wide lanes and varied landscapes and broad, tree-lined shoulders—feels more like an escape passage than anything else. It is a straight shot at freedom; it is the kind of road that deserves to be memorialized in an epic, throbbing Bruce Springsteen song.

Practically panting with anticipation, I evacuate downtown Charlottesville as quickly as possible and nose toward the interstate. Driving west on I-64, cranking the Band's *Stage Fright* and ignoring the thump-thump of fresh apples rolling around in the backseat, it is possible for a girl to lose herself. Pulling onto the on-ramp feels like gulping down a cold glass of water after a long, hot run. Today on 64, trees give way to trees, pickup trucks drag horse trailers, cars speed up and down endless hills. Ten miles from Stuart's Draft, the road curls to the left, and motorists are assailed with a big, panoramic view of the mountains, unfolding in varying shades of bruise. I shoot up and over Afton Mountain, through Waynesboro, pushing toward Staunton, then Roanoke—old Virginia cities, Civil War towns, all monuments, craft shops, and American flags. I pass "Nancy and Udean's Christian Tour Bus," plastered with orange stripes and smiles. Cows mull and chew, clouds cast misshapen shadows on the mountaintops, spools of hay sit fat and brown.

I sometimes think that if I had unlimited amounts of gasoline and energy, I would spend all of my time driving Interstate 64 back and forth between western Virginia and western Kentucky, starting in Charlottesville and ending in Louisville: it is one of the most breathtaking stretches of interstate on the East Coast. It is not showy, like Skyline Drive, or overrun, like most everywhere else.

A few hours in, I paw at the dashboard, slapping blindly at the glove compartment latch, trying to dig out a map of West Virginia. Assorted provisions flop out, hitting the passenger-side floor mat: Dunkin' Donuts napkins, cherry Life Savers, a Mini Maglite, a tire pressure gauge, several squished oatmeal-raisin PowerBars. Finally, I curl my fingers around a stack of poorly folded maps. My two most beloved U.S. highway maps (a giant 2006 book-bound Rand McNally road atlas, servicing the U.S., Mexico, and Canada, and a smaller foldout Michelin map of the southeastern U.S.A.) have already begun to feel quaint, archaic, and grandfatherly. Even the titles sound antiquated: the Michelin map is subtitled "Motoring and Tourist Map," as if "motoring" were still an appropriate and applicable American verb.

I am partial to actual maps over punch-and-print websites like MapQuest, which, I have learned, are occasionally wrong and generally loony (no one needs to know they'll be on an off-ramp for twenty-nine feet) and offer little to no context or geographic perspective—Mapquest spits out highway numbers, but there's no simple way of deciphering exactly which rivers you'll get to cross, which mountains you'll plow through, how close your vehicle will get to the Arkansas border, or which cities and towns and hamlets will speed by, hidden by off-ramps and highway trees. I feel safer with actual maps, more in control, less concerned about missing exits or taking foul turns. As Nick Paumgarten wrote in *The New Yorker*, "A map is a piece of art. It is also a form of language—a rendering of information. A good map can occupy the eye and mind longer than almost any other single page of data, including Scripture, poetry, sheet music, and baseball box scores. A map contains multitudes." No one ever suggests that a numerical list of turns and mileage possesses multitudes. Maps are the perfect marriage of romance and function.

I have already eaten two apples and am listening to a breaking-up WNRN, one of Charlottesville's commercial-free radio stations. Here, 64 doubles up with 81 South, and I wonder if I will get close enough to Roanoke to see the Mill Mountain Star, the red, white, and blue light installation balanced atop Mill Mountain, overlooking the city. I finally exit for gas in Lexington, Virginia, home of the Virginia Military Institute, Washington and Lee University, and the gravesites of both Robert E. Lee (his horse, Traveller, is also buried here, just outside Lee Chapel) and almost all of Stonewall Jackson, whose left arm is memorialized in Chancellorsville, Virginia, where it was mistakenly shot off by one of his own men on May 2, 1863.

Despite sitting well into the twenty-first century, Lexington is still crawling with Confederate pride. If you are in need of a Stonewall Jackson coffee mug or wall plaque, there are well-stocked souvenir shops offering Confederate-themed wares. Driving into town, I pass tractor dealerships and grocery stores, ice cream parlors and antique shops. There are plenty of American flags.

After filling up my gas tank, I park near the university, where tanned, blond people are playing volleyball, and wander into Smokin' Jim's Barbecue. The restaurant is decorated according to a vague firefighters-and-pigs theme (complete with giant, semi-horrifying pictures of actual local house fires in progress) and sells scoops of Carolina-style pulled pork barbecue, with little tubs of red sauce and puddles of coleslaw, all neatly divided on Styrofoam plates. After ordering a sandwich, I pull a can of warm soda from the fridge—it's not plugged in—and the woman behind the counter fills a plastic cup with ice. I'm sitting alone in the front room, and when the waitress brings me my food, she explains that I can turn on the television and watch whatever I want, pointing out a list of channels taped to the wall. I flip to an E! exposé on Tom Cruise, and chew.

Satiated, I wander down Jefferson Street to Goodart's Second Hand Shop, which is crowded with mounds of standard-issue, antique shop detritus: heaps of old shoes, cigar boxes, stacks of postcards and curling black-and-white photos, oil cans, glass jars, leather jackets, broken picture frames, and a few modern flourishes, like a pair of plaid skateboarding shoes and a full can of 2005-era Coke. In the back, I finger a banjo signed by Ralph Stanley, flip over violins, and scrutinize an upright bass and a stack of old, boxy record players. Thumbing through a wooden milk crate full of vinyl LPs, I pull out Dolly Parton's *Heartbreaker*, *The Great Roy Acuff*, Loretta Lynn's *You Ain't Woman Enough*, the Ozark Mountain Daredevils' *Men from Earth* (the cover of which features two unwashed, devious-looking men, wearing dirty overalls and oversized work pants, respectively, and leading three donkeys; someone has spilled something brown on the upper left corner), and, my crowning score, an original Sun Records LP of Jerry Lee Lewis's *The Golden Cream of the Country*. I hug the records to my chest. As I approach the counter, the shop's proprietor squints at my haul. "What are you going to do with these?"

Perplexed, I venture, "Mostly listen to them?" and begin tugging off each record's paper sleeve, scanning the vinyl for scratches.

"Are you gonna sell them? If you put these on the Internet," he declares, "you could get more money for them." He pauses. "That's a good T-shirt."

I glance down at my blue Martin Guitar tee and smile, handing over the stack of LPs, which I have topped off with a tiny, paperback book, circa 1948, of American folk songs. He unceremoniously places the book aside and begins adding up my bill for the records, which sell for two dollars each. He picks up the Jerry Lee Lewis record. "This is a Sun label pressing," he declares, voice slow and lazy, eyebrows half-raised. He looks about sixty years old, maybe a little younger, with gray hair parted in the middle. He is wearing an old flannel shirt and khaki shorts. "Five dollars for this one."

"OK." I nod. We're quiet. He's still holding the record. "I was in

Memphis not too long ago," I offer, now worried that maybe he's too attached to the Jerry Lee Lewis to sell it, even for five dollars. I am beginning to get the idea that not many things in the store are actually for sale. He looks up, squinting.

"The last time I was in Memphis . . ." He trails off. "That's a crazy story, you wanna hear that story?"

I nod again. "Memphis stories are always good stories."

He raises his hands. "I met a girl up in Washington, D.C., about your age." He's grinning now. "So I invite her down to Louisville to see the Derby with my son. And then she invites me down to Memphis," he says, voice dropping. "We were just having a good time. You know, just having a good time. She took me to Beale Street; I played blues with some blacks. They were sitting on a barrel in an alley. So we wake up in her apartment the next day. The phone rings, and she answers it and says 'Hello, honey,' and I'm thinking, 'Uh-oh,' OK. So then she says her fiancé is driving in from Tupelo to take her to lunch and I have to leave right now. I don't have a reservation or anything, you know, so I say, 'Take me out to 40.' I'm a thousand miles away from home, and Tennessee is long. So I get picked up by this guy in a '54 Chevy, and he's going forty-five miles an hour, and the engine's overheating, and we're pouring water all over it. Then I get picked up by a sailor from San Diego, and he drives real fast."

I get the sense that, maybe, he's making this all up as he goes along. I nod more, trying my best to seem sympathetic.

"We were just having fun." He shrugs.

He puts my records in a Wal-Mart bag. When I hand him a twenty-dollar bill, he gives me change from his wallet. On the counter, I notice a crumbling Bob Dylan book from 1974 and inquire about its origins. He tells me he spotted the book at the bottom of "a box of crap someone gave me." He seems convinced that, since it says "A Rolling Stone Book" (presumably an artifact from *Rolling Stone*'s early book publishing arm), it was actually published *by* the Rolling Stones. "I get a kick out of this guy," he says, pointing at the cover's black-and-white portrait of Dylan. "Totally," I agree, voice emphatic, head bobbing.

He tells me he plays bluegrass and blues, mostly on five-string banjo, which he also uses as a drum, and spends his winters bouncing around Florida, "staying with people I know, in different sorts of places," and recently recorded a blues CD with two of his friends. They're called the Three Amigos. He doesn't have any copies of the album, but he's happy to describe the cover art: "There are these three drunk olives, sitting on a bar stool. Like the three amigos. And there's this fly on the bar in a broken martini glass." He starts laughing. "It's crazy." He likes Delta Blues, Sonny Boy Williamson and Lightnin' Hopkins and Howlin' Wolf. He's going to Martha's Vineyard for two weeks in July, because his sister owns a house there, "in the Indian part." When I tell him I live in Brooklyn, he nods: "I have a friend in New York City. He had to learn karate because he was always getting mugged."

I pick up my bag of records and smile. "Thanks for everything."

"Have a safe trip," he mumbles. I put my sunglasses on and walk to my car.

Easing back onto I-64, I pass a colossal beige motor home, with "Roundup Ministries" scrolled on the sides in brown cursive, and its mission—"Roundin' up for the Savior!"—boldly looped across the back. This strikes me as a highly reasonable, if ambitious, undertaking, and I try to catch a glimpse of the driver as I speed by. Western Virginia roads have loads of good drivers, with fanciful faces and intent expressions, so many so that driving, here, I hardly need a radio for entertainment.

About twenty-five miles into West Virginia, I-64 develops curves, twisting up and down, a roller coaster without loops. Near exit 89, just shy of Charleston, I-64 inches alongside a coal power plant, which sits flat, a little village of tubes and warehouses, punctuated by giant black mounds. West Virginia is coal country, and roadside billboards regularly proclaim things like WE'RE FRIENDS OF COAL, I'M A FRIEND OF COAL, or, alternately, COAL KEEPS THE LIGHTS ON.

Billboards pile up: CARPETBAGGERS ANTIQUE MALL, APPALACHIAN BIBLE COLLEGE, SOUTHERN X-POSURE GENTLEMEN'S CLUB (thirty miles later, I see a new placard for SOUTHERN X-POSURE GENTLEMEN'S CLUB *PLATINUM*, and can't help but contemplate the details of the distinction), SUNBEAM BAKERS (a little girl, Norman Rockwell–style, with her hands clasped in prayer, accompanied by the caption NOT BY BREAD ALONE). In Charleston, I pass a Hooters billboard that inexplicably reads: A SLICE OF FLORIDA . . . RIGHT HERE . . . IN CHARLESTON! Meanwhile, Charleston's capitol building is immense, a giant gilded dome rising to the right of the interstate, as if to say, "We're no joke." The sun is high, ricocheting off the capitol. Gold on gold. I believe.

Country Rolls On:

Minstrel Shows, Race, and the Rise of Radio

Seven hours and four hundred miles later, I arrive in Lexington, Kentucky, and lug my bags into Lyndon House, a restored antebellum mansion on North Broadway. The innkeeper feeds me chocolate chip cookies and bottled water in the lobby and shows me to the Headley Room, a large, quiet space with Victorian-style furniture, a bathroom bigger than my bedroom in Brooklyn, and wireless Internet; as the innkeeper explains, the room was named after Joseph and Alise Headley, the affluent original owners of the house. Like Lyndon House, Lexington, a city also known as "the horse capital of the world," is oozing old southern charm, all mint juleps and white suits and slabs of pecan pie.

I nap for an hour (when I close my eyes, I still see highway) before Angela Hammond and I finally meet up in the John Jacob Niles Center for American Music, a room offset from the University of Kentucky's Little Fine Arts Library. While Hammond fires up her laptop, I stare at a series of chairs and doors, each meticulously hand-carved by John Jacob Niles, a Kentucky-born collector of American ballads and a famed, falsetto-wielding dulcimer player. Niles—with his high, supernatural pipes and meek strumming, his little round mouth and head of wispy white hair—is one of my all-time favorite players of southern American music, mostly because he is both impossible to listen to and impossible to not listen to. His voice is just that strange.

Niles recorded stacks of Appalachian standards, from the early 1900s through the 1970s (he died in 1980), but his mimicking of the female voice, in which he twists his vocal chords into weird, wobbling, vibrating shrieks, is his most paralyzing achievement. I run my fingers over a large wooden table, tracing the names of songs. "I Wonder as I Wander," Niles's most renowned track, loops along in big, billowing cursive.

Elaborate oil portraits of Niles line the walls of the room (he looks different in every one), and cases of handmade dulcimers and songbooks sit quietly, guarded by sheets of glass. Hammond pulls up her thesis, and I sit alongside her, eager to talk. Despite an enduring reputation as the whitest thing going, early country music borrowed heavily from African-American slave spirituals, early blues, and jazz; Hammond and I look at hillbilly cartoons, listen to interview clips by Mike Seeger, and chat about the folksinger Bradley Kincaid. Hammond suggests that RCA's acquisition of Charley Pride (the first and, some would say, only African-American country star—at the very least, the only African-American recognized by the *Grand Ole Opry*, who invited Pride to join in 1993) was really just a public relations scam. We talk about black musicians playing commercial country music, about how they were written out of its story, about what that means. About how American music is racialized and consumed, and how country music has, weirdly, become a genre comprised almost exclusively of white musicians. Still, African-Americans are very much a part of country music's history, and their exclusion from that canon is both tragic and telling.

When we're done, I thank Hammond and wander over to Tolly-Ho, where you can buy grilled cheese sandwiches, cheeseburgers, cigarettes, and milkshakes, all at the same counter. I eat my Oreo shake with a spoon and watch University of Kentucky students, cramming for midterms, swallow big club sandwiches without chewing. Angela Hammond is driving her thesis back to her home, just outside of town, and I am thinking about the ways in which we categorize sound, how race inevitably works its way in, and what the different names we slap on things eventually come to signify.

The next morning I will leave Lexington and drive south to Berea, Kentucky, making sure to first pass the Keeneland Thoroughbred horse track, with its impossibly green lawns and white picket fences and breathtaking expanse of farmland. On my way back to I-75, I pass upscale restaurants and fine bourbon distilleries, whizzing through another, wealthier, more gentrified arm of Appalachia. In Berea, I will have three cups of coffee with Loyal Jones, author, American music expert, and the (now retired) director of the Appalachian Center at Berea College, the very first nonsegregated and coeducational college in the South, where all students are handed full tuition scholarships, and at least 80 percent of the student body has been plucked from low-income Appalachian homes. Jones knows more about the traditional country, bluegrass, and folk music of Appalachia than almost anyone else I have ever read or spoken with, but the thing that affects me most about our conversation, after we wade through the socio-cultural implications and history of early country music, is his contention that this music comes from a tough place—rife with vicious stereotypes and severe economic disadvantages—and, accordingly, is beloved.

Country music wasn't born in Nashville—the genre is, as Bill Malone writes, "older than the south itself" and derived from the folk songs, ballads, and dances brought to America by Irish, Scottish, Welsh, and English immigrants. Early country music, as Malone notes, was "British at its core, but overlain and intermingled with the musical contributions of other ethnic and racial groups who inhabited the vast southern region." Coursing through the countryside, Celtic folk songs assimilated an impressive spectrum of traditions, eventually taking on the habits and peculiarities of Native American, German, French, Spanish, and Mexican music. I can hardly think of anything more innately American.

In the *Journal of American Folklore*, the writer and scholar Archie Green (known to some as the "Dean of Laborlore") notes that the term *hillbilly* appeared in print as early as 1900 and was used, mostly, as a vague catchall for rural, mountain-living southerners; as Malone discovers, *hillbilly* was first applied to musicians in January 1925, when a string band hailing from North Carolina and Virginia agreed to play under the name the Hill Billies. Whether *hillbilly* was taken as a nasty pejorative or a loving nickname depended, mostly, on how it was used. Malone notes, "Hillbilly music suffered and profited from a conflicting set of images held by Americans that ranged from stability and enchantment to decadence and culture degeneracy." That much hasn't really changed. Like Appalachia, the American South and its music are stuck in a loop of allure and dismissal, alternately romanticized and rejected, forced to contend with the repercussions of a history riddled with as much bigotry and intolerance as creativity.

These stereotypes aren't without a certain amount of substantiation. Beginning in New York City in the 1840s (and enduring through, appallingly, the 1950s), minstrel shows were considered high comedy for plenty of Americans: working-class white men dressed up as plantation slaves, slathered themselves with blackface, performed skits, and crassly imitated African song and dance. Minstrel shows simultaneously appropriated, parodied, insulted, and—occasionally and inadvertently—celebrated African-American tradition, while confirming existing racist ideas and, periodically, introducing brand new ones. Although it's tempting to grimace and dismiss minstrelsy as offensive, archaic, and ridiculous, its legacy is—unsurprisingly—slightly more complicated. As the music critic and author Nick Tosches points out, it's problematic "to imply that the blackface caricatures of minstrelsy were somehow more racist than the insidious stereotype of today's popular entertainment; as if to imply the playing of blacks by whites to be more demeaning or momentous an absurdity than the playing of Italians by Jews and WASPs, from *Little Caesar* to *The Godfather*, and every other manner of ethnic fraud upon which our popular culture has to this day been based." Likewise, Tosches is adamant about minstrelsy's tremendous influence on early American music, writing, "the impact of [minstrelsy] was profound upon the inchoate and gestative forms of blues and jazz."

Crucial elements of the minstrel show—the use of blackface, in particular—bled into medicine shows, which were horse-and-buggy operations designed to hock wacky elixirs, vying with song and dance routines for potential customers.* Some minstrel artists proved pivotal to country music history: the minstrel singer (and subsequent cult hero) Emmett Miller—who was born in Macon, Georgia, in 1900, boasted a curiously high, billowy falsetto (not unlike John Jacob Niles), and died, broke and soaked in whiskey, in 1962—is still considered a profound inspiration, vocally, for many country greats who followed, including Jimmie Rodgers and Bill Wills.

The musicians participating in early minstrel shows typically played fiddle, banjo, and some kind of light percussion (usually a tambourine or set of "bones," which is a shaker constructed out of two ten-inch racks of cow ribs and, when properly agitated, sounds a little like a snare drum), drafting a three-piece combo now familiar as the archetypical southern string band. Fiddles were brought over by Celtic immigrants, while the banjo evolved from a four-stringed West African gourd instrument introduced to North America by slaves in the 1830s. A fifth string was added to the banjo a few years later by Joel Sweeney, who also replaced the hollow gourd with a wooden hoop swathed in goat skin, leaving the body of the banjo to resemble a modern drum head. Mandolins, dulcimers, harmonicas, and zithers all eventually made their way south. Country music suddenly had its own particular arsenal of strummy noisemakers.

In the early 1900s, nearly all American music was being meticulously stylized for urban audiences, with little regard paid to the interests

---

*In 2005, Old Hat Records compiled an outstanding collection of medicine show music, from 1926 to 1937, appropriately titled *Good for What Ails You.*

and tastes of people living in rural areas. In cities, populations were denser and more easily accessed, and music executives (usually city-dwellers themselves) presumed that the gruff, untempered reality of raw country would be unpleasant, at best, to urban ears. But radio changed everything. Throughout the 1920s, with Atlanta's WSB and, later, Mexico's XERA (the million-watt brainchild of quack-cum-hustler Dr. John Romulus Brinkley) leading the brigade, station owners recognized that live traditional country music, aside from being cheap and plentiful, drew in armies of ready, rural listeners. On November 28, 1925, the Indiana-born DJ-turned-program-director George D. Hay launched a hillbilly radio show on WSM (a then-brand-new station broadcasting out of Nashville) known as *The WSM Barn Dance*, and, later, as the *Grand Ole Opry*. Nearly anyone who knew how to play was invited to participate (without pay—the show was commercial-free), and the *Opry* roster contained mostly amateur pickers, farmers and laborers who managed to squeeze out a few jams on Saturday nights. The *Opry*'s unpretentious, down-home, front porch aesthetics were a huge part of its appeal.

In 1926, a fifty-six-year-old, hat-and-tie-wearing banjo player named Uncle Dave Macon (advertisements pounded out by Nashville's beloved—and enduring—Hatch Show Print shop declare, "Uncle Dave handles the banjo like a monkey handles a peanut!") joined the *Opry*, bringing with him nearly eight years of professional entertaining experience in the vaudeville and minstrel traditions. As the folksinger Pete Seeger explains in the liner notes to the Uncle Dave Macon box set: "[Uncle Dave] brought dozens of old folk songs, vaudeville songs, blues, gospel songs, and comedy songs into the twentieth century. He was one of the first country stars to record, the first star of the Grand Ole Opry, and one of the first members elected to the Country Music Hall of Fame. Above all, he was an entertainer supreme, and one of the most accomplished banjoists in country history."

Along with black harmonica player DeFord Bailey and a mess of local string bands, Uncle Dave facilitated a soar in popularity for the *Opry*, proving to executives worldwide that raw country music could draw a considerable audience. By 1932, the *Opry*, working a fifty-thousand-watt clear channel, was broadcasting to the southeastern United States and shooting as far west as Texas. Now swamped with advertisers, the *Opry* was worming its way into the American vernacular, and new hillbilly-based programs, like Chicago's WLS's *National Barn Dance*, offered up a similar mélange of country-themed entertainment.

By 1930, federal census reports claimed that 12,078,345 American families owned radios; with its invisible, indiscriminate sound waves, radio effectively bridged the social and geographic gaps between rural and urban music listeners. Meanwhile, the *Grand Ole Opry* went on to become the longest-running program on American airwaves, creating dozens of fledgling stars. The Tennessee native Roy Acuff joined the *Opry* in 1938, after touring with Doc Hauer's medicine show, where he performed in blackface and developed impeccable stage skills. (That so many early country stars developed superior showmanship skills as members of vaudeville troupes is probably the element of traditional country that has endured best—contemporary country artists may not play as many banjos, but they still know how to put on a show.) Accompanied by his string band, the Smoky Mountain Boys, Acuff sang traditional mountain music, trying his best to keep his work as close to its rural roots as possible, shunning electric instruments, and, occasionally, singing off-key. Acuff was remarkably popular, responsible for much of the *Opry*'s still-growing success, and the natural choice for host when NBC began airing thirty-minute chunks of the *Opry* in 1939. Country music was assimilating and growing and changing; the sound that many long considered a plague of the hills was slowly and steadily eeking its way into nonrural American life.

Ain't That a Pretty Ole Mountain?

Appalachia, the Carter Family, and Early Country Music

*Appalachia, more than most of the regions into which the United States is
customarily divided, is a territory of images—a screen upon which writers, artists,
and savants for several generations have projected their fears, hopes, regrets, and
enthusiasms about America present and past.*
—John Alexander Williams, *Appalachia: A History*

✢ ✷ ✤

Germany's Bear Family Records, the self-proclaimed "world's greatest
record label for American vintage country music and rock'n'roll," is the
oft-cursed and unrelenting financial foe of nearly all well-intentioned
record collectors. Bear Family's big, wickedly comprehensive box sets
typically sell for upward of three hundred dollars and come packed with
riveting images, poetic liner notes, and, occasionally and spectacularly,
every single available recording by a given artist. That sense of comple-
tion—of comprehension, of chronology—is so stupefyingly satisfying
that Bear Family box sets always sit proud, positioned prominently in living rooms across America, destined to impress well-heeled visitors and ir-

ritate unsympathetic spouses. We hug them to our chests and growl at passersby.

Started in 1975, Bear Family is the brainchild of the former wine trader Richard Weize—the label's name is supposedly derived from an 1898 encyclopedia entry accompanied by an engraving of a female bear with two nuzzling cubs, an image reproduced on Bear Family CD faces—and, aside from being a weirdly apt encapsulation of Germany's unapologetic Americana fetish (Bobby Bare, Jr., told me that Germans often arrive at his shows dressed like cowboys, complete with hats, boots, and faux holsters), Bear Family Records is one of the most begrudgingly beloved reissue labels still operating. As Weize writes on the label's website, "I wanted to do it differently, based on our company credo: exclusive, LP-sized box sets, with extensive and well researched books containing rare pictures and ephemera, and a detailed and reliable discography. Every company calls its box sets 'collectors' editions,' but ours are truly the ultimate collectors' editions." Never has a company taken such pride in producing ridiculous products for economically irre- sponsible audiophiles.

Bear Family's collection of songs by country music forerunners the Carter Family, formally titled *The Carter Family: In the Shadow of Clinch Mountain*, weighs more than six pounds and is packaged in a perfect 12.5-inch-square box. The cover features a soft black-and-white photo of the vocalist A. P. Carter, his wife, Sara, whose hands rest gently on an Autoharp, and his sister-in-law, Maybelle, who is clutching a guitar. The trio's expressions are flat and quixotic, their thin lips curled into half smiles, half sneers. Inside, twelve CDs are stacked in groups of three, lay- ered neatly beneath an LP-size hardcover book authored by Charles Wolfe and featuring a handwritten introduction scrawled by Johnny Cash.

It is half past nine on a cloudless Thursday morning, and my Carter Family box is thrown open, splayed across the crumb-riddled rear passenger seat of my car; I periodically snake my neck over my right shoulder, clucking to myself and checking to make sure nothing is getting tossed around or scuffed up. While a six-and-a-half-pound CD box set is not the most practical thing to pack in one's suitcase, I am driving from Lexington, Kentucky, to Hiltons, Virginia, to see A. P. Carter's grave, and, like an autograph hound clutching a headshot and hovering nervously outside a stage door, it feels like the only appropriate thing to offer. Here, look, this is what you made. I carried it for three hundred miles. I can't imagine being here without it.

The stretch of Kentucky 15 that cuts through the eastern Appalachian Mountains from Lexington toward Bristol, Virginia, is a relatively narrow, two-lane, blue-line highway, relentlessly squiggling, jerking up and down over the foothills of the range. On maps, the Appalachians unroll southwesterly from Newfoundland, Canada, winding down, 1,500 miles later, in central Alabama, with foothills eeking into northeastern Mississippi and forming a natural barrier between the eastern seaboard and the Midwestern United States. The first time I see a full topographical map of the range, sliced into squares and scrupulously reassembled on a living room wall, I stop breathing. Notoriously impenetrable and marred by heavy forest growth, the Appalachians are dark, chilling, and massive. Centuries ago, the mountains famously halted British colonialists' westward expansion, trapping them, at least for a bit, in the coastal plains. I am sympathetic: when you see the Appalachians, you stop. And if you are smart, you turn around.

Despite the range's size, the cultural term *Appalachia* is applied only to the stretch of mountains blanketing rural Virginia, West Virginia, Kentucky, Tennessee, and North Carolina. This particular slice of the Appalachians is also hideously misunderstood by most Americans, enduring only as the tireless punch line for hillbilly jokes and incest digs, all corncob pipes, deviant sexuality, extra toes, and mental reenactments of key scenes from *Deliverance*. Even for relatively enlightened folks, the reigning iconography of Appalachia is an old white man with three teeth and a fiddle, crouched on a porch, square dancing around a giant jug emblazoned with a skull and crossbones. The pre-twentieth-century geographic isolation of the region may have led to loads of unshakable stereotypes, but it also bred a rich, multifaceted culture, steeped in song, self-sufficiency, and bone-deep faith. There is no other way to navigate this kind of land.

Along 15, the mountains are thick, unsolvable, and almost grotesquely overgrown, so coated with layers of green that it's hard to imagine anyone ever deciding it was a good idea to build a highway here. I squint out the window, taking inventory: modest single-family homes nudge up against rusting trailers, dilapidated cabins, burned-out cars, and broken-down school buses. My windshield yields a steady stream of one-story occupancies, punctuated only by mysterious backyard fires, gas stations, trampolines, above-ground pools, truck parts, liquor stores, tobacco outlets, and gated dirt roads with black and orange NO TRESPASSING signs. Tiny unpaved driveways, with names like 10 Mile Creek Road, Walton Mountain Lane, Grapevine Circle, Scuddy Bridge Road, and Holiday Place point uphill to well-concealed destinations. Periodically, bits of mining machinery pop up, sticking out from the earth, casting violent, prehistoric shadows.

In eastern Kentucky, coal is king. The Eastern Kentucky Coal Field (comprised of eighty individually named coal beds) rolls over nearly the entire eastern edge of the state, extending 10,500 miles from the Appalachians westward and encompassing thirty Kentucky counties from the Cumberland Plateau to the Pottsville Escarpment. This is the region's lone national industry; men sink into the earth and pull up lumps of glassy black rock, which are then pulverized and set on fire and used to run machines. It is mean, dirty work. Driving, today, I half-fear if it is the mountains' way of punishing us for the hubris of thinking we could unpack and thrive here.

There is something undeniably furtive, something cagey and secretive, about Appalachia's thickness and insularity. As Mark Zwonitzer and Charles Hirshberg write in their mesmerizing Carter Family biography *Will You Miss Me When I'm Gone?*, in Appalachia "every big valley rolls and folds into itself, forming valleys within valleys, haunts and hollows that can't be seen even from the highest perch in the county, on top of Clinch Mountain, 3,200 feet up." Appalachia is inherently obscured; the region's maze of peaks and dips conceal thousands of unspoken mysteries, treasures, ghosts. Appalachia, I decide, may be America's greatest living poem.

I wrap my hands tighter around the steering wheel, silently berating myself for feeling so spooked by the landscape. As a kid, I logged plenty of hours careening through the Hudson Highlands, eating Fig Newtons from my father's pockets, charging up Anthony's Nose, throwing pebbles at the Bear Mountain Bridge. But I've never seen mountains like these before, and when I finally stop feeling frightened by their scope, I can begin to appreciate their massive beauty. Appalachia's reticence may be unnerving to the uninitiated, but this particular slice of Appalachia is also truly stunning, all dense undergrowth, colossal green trees, and hills that go on forever.

Americans are conditioned to associate pretty landscapes with wealth, but sunsets don't buy groceries, and Appalachia's breathtaking geography does little to alleviate the basic problems of its inhabitants. According to 2002 U.S. census numbers, the median per capita income in Harlan County was $17,354, just 56 percent of the $30,906 national average for 2002. In neighboring Perry County, the median income was $20,926, or 68 percent of the national per capita income. As of 2000, Harlan County was declared 95.6 percent white, while Perry County counted off at 97.3 percent.

In the last two decades, ritual abuse of OxyContin and other prescription painkillers has scratched up and bled out eastern Kentucky, debilitating and paralyzing its citizens. Now, driving southeast toward the Virginia border, chugging past Hazard (the Perry County seat and subject of a 2001 *Newsweek* cover story titled, "How One Town Got Hooked"), it becomes difficult to tell which trailers are functional homes and which double as amateur drug labs. I'm equally struck by a gaping lack of adolescent distractions: strip malls, when they appear, are dilapidated and depressed, and none of the typical trappings of urban or suburban neighborhoods—three-level shopping malls, movie theaters, music venues, bowling alleys, record stores, baseball fields, dance studios—ever appear. The idea that, in lieu of viable options, the children of Harlan County might turn to recreational chemical abuse for entertainment is not particularly earth-shattering. They swallow fistfuls of pills because it is less boring and less scary than staring at the mountains all day.

According to the National Drug Intelligence Center, the number of oxycodone treatment admissions in Kentucky increased 163 percent between 1998 and 2000. Unsurprisingly, the mining industry is not innocent in Kentucky's big prescription problem. Miners are often required to spend hours hunched down, curling into harrowingly narrow mine shafts. Vials of painkillers are routinely dispensed by camp doctors in order to keep the miners functional. "Self-medicating became a way of life for miners," the NDIC report notes, "and this practice often led to abuse and addiction among individuals who would have been disinclined to abuse traditional illicit drugs." And even for those predisposed to recreational medicine, scoring those kinds of drugs (crack, cocaine, heroin, LSD) isn't particularly easy in rural Appalachia. In an interview with Lexington, Kentucky's *Ace Weekly* newspaper, Dr. Phil Fisher, director of the Appalachian Pain Foundation, explains: "This is an isolated area where it's hard for people to get real street drugs." Meanwhile, the *Newsweek* story is packed with tales of grandmothers hocking their prescriptions, of kids snorting and injecting the drug, gathering in parks for

"Oxy parties." Stories and statistics about exponential increases in domestic violence and burglaries are disturbingly plentiful. It is hard not to hurt for all of it.

Eventually, weeks after I leave Kentucky, I will become preoccupied with drug addiction in eastern Appalachia, sneaking peanut butter sandwiches into the New York Public Library and reading old newspaper articles, digging up magazine features, wincing and sighing and chewing my hair. In a 2005 piece broadcast on NPR's *Morning Edition*, Cheryl Corley reported on the opening of a series of public hearings administered by the Mine Safety and Health Administration, an agency of the U.S. Department of Labor, designed, supposedly, to thoroughly explore the drug and alcohol abuse committed by miners—although I suspect their investigation has less to do with quality of life and more to do with streamlining miners' efficiency underground. Armed with a microphone, Corley bravely records her descent into Hazard's Elkhorn Number 4, operated by Perry County Coal, detailing, over echoing pings and machine clanks, how confined spaces and huge, lumbering pieces of equipment leave very little room for human error. "The ceiling drops lower with every step," Corley notes, before observing a man sitting "on his haunches, pressing buttons on a small control box." The Kentucky Department for Natural Resources Mine Substance Abuse Task Force's final report, released in December 2005 (by the end of the year, twenty-two miners had been killed while working in the United States, eight in Kentucky), explains that while "it is not unreasonable to presume that the substance abuse problem in the mining population is at least reflective of the substance abuse problem within the community in which the miners reside," testimony still indicates "that drug dependency can develop from the legitimate use of prescribed painkillers." This particular cycle of abuse is not especially mysterious, but it is still tragic. If miners do not die while eyeballs-deep in coal, they seem destined for a life chopped up by chemical dependency.

In 1976, the director Barbara Kopple unveiled *Harlan County U.S.A.*, a stunning, Oscar-winning documentary film about the 1974 Eastover coal mining strike in Harlan. The film opens with footage of miners shooting down some kind of hideous human conveyor belt, hands first, helmet lights glaring at the camera, lunch pails tucked between their legs, climbing off and scurrying through ghastly, tiny tunnels, like ants in an ant farm. In go the miners, out comes the coal.

In May 2006, Criterion reissued the film on DVD, and Rounder Records released the accompanying soundtrack, which features classic mining songs performed by a variety of artists, from Norman Blake to Doc Watson to Merle Travis to Nimrod Workman, whose grizzly a cappella lament, "Coal Black Mining Blues," is one of the most impossibly heartbreaking songs I've ever heard, all clipped syllables and head-shaking fervor. Workman spent forty years in West Virginia mines, predictably contracting black lung, but, via some kind of tremendous, divine intervention, also managed to live to age ninety-nine. There is lots of spectacular singing in *Harlan County U.S.A.*, more singing than talking. Men and women employ their voices as weapons, chanting primordial fight songs, wonderfully unconcerned with whether or not they're on-key, or sound nice, or can follow a tune. Here, it is less about the sound, and more about the message and the act; they are chanting down gun thugs hired by the mining companies, singing for their lives. (Not long after I return to New York, five Kentucky miners are killed in an explosion at Darby Mine Number One, deep in Harlan County. Even though three of the miners initially survive the blast, they die, one by one, huffing poisoned air. A miner's widow tells *The New York Times*, "It makes me upset that he smothered to death." There is some minor media coverage, but it is mostly overshadowed by Kentucky Derby–victor Barbaro, a spectacular brown racehorse who injured his leg running, undefeated, in the Preakness Stakes. Folding up the newspaper and dropping it into the recycling bin, I listen to "Coal Black Mining Blues" and want to cry, for dead miners and fallen horses and all the other wild and impossible and horrifying things that Kentucky has thought up for us.)

Near Vicco, I pull over to a tiny roadside stand fronted by a tall, dirt-encrusted sign reading BANK'S DAIRY BAR. There is no one else around. I order a large soda and something called Corn Nuggets from a pleasant woman at the window. I am rewarded with a small wax paper envelope, stuffed with ten yellow-brown deep-fried chunks. I bite into one and uncover a sweet, gooey center, with whole kernels of corn swimming in some sort of honey-butter sauce; it is, I deduce, a ball of battered and fried creamed corn. They are crunchy, piping hot, and simultaneously the best and most disgusting things I've ever chewed on. I lick my fingers and watch a fire burn in the front yard of the big brown house across the street. Clouds trudge in and obscure the mountaintops. Everywhere I look is green.

Sipping my Coke, I continue tracking Kentucky 15 to Interstate 81 to Interstate 26, following the road until it ends and curling onto Highway 23, shooting north to Gate City and onto Alt-58/421, which snakes through some of southwestern Virginia's most spectacularly unspoiled countryside, all one-room Baptist and Pentecostal churches and lazy herds of cows. I am listening to Christian radio preach abstinence, shouting hard about the steadfast refusal to "give oneself physically" before marriage, and silently admiring stoic farmhouses and picturesque creek beds. I turn left onto Highway 709 in Hiltons, and swish onto A. P. Carter Highway, where the side roads begin to assume familiar names—Sunnyside, Weeping Willow. These are Carter songs.

The legendary folk guitarist John Fahey has described the Carter Family as sounding as if they were dead, their bodies coming out of the grave to sing the choruses like zombies. Today, switching off the car radio and sticking in disc one of the Bear Family set, which opens with 1927's "Bury Me Under the Weeping Willow," I hear what Fahey heard: there's an otherworldliness to the Family's flat, eerily expressionless harmonizing and quick rhythms. It is something half-devilish, half-serene, as if—just like the mountains that bore them—they are hiding all sorts of secrets. The Carter Family sound is organic and creepy and completely engrossing, rolled in dirt with twigs sticking out everywhere. These songs, sung this way, tangle themselves up in our subconscious, becoming part of our skeletons, spooning our DNA, settling in for good.

It has everything to do with where these songs came from, which, it turns out, cannot be established with any precision. The Carter patriarch A. P. Carter routinely pilfered and "fixed up" traditional Appalachian folk songs for the Carter Family repertoire, snatching rhythms and choruses, rewriting and reimagining ancient tracks. It sounds opportunistic and self-serving (and maybe even a little bit lazy) now, but by sneaking these songs under the Carter umbrella, A.P. made them functional and relevant. Unlike many traditional performers, the Carter Family succeeded because they ultimately learned, as Zwonitzer and Hirshberg explain, to "negotiate the gap between the insular culture of preindustrial Appalachia and the newly modern America." A.P. did so, mostly, by mining the mountains for honest, striking portraits of universal American strife, cleaning up the tunes, and reappropriating their essence for radio. Consequently, A.P. endures as one of American music's most prolific and important folklorists, having rescued (and, OK, inadvertently slapped his name on) dozens of songs that, presumably, would have otherwise disappeared.

As the late Joe Carter, one of A. P. and Sara Carter's three children, explains to the folklorist Kip Lornell: "Different people would have a song, or part of a song, and my dad would get a hold of it and finish it or whatever it needed, dress it up, polish it up, maybe even put a tune to it. A lot of the songs were old songs. They came from old country people who just kept singing them down through the years. They were just there for the taking, you might say." Or, as his daughter Janette describes, also to Lornell: "Usually when he went to collect he didn't take any instrument at all, he would just let them sing and get the tune in his head. If there was a verse or two, he would write that down on a paper. But mainly, first thing, you had to get the tune, if it had a tune. If it didn't have a tune, you'd get the words and make up a tune." From the beginning, Victor Recording Company's Ralph Peer, who eventually signed A.P. to his Southern Music Company, credited A.P. as the sole composer of the Carter Family's songs, even though chances are, most of the cuts were also legally credited to their original composers.

A. P. Carter was possessed by the acquisition of song, often ditching his growing family to roam Appalachia with his unlikely songcatching partner, Lesley Riddle, a perennially overlooked black singer and guitarist who frequently accompanied A.P. into the hills (and handed over at least twelve cuts from his very own songbook). Together, they trudged through fields and into homes, sniffing out rhythms, transcribing new tracks. Before the Family's professional dissolution in the early 1940s, A. P., Sara, and Maybelle Carter would successfully arrange, record, and preserve hundreds of Appalachian folk songs, perform countless live radio shows (including a long-running stint at the Mexico border station XERA), and earn the respect and adoration of loads of like-minded fans.

It has been almost one hundred years since A. P. Carter slunk off into the mountains, and musicians are still singing these folk songs the way the Carter Family sang them, because it is the only way they know how: they steal syntax and imagery and mountain rhythms, sneaking in tropes about railroads and mountain poverty and hoping that no one will notice. The single most triumphant thing about the Carter Family discography is how versatile its contents are, how you can play any disc for any person at any time and they will always leave humming its tunes. Good, functional folk songs are timeless: they're effortless to sing, imminently adaptable, and, if you listen hard enough, relevant to nearly every detail of American life, rural or otherwise. The Carter Family's material is comprised of real, proper folk songs, absorbed through the skin, howled around campfires, performed for children, whispered into pillows.

A. P. Carter was born on December 15, 1891, to Mollie Bays and

Robert Carter, in Poor Valley, Virginia (in an area now known as Hiltons), in a one-room log cabin burrowed deep into Scott County, the belly of Appalachia. Robert Carter was a notorious gossip, with little land or ambition; Mollie Bays was a tough, ferocious woman, determined to protect and provide for her family. As Zwonitzer and Hirshberg explain, Mollie, like all the women of Poor Valley, "had to be able to make corn bread, worm tobacco, teach her children Christian prayers, plow a straight row, put up kraut and beans for winter, sew a proper school dress, tan hides, keep a house clean and a cornfield free of weeds." Or, as the idiom goes: "A man's work is sun to sun, a woman's work is never done."

On all accounts, A.P. was a weird, shaky kid, struck with a palsy that left his head perpetually bobbing and his two hands stuck in constant motion. The tremble didn't stop with his fingers: A.P.'s tall, overstretched body coursed with a relentless, mysterious energy, rendering him incapable of sitting still for very long. Even his voice quavered, stuck in a now famous trill, twitching and jerking out of his mouth. Turning back to the mountains—seeking solace, like the ancient Greeks, in the life-altering potential of natural phenomena—Mollie believed that A.P.'s condition could be easily chalked up to a storm that blew through during her pregnancy: while gathering apples, a fruit tree Mollie crouched under was snapped in half by lightning, shooting a line of flame all around her, and, ostensibly, scaring the shit out of her unborn child. Supposedly, A.P. never recovered from the fright.

A.P.'s voice earned him notice in church, and he was promptly plucked from the pews and declared the newest member of Mt. Vernon United Methodist Church's illustrious quartet. Still, despite all that talent, singing wasn't a particularly viable way for a young man to make cash. In 1911, a twenty-year-old A.P. headed off to Richmond, Indiana, taking a carpentry job for the railroad company; unfortunately, he returned shortly thereafter, struck with typhoid and a wicked case of homesickness. In 1914, working as a salesman for the Larkey nursery, selling fruit trees and flowers, A.P. met sixteen-year-old Sara Dougherty and heard her sing for the very first time. He was instantly smitten with her smooth, lilting voice. On June 18, 1915, they were married, and by 1925, they were performing music together.

In March 1926, A.P.'s younger brother, Ezra, married Maybelle Addington, a native of Midway, Virginia, and the daughter of a farmer-cum-moonshiner. Maybelle was a tremendous guitar player, mysteriously capable of picking out both a song's chords and its melody at the very same time. Her technique was so seamless that when she played, it sounded more like two separate musicians, strumming in perfect unison. As Maybelle explains, "I started trying different ways to pick it up, and came up with my own style, because there weren't many guitar players around. I just played the way I wanted to and that's it." (Her unmistakable style would later be known as the Carter scratch.) Soon, A.P., Sara, and Maybelle began playing together, and on July 31, 1927, A.P. dragged his eight-months-pregnant wife and sister-in-law twenty-six grueling miles to Bristol (a border city straddling Tennessee and Virginia) to participate in Ralph Peer's now famous Bristol Sessions.

Peer, under contract with Victor Records, had placed an ad in the local Bristol newspaper, announcing that Victor would be bringing a recording machine to Bristol for ten days, and that Peer was looking for local talent, promising fifty dollars a song. It took A.P., Sara, and Maybelle an entire day to make it down the mountain and into town. The Carters, dressed in their very best Sunday outfits, recorded an impressive six songs for Peer. They returned to Poor Valley triumphant, each gripping a wad of cash. Peer was impressed by the Carters, but was also concerned that a woman, Sara, was carrying the lead vocals.

Initially, Victor passed on the Carters, and in October 1927, released records by eleven different artists culled from the Bristol Sessions, including songs by the Mississippi-born "blue yodeler" Jimmie Rodgers, whom many consider the first country star. But Peer changed his mind, and in November a double-sided 78 of two Carter tracks ("Poor Orphan Child" / "Wandering Boy") landed in stores, followed, in early 1928, by another ("The Storms Are on the Ocean" / "Single Girl, Married Girl"). The latter sold and sold and sold. As Janette wrote in her memoir, *Living with Memories*, "No wonder the Carter Family was a success! Mother could sing like a lark. Daddy with his unusual bass voice could sing high or low—his range was unbelievable! And Aunt Maybelle, with those small, lovely hands all over a guitar, could bring out music no one else could ever master or believe."

Ralph Peer wanted the Carter Family in New Jersey by May, to record new songs at a proper Victor recording studio. By this time, hill-billy music, marketed and performed by rural people, and pitched along by the success of several hillbilly groups—anchored by Jimmie Rodgers's ever-swelling popularity, as well as that of the notorious banjo master Charlie Poole, whose North Carolina Ramblers had begun releasing 78s for Columbia Records' black label—was proving itself a viable commercial medium. Urban audiences were romanced by the notion of the big-footed, overall-wearing backwoods yelper, a mostly inaccurate caricature of Appalachian culture that record executives, including Ralph Peer, eagerly helped establish and perpetuate. The Carter Family became a sudden and unexpected commodity.

There's something eerily prescient about the way Sara sings the Family's first hit, "Single Girl, Married Girl," a defeated, protofeminist reflection on couplehood. Maybelle strums encouragingly, while Sara's voice stays heavy with resignation: "Single Girl, Married Girl" is a bleak portrait of marriage, a swan song for a woman's relinquished freedom. As neatly detailed in the 2005 PBS documentary *The Carter Family: Will the Circle Be Unbroken?*, Sara Carter wasn't particularly passionate about her husband's lofty musical pursuits, and understood music—both hers and her family's—as little more than a simple and convenient means for providing for her children. Unsurprisingly, Sara's relationship with A.P. floundered as he grew increasingly infatuated with his budding career, combing the hills for new songs and pounding out arrangements, while Sara was saddled with the couple's domestic responsibilities. Slowly, their marriage began to dissolve.

In 1931, A.P. solicited his twenty-six-year-old cousin, Coy Bays, to escort Sara around the valley, presumably to alleviate the strains of A.P.'s emotional and physical absence. As these things tend to go, Coy and Sara fell in love. When their affair became uncomfortably obvious to the rest of the Carter family, Coy began packing his things for a trip out west. By February 1933, Coy was banished from Clinch Mountain, and, weeks later, Sara left Poor Valley for her birth home on the other side of the mountain. As Zwonitzer and Hirshberg contemplate, Sara's flight may have been a result of frustration over her violent separation from Coy, embarrassment over her now quite public affair, or a fear of repercussion from A.P. (Sara would later testify that A.P. had threatened her with physical violence). In the decade following, the Carter Family's popularity continued to swell, and A.P. and Sara established a taut working relationship, despite the fact that their divorce was finalized in 1938. As Janette writes, "Music meant my mother and daddy together. When there was music and singing there was no quarreling. I felt that through music, I was surrounded by love."

In 1939, after Coy heard Sara dedicate a song to him on the radio, they found each other again, as lovers tend to do, and married. The Carter Family officially disbanded when Sara left Poor Valley and moved to California, in 1942, to begin a new life with Coy. Maybelle continued to perform, often with her children, and A.P. retreated to Clinch Mountain, opening a general store.

Contemporary Hiltons, as far as I can tell, consists of a Shell station, a thrift shop, and a few little stores tucked into a roadside plaza. I roll past the Carter Family Fold, A. P. Carter's cabin, and the Carter General Store, chugging up toward Mt. Vernon United Methodist Church. Eventually, I spot a white plastic sign. Rectangular and weathered, the sign features a blue stripe and two white crosses, each accented by a tiny wisp of red. This is Mt. Vernon. The phrase HE IS ALIVE is posted in black block letters, announced plainly, impassively, like a movie marquee or a supermarket special. On the post, below the general information (est. 1906) and hours of service (Sunday worship at 9:45 a.m., Sunday school at 10:45 a.m.), I can see where the former pastor's name has been painted over with thin white paint, and the name of the current pastor, Randy Powers, has been carefully added, in diminutive black letters. I pull up a steep hill and park behind the church, where the cemetery unfolds, a mesmerizing patchwork of green lawn and gray stone. A man on a tractor is cutting the lawn around the gravestones, and waves. The smell of freshly sliced grass and mountain air is weirdly dizzying. I totter, temporarily drunk on Appalachia's ubiquitous and holy triumvirate: a cloud-free sky, thick, green trees, and a small white church glowing in the distance. The tractor disappears, and I am all alone. I gnaw my fingernails and zip up my sweatshirt.

A. P. Carter's headstone is fashioned out of hard, salmon-colored stone and stretches nearly three feet wide and two feet tall. There is a gold-colored phonograph record centered in the middle of the monument, with the words KEEP ON THE SUNNY SIDE engraved across the top. A few handfuls of music notes decorate each side of the monument, falling from staffs on the top corners to identical staffs below, drifting gently from song to song. Fragrant bits of severed grass gather in the crevices and along the highest ridge, twisting into a little green garland. The only other text reads A. P. CARTER / DEC. 15, 1891 / NOV. 7, 1960. Staring at the dates, I remember reading about how when A. P. Carter died, the local newspaper, the *Scott County News*, didn't even run an obituary. By 1960, A.P. was a mostly forgotten footnote, cherished only by country purists and historians. "They broke up, you know," Janette re-counts. "Maybelle and her children went their way, and Daddy didn't have anyone to help him much; he was just by hisself," she tells Lornell, her voice strong and perplexingly even. "My mother was living in Cali-fornia. And he just sort of slowed down there for a while."

I can't see or smell anything other than grass. Tipsy, I totter between the lines of graves, counting Carters: Etta, Robert and Mollie, Mattie Lee, James, Vangie, J.W., Jeffrey, Joe, three infants. I'm not sure how much time passes before I finally pull away from Mt. Vernon.

The Carter Family Fold is about half a mile back down the moun-tain, just past A.P.'s cabin and the General Store. In 1974, Janette Carter established the Fold to honor the memory of her parents and Maybelle; following Janette's death in January 2006, her son and daughter, Dale and Rita, dedicated themselves to preserving their mother's mission and their grandparents' legacy. Every Saturday night, musicians gather on its rickety stage to play old-time country, and bluegrass. Neither alcohol nor electric instruments are allowed; homemade snacks are served at the Carter Fold Snack Bar. I pull my car over and park in the dirt. The Fold isn't open any day except for Saturday, but construction crews working on the site have left the side door ajar. I'm not sure if I am allowed inside. Eyes darting, I wipe my feet on the mat, step over a bowl of dry cat food, and tiptoe through the doorway.

Sneaking past concert posters for early Carter performances and try-ing to make as little noise as possible, I creep into the auditorium. The moderate-size stage is decorated to resemble a living room, complete with wood-paneled walls, a big, brown, overstuffed couch, a potted plant, bookshelves, and dozens of framed photographs, including several shots of the Fold's most famous guest player, Johnny Cash. I sink into the couch and touch the waxy leaves of the plant. There is a wooden bench and a small piano and big portraits of Maybelle, Sara, and A.P. on the wall. Nubby brown carpet covers the stage floor, and a small picket fence separates the stage—which is low, barely a foot high—from the floor. Microphones are clustered in the center. I wander out into the audience, where fold-down chairs sit on a slight incline. They are numbered, marked with little silver-colored plaques. I sit there until I hear voices, at which point I sprint to the door, my empty seat thwapping back up, hard and conspicuous, echoing everywhere.

A. P. Carter's tiny log cabin is next door to the Fold. Outside, I shuffle through gooey Virginia mud and climb onto the porch, running my hands across an old wooden desk chair with chipping blue paint, eyeing the soft white curtains hanging in the window. The cabin was publicly dedicated in 2004, but it still isn't open to visitors. First constructed in the mid-1800s in Poor Valley, this scrawny brown cabin, which the Commonwealth of Virginia long ago declared a national and state landmark, was unreachable in its original location. Consequently, in 2002, in order to remain on the historic register, the cabin was dissembled and moved, offered up to the public as a gift. According to the Carter Family Fold's official website, "The restoration consisted of a costly and time-consuming procedure involving professional preservationists, archeologists, as well as craftsmen, carpenters, and historians. The cabin had to be taken apart meticulously board by board, brick by brick, moved, restored, and in the case of some items, replaced, and then rebuilt. Nothing but the most loving care on the part of everyone involved was given to the tremendously complicated project."

Janette's death marked the official end of the immediate Carter line, but plenty of historians have worked tirelessly to preserve their legacy, properly acknowledging the family's unmistakable role in saving and furthering American music. There are spectacular books and papers and magazine articles. There are tribute albums and PBS specials. There is the Bristol Birthplace of Country Music Alliance Museum and gift shop, which has several of the Carters' instruments and is located, perversely, on the lower level of the Bristol Mall, sandwiched between the Sears and the JCPenney. We are trying our best to remember.

A few yards from the cabin is the Carter General Store, where A.P. worked during the last fifteen years of his life. It's bigger than I imagined it would be, with a considerable porch and lots of peeling white paint. There is a little wooden sign hanging on the door that reads CLOSE in crooked red letters. A bouquet of pink plastic flowers has been arranged and nailed to a board alongside letters that spell out WELCOME. The construction workers have retreated to a cement-mixing truck across the street, and there is no one else around. I press my face to the dirty windows, straining to see into the dark space. Resigned, I sit on the porch steps. I hum to myself.

The Little Old Country General Store from Lebanon, Tennessee:

Cracker Barrel's Americana

Chewing my lips, I dump out a cup of pegs and start again, jamming gnawed plastic plugs into little, sticky holes. Shoulders arched and mug raised, I gulp coffee without glancing away from the board. I wipe my lips with the back of my hand. Last round, I was stranded with two pegs at the end, a showing that officially—though vaguely mockingly—rendered me "Purty Darn Smart." The Cracker Barrel peg game—known more officially as peg solitaire—is maybe the stupidest and most annoying sporting endeavor in the universe. I have sloshed coffee all over the front of my white tank top; the newspaper I brought in from the car sits, neatly folded and unread. And still: I cannot stop playing.

Before I can initiate a seventh attempt, a waitress smiles and lays down my breakfast plate: the Old Timer's Breakfast, which consists of two fried eggs, grits, Sawmill gravy, buttermilk biscuits with butter and preserves, hash brown casserole, and bacon. Most of the Cracker Barrel breakfast menu, and especially the section labeled Traditional Favorites, presents some sort of permutation on this particular lineup. Cracker Barrel is hardly slinging sophisticated cuisine—the restaurant deliberately eschews fancy-pants food styling or complicated recipes, apropos of its image and its demographic—but a Cracker Barrel breakfast is still impossibly enticing, all shiny, lulling fats, mass-produced carbohydrates and mild, soothing flavors. I don't care if it's sort of gross. It's also sort of delicious.

Unsurprisingly, Cracker Barrel is not particularly forthcoming with specific nutrition information about its meals, instead offering small, charming consolations on its website: Oatmeal is available on the menu. Sugar-free maple syrup is available. Decaffeinated Hot Tea and Coffee are available as additional beverages. Boiled Chicken Tenders are not printed on the menu, but are available upon request. No Sugar Added Apple Pie and No Sugar Added Vanilla Ice Cream are available. Sloppily buttering a biscuit, dipping half into a viscous puddle of bright yellow yolk, and stuffing it in my mouth, I admire the effort.

The clientele at this particular restaurant, where I've stopped en route from Hiltons, Virginia, to Washington, D.C., are, as far as I can tell, almost all above the age of sixty-five, and they hobble from table to table, gregarious and energized, greeting friends and inquiring about the quality of the food. Most diners are either incredibly thin or deliriously plump, and everyone is scarfing with gusto, cramming pancakes and sausage links into open mouths, swallowing and forking and nodding along to conversations in progress.

Despite popping up in forty-one different states (as of 2008, there are more than five hundred locations nationwide), Cracker Barrel is a predominantly southern and Midwestern phenomenon—there are only three Cracker Barrels within fifty miles of New York City, the closest being in Mt. Arlington, New Jersey. Likewise, there are no restaurants on the West Coast, and very few in New England. Florida, meanwhile, has fifty-five stores; Tennessee has forty-nine. In these regions, Cracker Barrel is known, mostly, as a roadside attraction. The restaurant advertises heavily on highways, with brown and yellow billboards gently suggesting motorists pause their journeys to EAT. SHOP. RELAX. Cracker Barrel acknowledges and facilitates their off-ramp steez: if you plug your origin and destination into the company's website, a program spews out directions that conveniently coincide with Cracker Barrel locations. Cracker Barrel also offers up a Books on Tape quasi-rental plan, wherein diners purchase a title at one Cracker Barrel, return it at the next Cracker Barrel, and are immediately refunded their purchase price (minus $3.49 per week of ownership).

Each Cracker Barrel restaurant is attached to an "old-fashioned" country store, which sells country music CDs, John Deere T-shirts, peppermint sticks, tin lunch boxes, old-fashioned candy bars (Valomilk, Sky Bar) and contemporary candy bars in old-fashioned packaging (Reese's peanut butter cups, Hershey's), Crayola crayons, scented candles, and a variety of objects festooned with woodland creatures. The general store is an essential bit of the Cracker Barrel experience (you have to meander through the store to get to the dining room, and stand in line at the store counter to pay your bill), and has been an integral part of the design since the chain's inception on September 19, 1969, when Dan Evins, a gasoline salesman from the tiny town of Lebanon, Tennessee, decided fast food offered inadequate respite from the newfound trials of interstate travel. According to Cracker Barrel's official history, "Dan began to think about all the things that would make him feel comfortable if he was far from home. Things like big jars of candy and homemade jellies. Potbellied stoves. Folks that let you take your time. Simple, honest country food. And a store where you could buy someone a gift that was actually worth buying." The original Cracker Barrel was erected on the outskirts of Lebanon; by 1977 there were thirteen stores, scattered from Tennessee to Georgia. The original stores sold gasoline as well as provisions and meals.

The company's history is written in cute, guileless, and unpretentious prose, riddled with words like *folks* and *cookin'*. Today, resalting my eggs, I survey the restaurant walls, which are haphazardly plastered with semirandom bits of Americana: old tin signs, farming equipment, fiddles, photos, flour sacks, egg beaters, coffee grinders, picnic baskets, fishing poles. Handmade, mostly obsolete artifacts from an American culture that doesn't really exist anymore, artfully rusted and hung from nails. Despite being both highly specific (everything is hand-cranked) and curiously vague (there's no particular time period suggested or evoked), the down-home, aw-shucks iconography of these walls is what most people conjure when confronted with the notion of "Americana."

For me, Cracker Barrel's collection is somehow both highly stylized and weirdly comforting, despite the plain fact that I've never before seen—let alone used or acquired fond memories of—a manual coffee grinder. *Americana*, employed as a marketing term, is more about evoking a fuzzy, formless warmth—think whole families pumping an ice cream maker on a wooden front porch and dreaming of strawberry sundaes, daughters balancing aprons full of berries, sons lugging over glass bottles of fresh cream, mothers and grandmothers tsk-ing and churning and shucking peas for supper—than any particular set of ideals or beliefs. We are buying into the artifacts of activities and emotions most of us have never experienced firsthand. These objects (cast-iron skillets, lard presses, butter churns), and not memories or facts, are the greatest players in the classic Americana myth.

Because I am innately suspicious of corporations, and because this particular design scheme is so ubiquitous (see the interiors of nearly all American-theme chain restaurants) and, I think, manipulative—I automatically dismiss the "antiques" draped over and around my breakfast as mass-produced reproductions, cranked out in factories staffed by underpaid workers, relentlessly prototyped and hand-selected by marketing committees, focus-grouped and standardized, boxed up, and sent along to new locations with a map and a hammer. But it turns out I'm totally wrong. All of the decorations featured in Cracker Barrel restaurants are actual antiques, hand-picked by a man named Larry Singleton, who took over the country store–décor business from his parents, Lebanon natives who were close friends of Dan Evins, in 1981.

When I first speak to Larry Singleton on the telephone, long after I've licked my plate clean, stopped in Washington, and chugged back up the interstate to New York, I'm simultaneously disarmed by his thick, almost impenetrable Tennessee accent and his tendency to actually use words like *folks* and *cookin'* in everyday conversation. Singleton is sweet and forthcoming, describing the company's beginnings casually and without pomp: "Part of [Dan's] family was in the gasoline distributorship—they sold Shell gasoline. And when he was young, he was always stopping at little country stores, little stations. It created an image for him; it made a neat connection. The interstates were just coming through this area in '69; they were just finishing the interstate between Nashville and Knoxville, and he was looking for an idea to sell gasoline on the interstate. My parents were in the antique business, and they bounced around the idea of an old country store with him. And they came up with ideas of what it should look like. [Dan and his investors] were considering moving a little old country store from an area east of here. They ended up just constructing one locally, and [Dan] asked my mom and dad to decorate the first one."

Singleton has spent the last twenty-five years combing through antique stores, hand-selecting pieces for Cracker Barrel's interiors. "We're still digging around and going to flea markets. We've done just about every way you can think. It started off with flea markets and antique shows. We bought lots and lots of stuff, and what that did is help us meet a lot of great dealers, and they would go to auctions and get pickers bringing stuff to them."

Every Cracker Barrel interior is different, although certain pieces pop up over and over again. Unsurprisingly, Singleton treats all his finds with an unpretentious, laid-back reverence. "We've got a store down in

Nashville, close to Opryland, that's got an old handmade tapestry of George Washington, framed. It's one my mom bought, thirty-five years ago. It's four feet tall by five feet wide, and you think about the ladies that did this in 1870, 1880—all the work! It's in a frame, and it was wired in a way that works like a security system. Someone thought to put a security system on it." Singleton giggles, delighted by good old-fashioned antitheft ingenuity. For the most part, Singleton doesn't over-think his work or spend too much time dicing apart different ideas about Americana. He knows it when he sees it.

"To me, it creates a connection to people, with memories," Single-ton says of his decorations. "It's hard to explain at times. People see things that they had or their parents or grandparents had and it really grabs folks. The things that we grew up with, the things we had when we were kids. They're not always made in America. A lot of the cast-iron or tin toys, the dolls, the marbles, the things that kids played with, they weren't made here. But they're part of our history. Home-grown, handmade. Those are the thoughts I think of when I think of Americana."

Even though I'm still vaguely wary, on both gastronomic and ideo-logical levels, of Cracker Barrel's tricky nostalgia trade, I am thoroughly charmed by Larry Singleton, who appears genuinely interested in mak-ing people feel at ease. For Singleton, Americana is synonymous with comfort, and the objects he chooses to fasten to the walls of Cracker Bar-rel restaurants are intended only to remind patrons of different, less com-plicated times. Singleton is peddling earnestness, industriousness, and faith, trying his hardest to "remind" us of a time when life was less vir-tual; the fact that our memories of these objects and eras are entirely fab-ricated has little to do with his endgame. Even if we've never baked our own bread or churned our own butter—even if we're deeply skeptical that "simpler times" have ever really existed for human beings on planet Earth—we still understand, immediately, what these tools are meant to represent.

Interestingly, Singleton's mission is not unfamiliar to Americana music purists, many of whom continue to believe that acoustic guitars and banjos are more authentic, more useful, and more uplifting than synthesizers and laptops. But applying these kinds of nostalgic ideas to art is more complicated than applying them to dining rooms. Because art that is unable to adapt to new landscapes is art that is not moving.

A Matter of Song!

John Lomax, Lead Belly, Moses Asch, and Folkways Records

Darting past cardboard boxes and heavy industrial shelving, I chase the Folkways archivist Jeff Place through the record label's main recording library, deep inside a Smithsonian-owned office building in northwest Washington, D.C. "It's like an archaeological dig. I'm in the process of organizing stuff. You try to attack the entire wall of tapes and recordings, but it's too daunting—you can't deal with it that way. You have to attack one thing at a time. You attack chunks. I end up being the head archaeologist on these digs, and then I publish my findings," Place explains, scratching his face. Place has shoulder-length brown hair and a thick, bushy beard; he reminds me of a better-looking, more cogent version of Jeff Bridges's Dude in the Coen Brothers film *The Big Lebowski*. "Even if you had ten lifetimes, you could never get close to touching what's in this room," Place continues. "I see my role as the gatekeeper. I know what's on that wall, I know what the radio guys call 'deep cuts.' I can take this stuff and put it on CDs and turn people on to artists that they don't know about." He smiles a little. I stare at a wall of movable metal shelving, the sort found in academic libraries, sliding back and forth on hydraulics, filling students' minds with grim notions of imminent, crushing demise. There is more music here than I can process. I understand how Place might be overwhelmed by his job.

Place heaves a cardboard box off a shelf and starts pulling out papers. He holds up a crinkled piece of notebook paper with handwritten lyrics. "Woody Guthrie." He grins. He goes back into the box and reemerges with an oil painting of a man who looks like Abe Lincoln. Guthrie has signed his name in the corner.

Folkways Recordings, which was started by Moses Asch and his assistant Marian Distler in 1948 and acquired by the government-funded Smithsonian Institution in 1987, currently releases 20 to 25 CDs each year, containing what Asch called "people's music," and what the Smithsonian interprets, broadly, as "spoken word, instruction, and sounds from around the world." Before Asch's death in 1986, Folkways released 2,186 records, ranging from instructional recordings to sounds of the natural world to traditional folk songs, culled from America and beyond. In the 1950s, among the tumult of the Red Scare and the squint of McCarthyism, Folkways established itself as one of America's premier independent record labels, the first thoroughly dedicated to documenting and preserving American folk songs, and the home to loads of influential (and often politically charged) American musicians. The label released records by Woody Guthrie, Doc Watson, Pete Seeger, Lead Belly, Ella Jenkins, and more; Folkways also protected and released traditional folk music from other cultures, becoming one of the first "world music" labels, and encouraged and nurtured new, experimental forms, including the work of the legendary avant-garde composer John Cage. Folkways is arguably the world's first socially and historically vital record company, and—as Jeff Place's song-littered work space demonstrates so vividly—its legacy is astounding.

The Folkways legend is, appropriately, a global one, reflecting the tangled ambitions of three white men—Moe Asch, John Lomax, and

Harry Smith—each preoccupied, in different ways, with preserving traditional American folk songs. Without their concerted efforts, our contemporary understanding of American folk music would be significantly less rich.

Moses Asch was born in Warsaw, Poland, in 1905, to the Yiddish writer and intellectual Sholem Asch and his wife, Matilda Spiro. Justly incensed by Poland's treatment of Jews, Sholem and his family ditched the country in 1912, leaving Moe to split his childhood between Paris and New York City. The second of four children, Asch distinguished himself by a burgeoning interest in radio technology; by the end of World War I, army surplus radio parts were plentiful, and Asch would cobble together his own radios from various scrap parts snagged in Lower Manhattan shops. Eventually Asch left New York to study electronics in Germany, returning to Brooklyn's Pineapple Street in 1925 and scoring a short-lived job with RCA. Despite having been told that engineering was "no place for a Jew," Asch was directed to catalog all the parts of RCA's first radios, called Radiolas. Asch eventually left RCA, took a job at a radio shop, and on March 18, 1928, married Frances Ungar, the child of Jewish immigrants. According to Peter Goldsmith, Asch's biographer, the very first piece of furniture the young couple lugged into their new President Street apartment was a phonograph. And in 1930, Asch opened his own store, Radio Laboratories, on Driggs Avenue in Brooklyn.

Asch continued piddling around with wires and circuits, developing a magnetic guitar pickup, and eventually partnering up with the former hillbilly musician Lester Polfus, known then as Rhubarb Red, and later as Les Paul. Radio Laboratories cranked out an amplifier that could accommodate both AC and DC currents, and eventually sold twenty-five to the Gibson guitar company, which fettered them out to musicians eager to plug in at hotels and clubs with nonstandard power sources. In 1938, WEVD, a liberal noncommercial radio station (underwritten by *The Jewish Daily Forward*, a well-respected, mass-circulation Yiddish paper), hired Asch and Radio Laboratories to build a new transmitter. Once the transmitter was complete, WEVD asked Asch to stay on as a recording engineer, where he fulfilled the station's growing need for Jewish music, cutting discs in-house for airplay. Despite being located in the WEVD building, Asch's studio remained independent from the radio station, and Asch christened it Asch Recording Studios, declaring his company "the only organization that is active in the Jewish phonograph record field."

Soon, Albert Einstein, who had recorded several programs about the ever-increasing threat to Jews in Europe, invited Asch and his father to his home in Princeton, New Jersey. Asch remembers telling Einstein that he had an idea for, as the biographer Peter Goldsmith chronicles, "recording the authentic sounds of the world's people and making it available to the public."

Long before Asch conceived of his record label, nascent folklorists and entrepreneurial musicians (see A. P. Carter) were coming up with new ways to preserve, study, and perpetuate folk songs. In 1907, John Lomax, a University of Texas graduate and a master's candidate at Harvard, fulfilled a regional literature assignment by offering his professor, Barrett Wendall, sheets of lyrics to ancient cowboy songs and frontier ballads— words Lomax had been collecting since his boyhood in rural Bosque County, Texas. Wendall, along with his colleague, the Shakespearean scholar George Lyman Kittredge, encouraged Lomax's scavenging, figuring Lomax could make sizable contributions to the still-burgeoning field of folklore studies. Lomax composed and mailed a letter, endorsed by both Wendall and Kittredge, to a thousand newspaper editors in the American west; in it, Lomax asked the editors to implore their readers to send in lyrics to native ballads. Around the same time, Wendall and Kittredge also helped Lomax secure funding for his first bout of fieldwork, and Lomax ventured into the American wilds, aiming to collect as many old songs as possible.

Despite his considerable collegiate backing, Lomax was eager to eschew the academic trappings of folklore studies, which traditionally focused on lyrics, ignoring or dismissing both the musical and social context of the songs. As Goldsmith notes, "The collection of oral ballads—indeed folklore as a whole—was at that time a quaint appendage to the study of 'great' literature, occasionally useful for the light it shed on the process of literary creation and dissemination." But Lomax wasn't terribly interested in song-as-staid-artifact, taking trouble to transcribe musical notation for as many ballads as he could, so that they would be read as they were sung. Eventually, Lomax secured the backing of President Theodore Roosevelt, who wrote an endorsement of Lomax's first book, 1910's *Cowboy Songs and Other Frontier Ballads.* Asch would later cite *Cowboy Songs* (and President Roosevelt's introduction) as confirming, for him, the artistic and cultural validity of American folk music.

Along with the University of Texas professor Leonidas Payne, Lomax founded the Texas Folklore Society in 1909 with the mission of gathering a significant body of folklore—for future analysis and study—before it was eradicated. Soon after, Lomax accepted an administrative job at the University of Texas; in 1917, Lomax, along with six other faculty members, was fired as a result of a political scrap between the Texas governor, James Ferguson, and the university president, Dr. R. E. Vinson. Distressed and disappointed, Lomax abandoned his song hunting, moved to Chicago, and, like so many dejected artists, took a job in another, less creative field—in this case, banking. But in June 1932, spurred by the death of his father, Lomax pitched a book to New York's Macmillan Publishing Company, proposing an all-inclusive anthology of American ballads and folk songs. Lomax's proposal was accepted, and he traveled to Washington, D.C., eager to browse the holdings in the Archive of American Folk Song, which had been founded for the Library of Congress just four years earlier.

Lomax managed to work out a deal with the library, borrowing equipment and blank discs in exchange for returning with new recordings, which were then incorporated into the archive. Over the next ten years, Lomax would work closely with the library; in 1933, after scoring a grant from the American Council of Learned Societies, Lomax took on song hunting full-time, employing the library's resources and bringing along his eighteen-year-old son, Alan (who ultimately became the archive's first paid employee, enjoying the title Assistant in Charge). For their first official field trip, Alan and John swept through Texas prisons, capturing work songs, ballads, and blues. In the Library of Congress Music Division's 1933 annual report, Lomax described his interest in prisons as places where, "thrown on their own resources for entertainment, [prisoners] still sing, especially the long-term prisoners who have been confined for years and who have not yet been influenced by jazz and the radio, the distinctive old-time Negro melodies." In July 1933, Lomax installed a 315-pound acetate disc recorder in the trunk of his Ford sedan, pulled up to the Louisiana State Penitentiary in Angola, Louisiana, and recorded a black twelve-string-guitar player named Huddie Ledbetter, imprisoned for attempted homicide (and convicted, in his home state of Texas, of murder), and known to his fellow inmates as Lead Belly.

The Lomaxes were entranced by Lead Belly's playful, lilting voice, which sounded strong, solid, and, occasionally, a bit menacing—much like Ledbetter himself, who, despite his charm and talent, still remained a ward of the state of Louisiana.

In 1934, Lead Belly was officially pardoned and released from prison. The exact details of his departure remain ambiguous: some continue to claim that John and Alan Lomax lobbied the Louisiana governor, O. K. Allen, for his early release, their "petition" consisting of a disc with two songs—Ledbetter's famous rendition of "Goodnight, Irene" and a specially crafted B-side, appropriately titled "Governor O. K. Allen." Lomax later wrote, with vague detachment, "Through a twist of circumstances, just a month after our second visit to Angola, Lead Belly was set free." In 1935, Lead Belly confirmed that he recorded a song specifically for Governor Allen (and appeared to believe it was his golden ticket out), but in 1939, the Angola warden, L. A. Jones, wrote, in response to a query from the New York Department of Probation, that the singing-for-a-pardon tale had "no foundation in fact. He received no clemency, and his discharge was a routine matter under the good law which applies to all first and second offenders." Regardless of how Ledbetter actually got out of jail, the notion that Lomax was Ledbetter's "savior"—and that a white man could still effectively bargain for a black man's life—became widespread. Later that year, the folklorist Lawrence Gellert wrote, in *New Masses*: "[Lomax] could go straight to the Governor of Louisiana with a phonograph record by Leadbelly—and presto—a pardon! Between gentlemen—a 'nigger's' lifetime—a matter of song!"

After his release, Lead Belly followed the Lomaxes back to Texas, where he was given the questionable job of driving their car and operating their recording equipment (the racial dynamics of this particular appointment have never really helped ease concern about John Lomax's agenda, although some sources claim that it was Lead Belly who first approached Lomax about the gig). Meanwhile, John Lomax took to "promoting" Lead Belly, parading him around universities (supposedly, Lead Belly's lurid past—A black murderer! Singing songs!—was destined to play especially well to mostly white, academic audiences). Lead Belly, John, and Alan Lomax eventually settled into a house in Wilton, Connecticut; shortly thereafter, Lead Belly married Martha Promise, whom he had known since he was twelve years old. Word of Lead Belly's music had spread, and by 1934, Huddie Ledbetter was already a celebrity of sorts in New York City.

In January 1935, Lead Belly recorded six country-blues songs—his first commercial recordings—for the American Record Company, which released the tracks on the Perfect and Melotone labels. Meanwhile, the Lomaxes continued strutting Lead Belly around New England, now swathing him in "prison garb" (to be fair, white hillbilly performers were just as often encouraged to wear rural costumes, including ridiculous, too-short pants and overalls). Still, Lead Belly's questionably symbiotic relationship with John Lomax eventually soured, although he continued to communicate with Alan. According to Goldsmith, Lead Belly accused John Lomax of sensationalizing his image and refusing to pay proper royalties, while Lomax grew frustrated with Lead Belly's inability to be effectively managed. As Joe Klein writes, in *Woody Guthrie: A Life*, "[Lead Belly] left the elder Lomax after a year, chafing under his white paternalism, wanting to control his own money, and tired of having to wear his convict clothes 'for exhibition purposes,' as John Lomax put it."

Lead Belly's personal songbook—tracks culled mostly from traditional sources, and occasionally rearranged or, more accurately, re-remembered—was, in many ways, more influential than his musicianship, eventually providing fodder for lots of other folks' cash-making. "Goodnight, Irene" was famously covered by Pete Seeger's Weavers in 1950, Eric Burdon and the Animals claimed "House of the Rising Sun" in 1964, Creedence Clearwater Revival recorded "Midnight Special" in 1969, and in 1994, Nirvana took on the chilling "Where Did You Sleep Last Night?" for their much-celebrated *MTV Unplugged* session. All those covers make what happened to Lead Belly's priceless copyrights especially disconcerting.

In the United States, songwriters retain the rights to their work for twenty-eight years; when the first twenty-eight-year term expires, songwriters are allowed to renew the copyright for another twenty-eight-year stint. Accordingly, when a copy of a song is sold, a royalty is paid to the writer. Traditional folk songs are particularly sticky, copyright-wise, since plenty are uncredited in their original forms, and it's often difficult to discern how strongly an artist's interpretation changes and restructures the song—especially when that folk song is part of an oral tradition, meaning there's no actual original to compare all subsequent versions to.

As Goldsmith wonders, "Should the royalties simply not be collected? Or should they be awarded to the singer who taught it to the collector, to the collector who rescued it from obscurity, or to the performer who added a verse that *might* have been crucial to its eventual popularity?" (Goldsmith's italics).

The Lomaxes claimed the copyrights for the songs performed, composed, and remembered by Lead Belly, a move still debated and often lamented by contemporary folklorists. In 1937, the *Native Son* author Richard Wright complained, in an essay for the Communist paper *The Daily Worker*, of how John Lomax "beguiled the singer with sugary promises, telling him that if he helped him to gather folk songs from other Negro prisoners in various prisons throughout the south, he would make him rich." Wright described Lomax and Ledbetter's relationship as "one of the most amazing cultural swindles in American history," with Lead Belly consistently positioned as a "half sex-mad, knife-toting, black buck from Texas." As far as I can tell, Lomax never responded; when I ask Ellen Harold at the Alan Lomax archives if she knows if John ever publically defended himself, she gives a few suggestions for scholars to contact and archives to scour, then says, "My sense is that John A. would not have formally responded to a Communist publication at all, since he was politically quite conservative in his outlook. It would also be interesting, to put things in perspective, to see just how frequent such personal attacks on people were in *The Daily Worker*'s pages. I would imagine that it was not uncommon, given the polemical spirit of the times."

It's easy to skewer John Lomax for conduct that appears both highly manipulative and racist, but it's equally essential to remember that Lomax's advocacy of African-American folk music was extraordinarily brave given the pre–civil rights climate of the 1930s, and his methods—making audio recordings of folk songs, rather than paper transcriptions—were both revolutionary and essential. Plenty apologize for Lomax's missteps, including, unsurprisingly, the Association for Cultural Equity at Hunter

College (an organization founded by Alan Lomax), which writes, on its website, "The Lomaxes were among the first folklorists to make audio documents of rural artists; and this at a time when the laws and standards pertaining to recording and music publishing deals were in their infancy and the intellectual property rights of traditional singers in folk songs were considered highly questionable or non-existent. Both independently and in collaboration, John A. Lomax, Huddie Ledbetter, and Alan Lomax left an enduring legacy that helped to bring African-American folk song into the musical and cultural fabric of our lives. The fact that their relationship is sometimes characterized by villainy or victimization says more about our ongoing collective struggle to deal with a history of racial injustice than it does about these people and their actions."

No matter how much context I collect, I still can't decide if I think Lomax's methods were vile or colonialist or racist to the extent that they fully nullify his contributions. I understand that Lomax was caught up in the first wave of music marketing, and capitalized—to inappropriate ends, in appropriate ways—on the fact that Lead Belly's otherness made him a spectacle, easily fetishized by white academics and gawked at by others. But I'm so intensely grateful for these songs that I mostly try to reimagine Lomax's trip-ups as an object lesson for future generations of writers, folklorists, and anthropologists, who now pause and reconsider their own intentions and interpretations. (In 1987, when Paul Simon released *Graceland*, a singer-songwriter record infused with the mbaqanga music of South Africa, he was promptly, unapologetically, and famously accused of employing his own brand of neo-colonialism). Harry Belafonte, the Jamaican-American pop singer who first nudged world-beat rhythms onto U.S. charts, elegantly surmises the stakes (in a conversation with Michael Elridge): "With Lomax, and others who went around the world in that colonial fashion, there are aspects of villainy: Lomax was a racist, et cetera. And yet this work was done, and we have this collection, and I don't know who would have done it if he hadn't. Thomas

Jefferson and all those other slaveholders wrote a proclamation that has done much to design where mankind has gone in its evolution. Is all of that villainous, or is all of it positive? I don't think we should reject the good because there was some bad, or ignore the bad because there was so much good. I think it's both, and I think what we should do is talk honorably about both."

After Lead Belly's split with John Lomax and his adoption by left-wing activists (Fred Ramsey, one of his friends and protectors, later suggested that he was coached into singing protest songs), he ended up at Asch Recordings in 1941. The folksinger Pete Seeger would later integrate the story of how Albert Einstein confirmed Asch's decision to record Lead Belly into his famed between-song banter: ". . . and then over supper, Einstein says, 'Well, young Mr. Asch, what do you do for a living?' And Moe says, 'Well, I've just bought this recording machine, and I'm fascinated with what it can do. And in New York, I've met a Negro musician named Lead Belly who's a fantastic musician but nobody's recording him. They say he's not commercial. But I think this is American culture and it should be recorded. Down in the Library of Congress they record things and just put it on the shelf there and only a few people ever hear them.' 'Well,' Einstein says, 'you're exactly right. Americans don't appreciate their culture. It'll be a Polish Jew like you who will do the job.' "

As usual, Asch's interest in Lead Belly wasn't commercial in the broadest sense—as Goldsmith notes, Lead Belly's music was considered too dated and "Uncle Tom-ish" by black audiences outside of the rural South—but, rather, an opportunity to market an artist to a small, niche group: in this case, American leftists. Asch presented Lead Belly with a contract for six songs within a period of twelve months.

Lead Belly had recently performed a triumphant show at Greenwich Village's Little Red School House, a notoriously progressive private school for the children of politically charged parents, and Asch figured a good way to capitalize on Lead Belly's kid-buzz was to release a children's record. In the liner notes to *Play Parties in Song and Dance, as Sung by Lead Belly*, Asch thumbs-up the simplicity of Lead Belly's brand of folk, claiming that the music's ease and repetition make these songs naturally child-friendly. And despite the obvious weirdness of a convicted murderer singing goofy songs for kids—even leftist kids—*Play Parties* was a tremendous success.

Lead Belly would continue recording for Asch (as well as for other labels, including Capitol Records) and making decent money from touring until his death in New York City on December 6, 1949, on Ward R6 of Bellevue Hospital, after a debilitating fight with Lou Gehrig's disease. Lead Belly was buried in the Shiloh Baptist Church cemetery, in Caddo Parish, eight miles west of Blanchard, Louisiana, and one mile from the Texas border. In 1974, Max S. Hale, chair of the Harrison County Historical Survey Committee, began a crusade to bring Lead Belly's remains back to Texas, where he was born; Ledbetter's cousin, Blanch Love, balked, saying, "Don't stir 'im, he's dead and tired of bein' worried." The Caddo Parish coroner, seeing no just cause, refused to issue a permit for the move, and Ledbetter remains in Louisiana.

By modern standards, Lead Belly's discography was indisputably the work of a folksinger (despite stupid industry attempts—thankfully, none by Asch—to seduce Ledbetter into singing blues songs). In the early 1940s, "folk music" was considered the exclusive terrain of backward-acting rural southerners, and songs recorded by black artists were known only as "race records," regardless of their content. The contemporary concept of folk music—confessional, ostensibly literary acoustic music made without consideration of commercial appeal—was just beginning to develop in New York City, starting at the Greenwich Village institution the New School, with the establishment of an annual folk festival known, cringingly, as Dances of Many Peoples. As Goldsmith explains, organizers at the New School "sought to create an egalitarian music by . . . casting off cultural particularism in favor of an internationally inspired, universal music form that would be comprehensive to all." That folk music in the 1950s, and '60s ended up becoming an insular, politically charged, mostly urban genre remains a particularly perplexing irony, given the New School's mission (and the genre's uninhibited front-porch roots).

The major labels—then Columbia, Decca, and RCA records—occasionally squeezed out a "world music" album for a tax write-off, but Asch's intentions were pure. As Goldsmith explains, Asch "did not select recording artists with the greatest commercial potential in the broadest possible market; rather, he chose those who were guaranteed to meet the needs of a previously ignored portion of the market, one that was small but well-defined." Still eager to expand his business, Asch hired Marian Distler, a twenty-two-year-old Jewish leftist and recent Hunter College graduate who began as Asch's secretary, but soon proved indispensable to his work.

After the December 1941 bombing of Pearl Harbor, shellac became a highly rationed substance, and record manufacturers were only allotted 10 percent of their previous intake. Because Asch produced so few records, his shellac allotment was laughable, meaning Asch Recordings was forced to temporarily shut down. Asch finally got back to work after sneaking some of the valuable polymer from the Communist party member Herbert Harris, who had pressed enough Soviet choral (and, occasionally, propaganda) records to score a significant allotment—which he no longer had much use for, given that the market for Soviet records was never particularly vast (Asch's connections to the Communist party are vague at best, but it seems likely that despite his business associates and leftist consumer base, he wasn't particularly political).

In the years following, Asch would record songs by the Oklahoma revolutionary Woody Guthrie, the sweet-faced Pete Seeger, the Harlem pianist James P. Johnson (the "father of stride piano" and mentor to Fats Waller), the folksinger-turned-movie-star Burl Ives, the jazz pianist Mary Lou Williams, the poet Langston Hughes, the tenor saxophonist Coleman Hawkins, and plenty of others; in January 1946, wanting an escape from his relationship with Harris, Asch founded a new company, known as Disc Company of America. In the February 25, 1946, issue of *Time* magazine, Asch was described as "the number one recorder of out-of-the-way jazz, cowboy music, and such exotic items as Paris street noises during the liberation, and little-heard Russian operas."

Unfortunately, Asch got into some financial trouble in 1947 and was forced to shut the Disc label down. In a 1978 interview with the *Folk Scene* writer Jim Capaldi, Asch sorted out the details: "[The bankruptcy] happened because I issued *Jazz at the Philharmonic* with [the bandleader] Norman Granz. Nat King Cole [, who performed on the record,] cost me $15,000. It was so expensive. I couldn't commercialize it, so I couldn't keep up with it. The Disc Company went bankrupt and then I started Folkways in 1947. The banks gave me a $3,000 advance because they knew the type of thing that I did would sell. So I started Folkways Records with $3,000. It was actually the high cost of the jazz records that caused the bankruptcy. Today Norman Granz is doing very well; he knew how to merchandise jazz." Granz went on to establish his own label, the famed Verve Records, in 1955, which would release records by Ella Fitzgerald, Nina Simone, Sarah Vaughan, Dizzy Gillespie, Count Basie, Charlie Parker, Lester Young, and more, while Asch moved on to a new venture, Folkways, where he would work until his death in 1986.

Asch was ostensibly unconcerned with chasing market trends, heralding fads, or securing a smash hit (in the Capaldi interview, Asch describes the majority of demo tapes he receives as frivolous, claiming, "most of them protest about love and stuff like that; I try to tell them, why don't you use this talent that you have for the people's use? I am not interested in pro-love or anti-love material," thus blatantly rejecting pop music's golden formula). Asch was also notoriously irresponsible about paying proper royalties (he repeatedly scrapped with Lead Belly over financial concerns), and it's not hard to find accounts of his generally unpleasant studio demeanor (Seeger diplomatically refers to Asch as "stubborn" on the back of Goldsmith's book). Likewise, plenty of Asch's recordings are of relatively shoddy quality, rendered with bare-bones equipment (most were recorded with one microphone) and without the aid of a proper producer, and eventually Asch became known for formally releasing demo tapes, regardless of their sound quality. As Jeff Place explains, "Most of the later years of Folkways consisted of people sending him tapes, from different studios, and some of them—some bluegrass records—were really well produced. But other people would record demos in their living room, with a little tape deck and a guitar, send it to him, and Moe would say yes, and put out the demo tape, not thinking twice about it. [Asch] hated stereo—he didn't like the sound of it."

Regardless, throughout the 1950s and '60s, Folkways' increasingly essential arsenal of Americana swelled, and Asch revised his marketing plan to focus on librarians, social studies classrooms, and museums—spots where, he imagined, his esoteric tastes would be fully appreciated. It's still difficult to discern exactly how strongly Asch felt about the music he was producing, and whether or not folk was anything more than an incidental focus for him, the only kind of music he deemed "serious" enough for his participation. "Moe Asch said he considered himself the pen with which these artists wrote," Place says. "So, frequently he would record people who were not that good, musically—not great singers—but [who] had words he was interested in. The people had to have something to say. He turned down Dylan, and his reason for that was that he thought Dylan didn't have anything to say. And of course, he was wrong on that one. And Joan Baez, too: he thought she was just a singer, that she didn't know what she was singing, that she wasn't special." Indeed, in the first volume of his memoir, *Chronicles*, Dylan writes, "I envisioned myself recording for Folkways Records. That was the label I wanted to be on. That was the label that put out all the great records." Dylan's desire was understandable: it is difficult to think about Americana music without thinking about Folkways.

Making Familiar Strange:

Harry Smith's *Anthology of American Folk Music* and the Birth of Smithsonian Folkways

The whole bizarre package made the familiar strange, the never known into the forgotten, and the forgotten into a collective memory that teased any single listener's conscious mind.

—Greil Marcus, "The Old, Weird America"

* ✹ *

Folkways' greatest legacy—and the record still most closely associated with the label—came early in the company's existence. In 1950, the twenty-seven-year-old Oregon-born anthropologist-turned-filmmaker Harry Smith landed in New York's Penn Station, broke, towing his colossal collection of rare 78s, and looking for cash. Smith, along with Fonotone Records' Joe Bussard, was one of America's first obsessive record collectors, a tiny, curled-up man with a craving for rare bits of shellac. The critic Robert Christgau would later describe him as "a strange, bearded little man from Portland, Oregon, who lived in places like

Berkeley and the Hotel Chelsea and spent his days painting, creating experimental films, scrounging money, making whoopee, and collecting stuff—quilts, paper airplanes, Ukrainian Easter eggs, phonograph records, anything." After a friend suggested that Smith approach Asch about unloading some records, the two men met, and in March 1952 Asch agreed to release a three-volume, six-LP anthology on Folkways; each of the *Anthology of American Folk Music*'s eighty-four tracks, most from the 1920s and '30s, was plucked straight from Smith's personal collection of 78s. According to Goldsmith, Asch later claimed that his only act of supervision was to provide Smith, who was now working from the Folkways office on 117 West Forty-sixth Street, "with a peyote button every few hours, from which Smith would draw some degree of inspiration."

All that peyote certainly amplified Smith's cosmological interests. Already heavily invested in the occult, and supposedly the recipient of a shamanic initiation as a young child, Smith's eccentric tendencies (that Ukrainian Easter egg collection numbered around thirty thousand) are evident in the physical trappings of the *Anthology*. Each of the three volumes boasted the same cover art—an etching by Theodore de Bry, plucked from a compendium on mysticism by the British physicist, astrologer, and mystic Robert Fludd. The picture, a sketched globe, anchored by a one-stringed instrument, with a hand bursting forth from the clouds to twist its lone tuning peg, was of something Smith called the Celestial Monochord, a protean instrument invented by Pythagoras in 400 B.C. The illustration was rendered in red (fire), blue (air), or green (water), and the globe was divided into sections, each festooned with Latin notations. Along the left edge of the globe, in thick block letters, song titles are listed numerically; along the right side, the names of the artists are similarly stacked, numbered, and pressed. As Greil Marcus writes in his essay "The Old, Weird America" (a name he would later give to a full-length book—originally titled *Invisible Republic*—about secret collaborations between Bob Dylan and the Band), the monochord, ostensibly tuned by the hand of God, "divided creation into balanced spheres of energy, into fundaments; printed over the filaments of the etching and its crepuscular Latin explanations were record titles and the names of the blues singers, hillbilly musicians, and gospel chanters Smith was bringing together for the very first time. It was as if they had something to do with each other: as if Pythagoras, Fludd, and the likes of Jilson Setters, Ramblin' Thomas, the Alabama Sacred Harp Singers, Charlie Poole and the North Carolina Ramblers, and Smith himself, were calling on the same Gods."

Certainly there is something strange and otherworldly about the *Anthology's* cover, its ancient Latin declarations rubbing up against the names of rural folksingers, art and tradition getting all tangled up in mythos and mysticism. Smith seems to be asking listeners to consider if all of this—cosmology, science, religion, music, art—is actually drawn from the same basic human impulse: to understand and make peace with God. On a more practical note, Marcus also observes how the *Anthology* was "dubiously legal" at best, considering its contents include forgotten songs released on still-active labels, including Columbia, Victor/RCA, and Paramount.

Smith's legendary twenty-eight pages of liner notes, which offer loads of priceless information about the songs' origins, are filled with small etchings culled from late-nineteenth- and early-twentieth-century catalogs (see "THE BANJO and description of its parts," a diagram of the instrument accompanied by dashes and explanations like "nut," "1st fret," "rim," and "bridge"). They also include tiny, occasionally disturbing synopses of each song, such as the entry for "Fatal Flower Gardens," a vocal duet with guitars performed by Nelstone's Hawaiians, that reads, "GAUDY WOMAN LURES CHILD FROM PLAYFELLOWS; STABS HIM AS VICTIM DICTATES MESSAGE TO PARENTS." Smith may have been trying to exercise his anthropologist muscle with bits like

"WIFE'S LOGIC FAILS TO EXPLAIN STRANGE BEDFELLOW TO DRUNKARD," but his notes read more like perverse snippets of poetry, or excerpts from an aspiring novelist's notebook.

The *Anthology of American Folk Music* was widely celebrated upon its initial release, and in 1997, Smithsonian Folkways (then just ten years old) reissued the *Anthology* on six CDs, with additional commentary by Greil Marcus, Jeff Place, and Asch, as well as observations on the original 1952 edition by Allen Ginsberg, Elvis Costello, John Fahey, Dave Van Ronk, Luc Sante, and others.

In 2003, the collection clocked in at 276 on *Rolling Stone*'s list of the 500 greatest albums of all time, and remains beloved. Homages are common: between 1999 and 2000, the producer Hal Willner and the musician Nick Cave staged a series of five-hour-plus concerts in London, New York, and Los Angeles, intending to celebrate Smith's work as an experimental filmmaker and musicologist by pairing contemporary artists with bits of Smith's films and the *Anthology*'s ancient folk songs: Beck, Beth Orton, Philip Glass, Van Dyke Parks, Elvis Costello, Wilco, Steve Earle, Lou Reed, Marianne Faithfull, and a mess of other contemporary rock and folk artists agreed to participate. *The Harry Smith Project* (2006) documents the concerts, pairing two CDs of live cuts with a DVD of concert footage—some featuring the legendary camera-stylings of D. A. Pennebaker and his team—and *The Old, Weird America*, a documentary about the endeavor. Meanwhile, in 2000, John Fahey's Revenant Records, in association with the Harry Smith Archives, released a "secret" fourth volume (presumably representing the missing element, earth), on two CDs or two LPs, which featured additional tracks by the luminaries the Monroe Brothers, the Carter Family, Robert Johnson, Bukka White, Lead Belly, Uncle Dave Macon, and Sleepy John Estes, most of whom also appeared in the first three volumes.

The Smithsonian reissue comes housed in an LP-size red canvas box with a picture of the celestial monochord pasted on the front—although now the lists of artists have been zapped from the cover, cracking the metaphysical continuum (they're still in place on the individual CDs). It remains beautiful. In a 1972 interview with Ethel Raim and Bob Norman, Asch talks about how people often feel compelled to travel with the *Anthology* in tow, declaring, "Pete Seeger just went to Asia. He took a plane and even with all that weight he took the *Anthology*. [Woody Guthrie's manager] Harold Leventhal went to India and took the *Anthology* with him." I empathize: there are days when I want nothing more than to tote the *Anthology* around New York City, stroking its cover and feeding its contents into my Discman, behaving ridiculously, using scratchy old folk songs as a romantic crutch, pouting and trying to remind myself that there is life beyond taxicabs, expensive purses, investment bankers, and blank-faced commuters—and that, perhaps ironically, all of this music was compiled here, in this ridiculous city.

The *Anthology*'s three volumes are organized thematically, parsed neatly into Ballads, Social Music, and the catchall Songs—the last is my favorite, packed with choice cuts from Mississippi John Hurt, the Carter Family, Uncle Dave Macon, Sleepy John Estes, and Blind Lemon Jefferson. There are days when I think that the rumbled chorus to Ramblin' Thomas's "Poor Boy Blues" ("Poor boy / Poor boy / Poor boy, long way from home . . .") is maybe the saddest thing I've ever heard. Strapped into my headphones, burning down sidewalks, sidestepping tourists and strollers, jogging away from open-windowed cars with rattling stereo systems, listening hard, I am acutely aware of how early American folk music sounds like nothing else on earth.

In 1985, an eighty-year-old Asch—conscious of his deteriorating health—pressed negotiations with the Smithsonian, and in August, the government secured funding for the purchase of Folkways and its archive. The Smithsonian acquisition was hinged on one condition: all Folkways titles must remain "in print" forever, with the Smithsonian agreeing to fulfill on-demand requests for Pete Seeger and Woody

Guthrie discs as well as obscure instructional manuals and, occasionally, *Sounds of the Human Body* or *Sounds of North American Frogs* or *Sounds of the Rainforest* (a popular 1950 release that many critics continue to believe was actually recorded in a New York City shower).

"The three thousand titles on the wall over there? You can get any of them on CD," Place explains, thumbing at the bookcases across the room. "We burn them one at a time. [Asch] treated it as an encyclopedia—the sounds of the twentieth century. All these different areas. And that was why it was so important to him not to take anything out, or drop things. We had to make everything available, no matter how obscure it was, and there's some really weird stuff over there, things someone might ask for once every ten years. There are instructional records for technologies that have been obsolete for fifty years. There are manuals to stenographer and dictation machines. Once in a blue moon someone will want one for historical reasons," Place says.

No matter how inconvenient, Smithsonian Folkways remains wholly dedicated to Asch's mission, augmenting ancient tapes with as much context as possible. "We're in the process of scanning all of the original record covers and all of the original liner notes," Place continues. "If you've ever looked at the original Folkways record covers, there's [a] classic styling, and there are young bands mimicking these covers [now]," he says, waving around a record. "We're going to print labels that have these little cardboard album jackets that wrap around, and then put the CD in it, and then put all the liner notes on the CD itself, so you can put it in your computer and read the liner notes. We're doing that for all three thousand. All the tracks are up for download now, through our global sound site, and Microsoft's music store, and iTunes. So you can get the most obscure track on that wall, and download it." He pauses. "For people who are into that sort of thing, the iPod thing. For me, I like to have the context with the music. To have a song, totally disassociated from an album, without anything framing it, that doesn't work for me really well."

Place, who concentrates mostly on rural American music, produces a good percentage of Smithsonian Folkways' twenty to twenty-five annual releases, and writes the text for their accompanying booklets. He won two Grammys in 1997, the year of the *Anthology* reissue, for Best Album Notes and Best Historical Album. Smithsonian Folkways generally seeks out artists who aren't likely to be picked up by other labels. "We're not too good with active musicians, people who are really out there, professional musicians with tour schedules who need press and need to have their CDs sent out." Place sighs. "That's not our bag at all. Most of the people [we release] are very local folks. We're nonprofit. There was an issue at first, with people complaining: Why is the government taking on this thing, this nonprofit, to compete in a private industry? So we carved out this niche of things that nobody else is going to want to do. And we do fat booklets, with lots of historical information— someone has to warrant having a giant historical workup; someone has to deserve that kind of treatment. So it's not going to be somebody brand new. There are too many other people doing that; there's no reason [for Smithsonian Folkways] to do that."

Accordingly, Smithsonian Folkways relies on experts and fetishists for new content. "There's an incredible network of folklorists. A lot of them work for their state's folklore agency, where there is one, or for an arts agency, or they freelance. These people have already been everywhere there is to be in their state. There's no going out and discovering someone unknown—it's just not gonna happen," Place asserts. His voice is emphatic, and I nod—clearly, there's little chance of striding off into the wilds of western Mississippi and trotting back with an undiscovered-but-profound blues singer in tow, and the days of imperialistic song-collecting, Lomax-style, are pretty much done.

"Generally," Place continues, "I call people up, the experts in certain states, and they already have the field recordings and interviews, and they hand that stuff over. Some people bring projects to us, archival projects. Or independent labels, niche labels, forty years from now, when the person who is running it isn't into it anymore, and tapes are sitting on the shelf—those are the kinds of things we're looking for, to take on and bring into our mix. And if the person hands over the intellectual property rights, then we're able to disseminate it. We're always looking. I've been talking to this guy who has a labor union record label, and I just got all this stuff from him," Place continues, nodding at a stack of cardboard boxes, not far from his desk. "And if we don't have contact information, we [make] sure we can track information down. Every time I work on a record I try to track down every last person involved, or a family member, even if I have to go to online folk chat rooms and spread it around, finding out who so-and-so's granddaughter is, so we can get royalties to the right people."

Smithsonian Folkways may focus on historically significant artists, but Place doesn't believe that the genre is dead. "Folk has changed. You look at other ethnic traditions, like polka—it's become more electrified and changed and modified; that's just how it works." He shrugs. "But I'm pleased by the [contemporary] stuff I've heard in the last ten years. That they care enough about the tradition to go back and really understand it—bands like Freakwater are doing these great ballads, and they're totally different, way out of left field, but I can get into it. When I first started working here, there were definitely people of the mind that tradition should be frozen in stone, you shouldn't play with it, it's not legit. But I'm not of that mind at all—music changes and evolves; it always has."

I understand Jeff Place's mission in the same way I understand what the Lomaxes and Asch and Smith were ultimately getting at: for better or worse, these men are keepers and disseminators of song, and the results of their work are immeasurable.

Place's capacity to understand the mechanics of change is equally essential. After I leave Washington and drive back to New York City, I will attempt to pinpoint Folkways' old address on West Forty-sixth Street;

since its move to Washington in 1987, the label's old digs have been converted, as far as I can tell, into the parking garage of a giant Comfort Inn. The rest of the block is runoff from nearby Times Square—restaurants with neon signs and names like Rosie O'Grady, or comedy clubs with giant marquees and fourteen-dollar cocktails. It's hard to imagine where Harry Smith, slagging off on the *Anthology*, might have darted for a cup of coffee. But it is not American—not folk—to be surprised by change.

You Won't Find It So Hot If You Ain't Got the Do Re Mi:

Woody Guthrie, Ramblin' Jack Elliott, and the Folk Revival of the 1960s

A folk song is what's wrong and how to fix it, or it could be who's hungry and where their mouth is, or who's out of work and where the job is or who's broke and where the money is or who's carrying a gun and where the peace is—that's folk lore and folks made it up because they seen that the politicians couldn't find nothing to fix or nobody to feed or give a job of work.

—Woody Guthrie to Alan Lomax, September 19, 1940

Someday people are going to wake up to the fact that Woody Guthrie and the ten thousand songs that leap and tumble off the strings of his music box are a national possession, like Yellowstone and Yosemite.

—Clifton Fadiman, The New Yorker, 1943

* ✶ *

I'm steering my car down Coney Island's Surf Avenue, and the Atlantic Ocean is looming to the east, protected by fast-food shacks and gaudy boardwalk cast-offs, homemade signs pushing soft-serve ice cream, Italian ices, candy apples, fried clams, and fresh-roasted corn on the cob. I've been back in New York for less than a week. The water is slate gray and uninviting. Inland, the Cyclone, New York's premier roller coaster, whirs and clatters, its ancient wooden bones thwacking hard, like chattering teeth. Rows of sticky-faced kids, strapped into Deno's Freefall, shriek in perfect unison, relishing the plummet in three-second bursts. Hungry beach-goers line up at Nathan's, cramming hot dogs and crinkle fries into sunburned faces. I pass KeySpan Park, home of minor league baseball club the Brooklyn Cyclones, and at Twenty-second Street, the Carey Gardens housing projects begin to unfold, stretching from Twenty-second to Twenty-fourth Streets, between Surf and Neptune Avenues. Without them, the sea spray and too-short buildings and vans of toddlers would make Coney Island feel too distant, too autonomous, too uninhabited.

I park in a spot with a broken meter and shuffle onto the boardwalk, wincing as the boards shift and slip; immediately, I conjure a variety of cartoon scenarios, in which a screw falters and one end of the board shoots into the air, see-saw style, ejecting dumb-faced passersby into the atmosphere. I buy a strawberry shortcake at a stand in front of Shoot the Freak, and lean against a railing outside of the New York Aquarium's teaching annex, watching the ocean and pushing my hair out of my face.

In 1943, the folksinger Woody Guthrie moved into a one-bedroom rear apartment at 3520 Mermaid Avenue in Coney Island, two blocks from the boardwalk. Guthrie and Marjorie Mazia, the modern dancer who would eventually become his second wife, had already welcomed their first child, Cathy. Three years earlier, Guthrie had released his most renowned and enduring song, "This Land Is Your Land," a caustic, if widely misunderstood, response to Irving Berlin's "God Bless America" (a track Guthrie found pompous, complacent, and mostly ridiculous) and a note-for-note reinterpretation of the Carter Family's "When the World's on Fire," itself based on an even older gospel song. (Some will argue that "This Land Is Your Land" was actually inspired by the Carters' "Little Darling, Pal of Mine," which was, like "When the World's on Fire," a variant of the southern gospel standard "Oh, My Loving Brother.") At the same time, Guthrie's autobiography, *Bound for Glory*, was garnering effusive praise.

The apex of Woody Guthrie's personal and professional life, arguably, was at Coney Island in 1943. By the end of the next decade, Cathy will have died in a house fire, Guthrie will have left Marjorie and their three remaining children, moved to California and remarried, divorced again, returned to New York, and, finally, been institutionalized for Huntington's Disease (a rare, inherited neurological disorder with debilitating—and ultimately fatal—physical, psychiatric, and cognitive ramifications).

Where the apartment at 3520 Mermaid Avenue used to be, a medical park the color of manila folders now squats, ugly and useful. A sign reading SAUL'S PHARMACY AND SURGICALS hangs on the side of the building. There are bars on the windows. The original house was torn down many years ago, but I know from the single archived photograph of the building (taken for estate purposes sometime in the 1940s and dotted with little balls of white light, presumably from a flash gone bad) that it was a three-story brick town house, sporting three front porches, each with white wood railings, and with four steps leading up from the sidewalk to the front door. The house at 3520 sat down the block from a Jewish corner store, Sam's; Nora Guthrie, Woody's daughter, later told me she used to buy plums there. Today, I can only imagine Guthrie's tiny frame inside, hunched over a notebook, doodling dirty pictures, writing and rewriting songs, strumming his battered guitar, painting, scheming.

In 2000, Billy Bragg, a British punk rock singer with a penchant for protest songs, collaborated with the Chicago alt-country band Wilco on a two-disc series of previously unrecorded Woody Guthrie songs titled *Mermaid Avenue*, produced under the direction of Nora Guthrie. (In his 2004 memoir, *Chronicles*, Bob Dylan writes sneeringly, "These performers probably weren't even born when I had made that trip out to Brooklyn," referencing a voyage to Coney Island, where a hospitalized Guthrie supposedly promised Dylan a basement full of unpublished songs.) Both discs feature cover shots of comparable Coney Island homes rather than the real thing. Volume II also offers one of Woody's portraits of a giant, vaguely sinister-looking house cat, lounging on the sidewalk in front of the building. Nora reports that her father took an entire series of pictures of this particular cat, noting, "[He] must have been crawling on his belly down Mermaid Avenue."

Coney Island is a long way from Woody Guthrie's first home. Born on July 14, 1912, in Okemah, Oklahoma, he was named after soon-to-be president Woodrow Wilson. The son of Charley Guthrie, a cowboy-politician, and Nora Belle Tanner, a Kansas-born beauty with a knack for song, Guthrie's early home life was marked by a variety of perverse tragedies, many involving fire. When Woody was six years old, his fifteen-year-old sister, Clara, dumped kerosene down the front of her dress, struck a match, and set herself aflame following a frenzied argument with their mother over whether she could go to school to take an exam. (Nora had demanded she stay home to help with housework.) Clara died shortly after. Meanwhile, Nora was slowly succumbing to the perils of Huntington's (though the disease had been discovered and named in 1872, Nora was officially diagnosed only as having a rare form of hereditary madness).

In 1927, in an uncomfortable playback of Clara's death, Nora dripped kerosene on her sleeping husband's chest and lit a match, watching the flames crackle and rise. Charley woke up and smothered the fire, but not before suffering debilitating burns. Nora Guthrie was institutionalized and died three years later at Central State Hospital for the Insane in Norman, Oklahoma.

It's not especially surprising, then, that Woody Guthrie was described as a temperamental and emotionally unstable teenager, his demeanor typically alternating between charismatic and deeply glum. While his father recuperated from his extensive injuries—still covered in half-inch-high welts, Charley went to live with his half sister, Maude Boyston, in Panhandle, Texas—Woody, now on his own in Okemah, took a series of crappy jobs, from scavenging scrap metal to washing dishes to polishing brass spittoons to picking cotton to jig-dancing and playing harmonica in exchange for sandwiches. At sixteen, Woody hitchhiked south through Texas to the Gulf of Mexico, learning street songs from missionaries, bluesmen, cowboys, and ranchers. At nineteen, he left Oklahoma for the Texas panhandle, marrying sixteen-year-old Mary Jennings in 1933 (Mary and Woody would eventually have three children, Gwen, Sue, and Bill Guthrie). Along with Cluster Baker and Mary's brother, Matt, Guthrie formed the Corn Cob Trio, his very first band; they earned piddling gigs around town, playing dance clubs, parties, and informal radio broadcasts. Meanwhile, Guthrie started sitting in with other bands, contributing guitar, bones, washboard, spoons, double bass, and drums. According to Ed Cray, the author of the Guthrie biography *Ramblin' Man*, he "sang, danced, spun long yarns to keep the scant audiences in their seats and even drew cartoons." Guthrie was irascible, mischievous, charming, and naturally driven to perform.

By the mid 1930s, the Great Depression had ravaged much of America, and Guthrie found it increasingly difficult to find work in Texas. Between 1934 and 1939, a confluence of geographic and agricultural events (displaced buffalo herds, improper farm technique, drought, and overgrazed grass) shriveled up the famously fertile soil of America's Great Plains. Dirt rose into big, black clouds that puffed eastward. On April 14, 1935, a catastrophic "Black Blizzard" hit the south plains, ravaging the Midwest. Equipment was buried, farms were ruined, dirt fell in clumps. Guthrie, desperate for work, packed up for California, leaving his family behind. Nearly 15 percent of the Oklahoma population headed west to escape the Dust Bowl. In California, they and nearly all other Midwestern immigrants—regardless of their actual origins—became known as Okies.

Guthrie hopped freight trains, hitchhiked, and plodded along by foot, hustling for food and shelter, sleeping under bridges, stealing peaches from orchards, pulling fish from rivers, singing for beer, and, like Robert Johnson before him, inadvertently furthering the archetype of the Great American Traveler, streaked with dirt and full of stories (an image eventually appropriated and romanticized by everyone from Jack Kerouac to Bob Dylan). Guthrie begged cops for a night in jail in order to get out of the gutter, sold his sweater for a ten-cent bowl of chili, and swapped his guitar for more grub, hustling all the way to California. According to Cray, Guthrie finished his trip by coasting west on Route 66 with a "Japanese boy" driving a 1929 Ford Coupe, following the orange groves into Los Angeles. Guthrie rolled himself in brown paper, hopped and slept on a Southern Pacific boxcar, and headed south to Turlock, where he stayed with family for a few days before meeting up with his cousin Leon (known to most everyone else as "Jack" or "Oklahoma") and shuffling back toward Los Angeles.

Guthrie scored a quarter-a-night hotel room in L.A. and began performing at local bars. Jack arranged for an audition at KFVD, the only radio station in Los Angeles without a country-and-western show. The station owner, J. Frank Burke, Sr., a progressive who shunned California's increasingly conservative Republican party, left the management of the station to his son, Frank, Jr., who hired Jack and Woody for an 8:00–8:15 morning slot, which they named *The Oklahoma and Woody Show*. Their performances were mostly unexceptional—Jack favored bombastic cowboy songs, while Woody's tastes ran far scrappier, and their harmonies were rarely successful—but it provided an outlet for Guthrie's musical aspirations.

Jack worked construction with a Missouri man named Roy Criss-man, and dragged Guthrie to the Crissman house on May 12, 1937; Woody and Jack returned the following night with a guitar and kicked off a full-on jamboree with the Crissman family. Guthrie and Maxine Crissman, Roy's eldest daughter, enjoyed a natural synergy. As Cray writes, "Together they found what Guthrie would call 'the crossnote' . . . the sum of their two voices was greater than the parts." After Frank Burke, Jr., shuffled *The Oklahoma and Woody Show* to 11:00 p.m. (allow-ing Jack to work construction jobs during the day), he asked Guthrie to continue in the morning slot, and Guthrie implored Maxine Crissman to join him on-air, introducing her as Lefty Lou from Old Mizzou (Max-ine was left-handed, and Lou, apparently, was the only thing Guthrie could think of that rhymed with Mizzou). Frustrated over his inability to translate his radio show into a full-fledged, paid endeavor, Jack quit KFVD soon after, and Woody and Maxine took over *The Oklahoma and Woody Show*, too. KFVD was showered with letters of support for the duo. As Cray writes, "Woody and Maxine were different from the cow-boy singers who favored artificial 'buckaroo ballads.' Rather than sing of a west that never was, Woody preferred to re-create in song a west that had vanished." They were paid twenty dollars a week, with an additional fifteen dollars for every fifteen minutes of airtime bought by a sponsor; by November 1937, Guthrie had saved enough money to bring his wife out to California.

Off the radio, work was scarce and arduous. The mass evacuation of the high plains marked the largest migration in American history—by 1940, nearly 2.5 million people were forced to abandon their land. Of those, 200,000 headed to California, where they were greeted with un-mitigated disdain. The Los Angeles Police Department eventually sent 125 uniformed troops, dubbed the Bum Brigade, to dissuade Okies from crossing the border, stopping only after a successful lawsuit from the American Civil Liberties Union. California was suddenly and irrevocably jammed with work-seeking Dust Bowl refugees, and no one appreciated the congestion less than state natives. Migrants congregated in roadside camps, banding together to claw off packs of vigilante locals who tore the migrants' shanties to the ground, presuming all Okies were Communists. An excerpt from a 1935 *Collier's Weekly* outlines the scene: "Very erect and primly severe, [a man] addressed the slumped driver of a rolling wreck that screamed from every hinge, bearing and coupling. 'California's relief rolls are overcrowded now. No use to come farther,' he cried. The half-collapsed driver ignored him—merely turned his head to be sure his numerous family was still with him. They were so tightly wedged in, that escape was impossible. 'There really is nothing for you here,' the neat trooperish young man went on. 'Nothing, really nothing.' And the forlorn man on the moaning car looked at him, dull, emotionless, incredibly weary, and said: 'So? Well, you ought to see what they got where I come from.' " As Cray writes, "The Okies and Arkies, the Texicans and Jayhawkers, had become Woody's people. They were rootless, ground down, stripped of farms and jobs back east, shorn of their dignity in California."

Ed Robbin, another DJ at KFVD, was the first to introduce Guthrie to the notion of organized Communism when he invited him to perform at a party rally. Although Guthrie was a Socialist and union activist, sympathetic to the migrant plight and supportive of the party's mission, he never became a card-carrying Communist—instead, as Cray explains, Guthrie "took what he wanted of doctrine and brushed aside the rest." In May 1939, with the help of Robbin, Guthrie began writing a column, "Woody Sez," for the Communist paper *People's World*, but continued to shun all religious and political organizations, and refused to join up with any particular party or church. In a 1941 letter to Alan Lomax, in reaction to reader responses to a September 1940 newspaper article about himself, Guthrie wrote, "They called me a Communist and a wild man and everything you could think of, but I don't care. I ain't a member of any earthly organization."

That fall, Guthrie, young family in tow, left Los Angeles and returned to Texas, staying through Christmas and the close of the year. Still unable to find steady work, he looked east, buying a bus ticket to Pittsburgh (the farthest he could afford), leaving his family again. Once in Pittsburgh, Guthrie attempted to hitchhike the remaining three hundred miles to New York City, despite inclement weather. Half-frozen in a blizzard, Guthrie was serendipitously yanked from the snow by a passing forest ranger, who lugged Guthrie to his parents' house and pumped his stomach full of hot, buttered clam chowder. The next morning, Guthrie was offered three bucks and a ride to Philadelphia, where he caught a bus to Manhattan, finally arriving on February 16, 1940.

Alan Lomax first heard Guthrie sing, billed only as "Woody, a real Dust Bowl refugee," at a benefit for the Steinbeck Committee to Aid Farm Workers, and was instantly overtaken by Guthrie's scruffy appearance and charming performance. As the Guthrie biographer Joe Klein explains, "Alan loved everything about him, even the way he moved: the exaggerated way his arm swept around and his fingers came down to scratch the very top of his head like a steam shovel; the way he pooched his mouth and stroked his chin when he was thinking, the finger to the forehead when an idea came, and those eyes that seemed to take in everything and give out very little." Soon after, Lomax invited Guthrie to Washington, D.C., recruiting him to record songs and interviews for the Library of Congress. The recordings would eventually be released to the public by Elektra Records, twenty-five years later, as a three-LP set, advertised as including stories about "his family, early life in Okemah, Oklahoma, his 'gang,' home brew, ice cream freezings and house parties, Texas oil fields, Dust Storm of April 14, 1935, migration from the Dust Bowl, 'Pea Patch Poppas,' hard times, Pretty Boy Floyd, Jesse James, bank-

ers, hoboin' and freightrainin', railroad 'bulls,' government camps . . . "
and on and on. In the liner notes, Lomax dubs Guthrie "the most truth-
ful and most talented man of his generation."

Guthrie relished the sessions. In a September 19, 1940, letter to Lomax, Guthrie writes, "The Library of Congress is good. It has helped me
a lot by recording what I had to say and to copy all of my songs and file
them away so the Senators can't find them." Two days earlier, in another
letter, he jokes, "How's the skid row section of the poor folks division of
the Library of Congress? That's some joint." Guthrie was an easy interview and, as Klein points out, Lomax "knew what he was after and how
to get it." Now, listening to Guthrie's hardscrabble stories about root beer
stands and guitars and oil fields in the high, dry, windy plains, it becomes
obvious that storytelling was hardwired into Guthrie's brain—his narratives are musical, rhythmic, and effortless, recounted in a soft, lilting Oklahoma accent. They bleed into songs the way cream blends into coffee.

Back in New York, Guthrie sparked up a friendship with Lead Belly,
periodically crashing on the Murphy bed in the Lower East Side apartment Lead Belly shared with his wife, Martha. Guthrie was entranced by
Lead Belly's music, but, as Klein notes, "It was difficult to tell what Lead
Belly thought of any white man; he was unalterably servile in their pres-
ence, and addressed them formally as 'Mr. Alan' and even 'Mr. Woody.' "
Regardless, definitive echoes of Lead Belly's work—his plaintiveness, his
playfulness—pop up in plenty of Guthrie's songs from this era, and it's
obvious that Guthrie's admiration for the folksinger was entirely sincere.

Guthrie was beginning to embody what Lomax referred to as a
"New America," where, as Cray writes, "the working people expressed
themselves through folk culture," and, in Guthrie's case, fought to high-
light the plight of the poor. As Guthrie explained, "Usually I set down
and knock out a song in about thirty minutes or an hour, but in most of
them I've been going around humming and whistling it and trying to get
it all straight in my head what I want to say and why I want to say it and

usually when I decide who exactly the song is going to help out, if it's the right bunch I can really scribble her down in a hurry . . . I get my words and my tunes off of the hungry folks and they get the credit for all I pause to scribble down."

New York's intellectuals were interested in Guthrie's story—being poor, left-leaning, and a "real worker," he fulfilled, almost perfectly, a stereotype popular among folklorists and academics. No one was talking about Guthrie's potential impact on the sound of popular music; already, Woody Guthrie was more a symbol than a singer.

Guthrie's first marriage to Mary Jennings dissolved in 1941. He began performing with the Almanac Singers (Millard Lampell, Lee Hays, and Pete Seeger) and in 1944 started releasing records with Moe Asch. Accounts of Asch and Guthrie's first meeting vary but, as Peter Goldsmith explains, they were all based on some version of Guthrie sitting down on the floor, stating "Hi, I'm Woody Guthrie," and Asch replying, "So what?" with classic, Aschian irritability. Guthrie and Asch would go on to collaborate on more than three hundred songs.

From the very start, Guthrie raged hard against the machinations of a still-developing record industry—even one that was eager to position him as the definitive poster child for the workingman, despite the fact that, by the mid-1940s, Guthrie's only "work" involved sitting at home, writing songs. By the time he hit his professional prime, Guthrie (like Lead Belly) was deified by the urban left, worshipped by people in cities with university diplomas and progressive politics. In a 1946 letter to Asch, Guthrie wrote,

I have been doing a good bit of thinking all along about the whole business of folk songs, and ballads . . . There are all kinds of different positions you could take on this subject, I mean ranging from pure reaction to pure union; from purest capitalist uses, to the uses, we will say, that fight for socialism. I have always taken the side that I thought would help the workers in the lowest places to know their real fighting history, and to be proud to take their place, each in his own part of the fight. I have always said in my songs and ballads that this old world is a fight from the cradle to the grave. I never sung nor made songs just to entertain the upper classes, but to curse their clowing, reckless racketeers, and to warn the nervous ones that live and die by greed. Not all of us folk and ballad makers and singers stand where I stand. Not all of them see the world as I see it. Some would rather be a "character" and be photographed and filmed, broadcast and recorded, and paid big money by the big money side. They would rather occupy a certain social position, be well known, to play the games of publicity gangsters, and to enjoy the crowds that clap and yell when you tell them directly or indirectly that this old world is okie-dokie, she is all right, she is a nice good place to live on, and if you kick or argue, or make too much noise with your mouth, then you are just a native born kicker, and a griper, and you are kicked out by your own inability to "cooperate" with the high moguls.

Guthrie may have been striving for "the workers in the lowest places," but his audience was considerably more bourgeois. As with Lead Belly before him, the loyal following Guthrie ended up with was New York leftists. By the start of World War II, Americana music had begun to be romanticized and urbanized, transforming into a lifestyle choice with its own wardrobe and vocabulary, and taken away from the rural audiences that it was originally conceived for. The more that Americana music was adopted by the liberal left, the less accessible it became to the downtrodden. Folk music would never operate in the same way again: a document of daily life had become a political, social, and, later, commercial tool.

In a 2004 book review of *Ramblin' Man*, the critic Robert Christgau writes, "Those who resent Guthrie's doctrinaire leftism and staunch artistic populism are free to disparage his pretensions to authenticity and his claim to speak for the common man . . . He delighted in shocking and sometimes exploiting genteel progressives who took him up as a true working man, rustic wit or son of the soil. He mythologized himself compulsively and shamelessly." Guthrie was instantly treasured (and embellished) by the left because, as Christgau points out and Lomax celebrated, he was a "theory come true for several generations of folklorists, as well as the embodiment of folk music as the Popular Front conceived and promulgated it."

Still, Guthrie appeared comfortable with his newfound populist renown, and he fulfilled the role as best he could. Guthrie's underdog mythology—as the creator of dirty, authentic, by-and-for-the-people folk songs, an activist purring little-guy anthems for a theoretical audience of peers—was very much his own creation. Temporarily shacking up with Alan Lomax and his wife in Washington, D.C., Guthrie insisted on sleeping on the floor and eating his meals at the sink; Lomax's sister, Bess, later described Guthrie's antics as "annoying . . . Pretending he was such an ignorant country boy that he didn't know how to behave properly in public . . . Everybody knew it was an act."

The Woody Guthrie Archives are located on the twelfth floor of a sizable office building on West Fifty-seventh Street between Broadway and Eighth Avenue, just a few blocks from Central Park, and sandwiched between a Gap and a Duane Reade drug store. Here, at lunchtime, men and women in business suits troll delis and salad bars, toting plastic bags of semihot food back to their desks. Tourists, chugging north from Times Square, shift their backpacks and cameras, hastily navigating Columbus Circle's convoluted arteries. Nannies lug cloth sacks stuffed with organic produce from Whole Foods, exasperated, waving for cabs. It is an especially unromantic slice of Midtown Manhattan, corporate and bland, the kind of neighborhood most reasonable people evacuate by 7:30 at night.

It is my own fault that I am deeply disappointed by the Archives' location: deep down, I know it would not make more sense for Woody Guthrie's precious papers to be blowing free down Surf Avenue, getting caught in trees, smacking up against clam-stand sneezeguards, floating, yellow and damp, over gray waves. Nor would it be practical for Guthrie's legacy to be stacked in cardboard boxes in a Bowery basement, unsorted and unregulated, accessible only to sheepish, disheveled people in coveralls with a copy of *The Daily Worker* tucked under one arm.

I ride the elevator up, wander down a white hallway, ring a doorbell, and get buzzed into a tiny room with red and white linoleum floor tiles and countless boxes of papers, organized, cross-referenced, and lined up neatly on shelves. I am introduced to an extraordinarily helpful archivist, and, after signing some security forms, I am handed a pair of white gloves and a little metal stick so I can flip through Guthrie's papers without ever having to touch anything with my bare, sticky hands. The deeper I get into Guthrie's letters and journals, the more inappropriately privy I am to his sexual perversions, insecurities, doodles, dreams, and fears, the stranger it seems that I am learning these stories while wearing little white gloves, slouched over in a quiet, clean room in a Midtown Manhattan office building, swatting at journal pages with a little metal stick, trying not to make any noise. Three hours in, I decide that the Woody Guthrie Archives may be the most miraculous seven hundred square feet of space in all of Manhattan.

Guthrie's letters and journal entries are alternately upsetting, hilarious, true, despicable, and poignant. Clutching these papers in a gloved hand, it's hard not to start mulling big questions about genius and madness and poetry and the horrifying effects of neurodegenerative psychosis. By the late 1940s, Guthrie was beginning to show signs of illness, and his writings and his actions reflect that shift. During a 1948 separation from Marjorie, Guthrie began mailing dirty letters to Maxine Crissman's twenty-eight-year-old sister, Mary Ruth, detailing potential sexual escapades. Guthrie also included cutouts from local newspapers, circling descriptions of violent murders. Guthrie's misbehavior could be chalked up to his burgeoning Huntington's, which is often accompanied by psychotic breaks and hypersexuality, but the letters frightened Mary Ruth. She consulted with Maxine, who brought them to the Los Angeles Police Department.

In January 1947, Elizabeth Short (later known as the Black Dahlia) had been disemboweled and dumped in L.A.'s Leimert Park, and the LAPD were desperate for suspects. The police told the Crissmans that they wanted to question Guthrie about the murder. Although he was quickly exonerated, joining the thousands interviewed, hundreds considered suspects, and nearly sixty people who confessed to the crime, the letters were handed over to the U.S. Postal Service, and in August 1949 Guthrie was indicted for sending obscene material through the mail (at the time, Marjorie was pregnant with their fourth child). That October, Guthrie pleaded guilty and was placed in a psychiatric counseling program at the Quaker Emergency Services Readjustment Center in downtown Manhattan, where he was treated for "sexual behavior disorder." Guthrie left the clinic prematurely and, accordingly, was sentenced to six months in prison, serving only ten days before a judge reconsidered and released him.

Guthrie would drift in and out of psychiatric hospitals until his death on October 3, 1967, at the Creedmoor State Hospital in Queens, New York. He was too sick to appreciate or comment on the so-called folk revival of the 1960s (which the scholar Robert Cantwell loosely frames as the seven years between the Kingston Trio's 1958 cover of the old-time classic "Tom Dooley," and Bob Dylan's controversial electric appearance at the 1965 Newport Folk Festival), wherein folk music—once the product of the poor, and then the terrain of overeducated political activists—became a relatively viable commercial pop form. In his book *When We Were Good*, Cantwell describes the folk revival as a series of transformations that took place "when the carriers of a superannuated ideological minority found themselves celebrated as leads of a mass movement; when an esoteric and anti-commercial enthusiasm turned into a commercial bonanza; when an alienated, jazz-driven, literary bohemia turned to the simple songs of an old rural America."

American Socialist and Communist groups had been employing folk music as a promotional tool for some time—but the 1960s saw folk reach previously unimagined success as a vehicle for political change. Cantwell goes on to describe "Tom Dooley" going gold and Dylan wailing electric at Newport as "the boundaries between which a longstanding folksong movement, with elaborate political and social affiliations, emerged out of relative obscurity to become an immensely popular commercial fad, only to be swallowed up by a rock-and-roll revolution whose origins, ironically, it shared."

Woody Guthrie dramatically influenced a new wave of American folksingers, revolutionizing the genre and finalizing a shift in folk music's supposed audience. Guthrie enjoyed his share of acolytes, most of whom were so overwhelmed by his history, demeanor, and songcraft that their adulation eventually devolved into mimicry. Interestingly, Guthrie's two most ardent followers—Elliott Charles Adnopoz, better known as Ramblin' Jack Elliott, and Robert Zimmerman, better known as Bob Dylan—are also two of folk music's most rabidly self-mythologizing figures, constantly diddling with their own identities and backstories. Dylan has since gone on to define (and redefine), the modern folk canon, and his once-removed muse, Jack Elliott, is, at seventy-five, still touring folk clubs, dressed, as always, in a kerchief and cowboy hat.

When I first meet up with Elliott, it's backstage at B. B. King's Blues Club & Grill in Times Square, a cavernous club with a ten-dollar drink minimum and a roster that includes jam bands, overpierced nü-metal acts, rappers, and various aging blues and soul singers. I'm waiting in an office chair in a big gray corridor, staring at a silver coffee decanter and a stack of paper cups. A glass carafe of milk sits in an ice bucket; an orange paper pumpkin has been half-taped to a white wall, alongside a graffiti-accented fuse box. I can hear line cooks bickering in Spanish; a man dressed all in black, wearing a tie and headset, is seated by the backstage door, rifling through a stack of printouts. Gaynell Rogers, Elliott's manager, pops out of a dressing room, smiles, and beckons me inside; Elliott is seated on an old couch, wearing faded blue jeans, a green, pearl button shirt, and khaki-colored cowboy hat. A waitress walks in holding a small cocktail glass of Jameson's. Elliott perks up, taking the glass and thanking the waitress. "I thought you were going to bring a whole bottle," he says, smiling.

Elliott has tied a faded red bandana around his neck. His hair is white. Even at seventy-five, Elliott is striking, magnetic, and sweet. He likes to talk (and talk) about boats and sails and trucks and horses, and works circuitously, using questions as vehicles for more stories, peppering his narrative with rich, colorful descriptions (Elliott never got "the lead out of his ass," someone has "a face like a St. Bernard dog," others have delirious accents). Questions about music snake back to nautical knots, which he demonstrates with his hands, lacing his fingers together, looking up at me and grinning. Later, when he strides onstage, the venue will go silent; Elliott, guitar slung low around his neck, is a transfixing storyteller, charming and conspiratorial and humble, straddling a stool and hollering classic folk songs.

Elliott's father was an esteemed New York doctor ("I was supposed to be a doctor," Elliott will later muse onstage. "The smell of ether and babies crying, nah," he'll say with a snort), but Elliott ditched his family—and Brooklyn—as a teenager, joining the rodeo instead. "I was fifteen. I didn't go with any big plan," he explains. "I made my parents so upset—they didn't know where I was." Soon after, he changed his name to Buck Elliott. "I never liked that name, Elliott," he says, sneering. "It's a faggoty name. But Elliott on the end is OK, as a family name. I even got an Elliott tartan when I was in Scotland. But I can't wear a kilt. I don't have the legs for it."

Despite a mesmerizing performance style, Elliott was never much of a songwriter ("I think I wrote four songs in forty years," he says, smiling), and, consequently, is probably still better known for his relationship with Guthrie than his own discography. Even now, Elliott's face softens when asked about Woody. "The first card Guthrie sent me was written in crayon, in green or blue crayon, and said 'Dear Jack.' Then you had to rotate it or turn it upside down or move it around, and upside down, in different colored letters: 'Fuck you. Woody.' I wish I had saved it." He grins.

"I heard [Guthrie's] records [before I met him]. I used to hang out with an old sailmaker. He sailed around Cape Horn twelve times. And he mentioned something to me about the music of Woody Guthrie, because he knew that I was fooling around with a guitar a little bit, and I liked cowboy stuff. This was late 1946, early '47. Right before I ran away from home." Elliott nods. "I came back and started playing guitar. I was hanging out with other musicians who would play in Washington Square Park. Tom Paley was the greatest. Tom was going to Woody's house [in Coney Island] and I asked him if I could come along and play and hang out. He said, 'Buck, I can't invite you. Woody lives in a three-room apartment, and there are gonna be about nine people there—it's too crowded and there won't be anyplace to sit down. I can't invite you, but I'll give you Woody's number. He's a friendly guy—call him up. He'll invite you over. Just tell him that I gave you the number.' So I waited about a week for things to cool off. And then I called Woody, and he answered and said, 'Horse and mule barn.' He liked funny ways of answering the phone. So I said, 'Is Woody Guthrie there?' and he said, 'This is Woody Guthrie, speaking,' and I said, 'Hello, Woody, my name is Buck Elliott and I'm a friend of Tom Paley's and he gave me your number and I've been listening to some of your records and I like your music and I've been picking guitar for a couple of years, fooling around in rodeos and hitchhiking around, and I like the way you play and sound.' So he says, 'Come on over to the house one of these days here, Buck, bring your guitar, and we'll knock off a couple of tunes together.' And I thought, Gee, that's great, that sounds like an invite. 'OK,' I said. And he said, 'Don't come today, I got a bellyache.'

"And it turned out he had a very serious case of appendicitis. In fact, he almost died," Elliott continues. "They caught it just in time and were able to operate. And he was staying in the hospital right across the street from his apartment. So a couple of days went by and I thought I better call and see how Woody was doing. And his wife, Marjorie, answered and said that Woody was in the hospital. So I said, 'Can I visit him?' and she said, 'Not for a while, Buck, because he's very doped up, on pain pills and all that. He needs a while to simmer down.' So I waited about two or three more days, and then I was afraid to call and get refused again. So I thought, He's gotta be good by now, so I just went over there. And I brought my guitar. He was barely able to speak. I was premature. And I said, 'Would you like me to play you a song?' and he said, 'Better not make any noise—that guy in the other bed over there just got off the operating table.' "

Elliott rambles on, talking about how he went across the street to Guthrie's apartment, met Marjorie and the children, and hitched a ride home on the Belt Parkway "with a big Irish lady" in a Cadillac—his first time ever in a Cadillac—who was on her way to christen a brand new tugboat in Oyster Bay. He talks about a party in Connecticut, about driving to California, about how old the car was, about U.S. Route 40, about the weather that winter, about his cousins in San Francisco, about playing songs to Market Street winos, about ship model makers, the Anchor Saloon, the Harbor Hotel, and a man named Eric Swanson. Rogers gently reminds us that Elliott has to go onstage soon. I still don't know anything about the first time Elliott played guitar with Guthrie, but, as we hug goodbye, I'm not so sure it matters.

My understanding of Woody Guthrie gets more and more fragmented the further I dig, dissolving into a disjointed series of images and jokes, women and songs, ideas and fibs, friends and enemies, neurons and

DNA. It is easier to understand his life as a series of anecdotes, a collection of short stories, many put to music, some saved in pictures.

The Woody Guthrie Archives houses one of Anneke Guthrie's scrapbooks—Anneke and Guthrie were married in 1953, after his divorce from Marjorie was finalized. Anneke was twenty years old, a potter, prone to wearing no shoes, and exceptionally pretty. They separated one year later, officially splitting in 1955, after the birth of Guthrie's eighth child, a daughter whom Anneke put up for adoption before leaving the country (the girl was later killed, in a car crash, at age eighteen). It is a monstrous brown book with "Book #6: Tall Tales Heroes Funny. None of these actually, but a collection of pictures, some good and some bad, depending on a lot of things, of course. But open—and here they are," scrawled across the front. The book documents Woody, Ramblin' Jack Elliott, and Anneke's March 1953 roadtrip from New York City to Jacksonville, Florida, in Ramblin' Jack's rickety Ford Model A, which he salvaged from a junkyard for twenty-five dollars. "Woody spent fifty dollars trying to keep it running, so I gave him the car when we got down there." Elliott laughs. "In those days, Model As weren't considered antiques yet—they were just old cars. It was a 1931 Model A. The car was twenty-two years old, and I was twenty-one years old. Anneke wrote with soap in the lower right-hand corner of the windshield, 'Moooove, old A-bone!' It was my second car."

Small black-and-white pictures of the trio partaking in standard roadtrip behavior—playing guitar and banjo, sitting in the car, driving, breaking down, "sampling southern cola—tastes the same," smoking, cooking breakfast, picking their teeth—are accompanied by self-deprecating captions. Some photos have been ripped out. Some photos feature Guthrie's naked ass. Shortly after the group arrived in Florida, Jack left for Texas. "I left after a week because I realized I wasn't very welcome. Woody was forty-two and I was twenty-one and his wife was twenty-one. Anneke and I were the same age and Woody was an old guy.

So he felt that there was a little danger of something going on. Which of course there wasn't—I just worshipped him, I loved him. I couldn't imagine doing something like that. But he was getting more grumpy every day, so I just picked up on the hint and decided I wasn't welcome, and I gave him the car and left. I hitchhiked to Texas, got a ride in a big semi, and the guy let me drive the truck. I only went to Texas because [the driver] said he would let me drive it. I was really heading for New York State. I met that truck driver again about thirty years later. He lives in Houston—he was retired when I met him the second time. But he remembered me." Elliott beams.

The Archive also possesses a folder of black-and-white photographs of Elliott and Guthrie playing together in Washington Square Park in June 1954, thirteen years before his death—already, Guthrie, bearded and gaunt, looks impossibly ill, his guitar tied to his neck with white string, a long cigarette dripping from his lips. Onlookers, lounging on fountain steps in white T-shirts and Ray-Bans, look mostly unimpressed. In one shot, Guthrie lies flat on the ground, left leg bent, his guitar balancing on his chest, black motorcycle boots sticking out from the cuffs of his pants. He barely looks alive. Elliott remembers the famed New York crime scene photographer Weegee snapping pictures of Guthrie. "I asked him to not take any more pictures. Woody wasn't looking so good. Nobody else recognized him."

The summer of 1954 was particularly rough for Guthrie; he had been arrested twelve times in six weeks, ambling from California to New York, trespassing in freight yards, drinking heavily (likely to conceal his encroaching chorea), hitchhiking, neglecting basic personal hygiene, and getting picked up on vagrancy charges. That September, Guthrie checked himself into the Brooklyn State Hospital. Twenty months later, he left, borrowed ten or twenty bucks from his manager, Harold Leventhal, and was found in Morristown, New Jersey, taking a leisurely, dazed stroll down the highway. Morris County police officers arrested Guthrie for trespassing; the medical reports from the New Jersey State Hospital at Greystone Park note that Guthrie "had a silly little smile on his face at times." He was institutionalized with schizophrenia and would remain at Greystone for nearly five years.

As Cray explains, Ramblin' Jack Elliott had been living in Great Britain for the previous six years and, by his own admission, playing "Woody Guthrie songs exactly the way that Woody did" (even Guthrie snickered, "Jack sounds more like me than I do"). In early 1961, a nineteen-year-old Bob Dylan, abandoning a half-finished degree at the University of Minnesota, showed up at Marjorie's door. Fourteen-year-old Arlo Guthrie liked Dylan and brought him along on a visit to Woody; awed and humbled, Dylan immediately wrote "Song for Woody" in a drug store on Eighth Street in downtown Manhattan, setting his words to the tune of Guthrie's "1913 Massacre." Dylan later admitted, "Woody's songs were having that big an effect on me, an influence on every move I made, what I ate and how I dressed." Not long after, Dylan began mimicking Jack Elliott's interpretation of Guthrie, latching onto, as Cray notes, every detail of "appearance, manner, and gesture"—one young, middle-class Jewish man appropriating the already-appropriated shtick of another.

Guthrie was discharged from Greystone on April 4, 1961, and moved back to Brooklyn State Hospital. By early 1966 he weighed less than a hundred pounds and was transferred to Creedmoor, where he died in 1967. Of Guthrie's eight children, three (Cathy, Bill, and his daughter by Anneke) died of other causes before they could be tested for the Huntington's gene. Three (Nora, Arlo, and Joady) are disease-free. His two oldest (Gwendolyn and Sue) each succumbed to Huntington's at age forty-one.

Since Guthrie's death, he's been recontextualized and, in some cases, reanointed by scads of modern artists (from Jay Farrar to Lou Reed to Nellie McKay), both on tribute albums and unlikely new recordings: the

Klezmatics, a New York–based klezmer band dedicated to melding traditional Yiddish culture with contemporary global sounds, released *Wonder
Wheel* in 2006, a collection of unreleased Guthrie songs (like the *Mermaid Avenue* records, the band borrowed only lyrics, not music) produced by Nora and nominated for a Grammy award. Likewise, in 2003,
the German singer-songwriter Hans-Eckardt Wenzel recorded fourteen
songs with previously unpublished lyrics; in the record's liner notes, Nora
writes, "Woody, and his songs, are lifted up out of the dusty pages and
thrown back out into the street where they belong because my father's
songs are always street songs and street people's words. It's truly amazing
for me now to watch these two new friends, Wenzel and Woody, rambling together along streets of Germany."

In 1967, Woody Guthrie's ashes were tossed into the Atlantic
Ocean, from a jetty between Seagate and Coney Island. A bronze plaque
sits in a cemetery just outside Okemah, alongside the grave of his sister,
Clara, but I suspect that Guthrie is, in fact, rather pleased to be bobbing,
eternally, in the bleak, scrappy waters of Coney Island, mingling with
used condoms and car parts, shoelaces and beer bottles, toothpicks and
coffee cups, floating proud amongst the plain old garbage of plain old
people—the stuff of folk song.

The New, Weird, Hyphenated America:

Indie-Folk and the Next American Revival

Trying to isolate the cultural moment when Williamsburg, Brooklyn, went from titillating to exhausting is like trying to define the tipping point wherein employing a piece of urban slang or quoting from a certain film shifts from being relatively witty to completely humiliating. Williamsburg itself "jumped the shark" (check the multilevel irony!) at some indefinable moment between 1998 and 2006: After a dizzying shower of newspaper trend pieces, condo developments, $4200-a-month lofts, and glossy photo shoots, the neighborhood lost its artistic cache, becoming less the terrain of trailblazing bohemians and more a haven for bond traders with iPods. Williamsburg's fall from grace was so inevitable—so patent and well-documented and agreed-upon—that it's a cliché to even point it out. By now, barbs about trucker hats and faux-vintage T-shirts and pre-frayed Converse are cringingly ubiquitous. Williamsburg is a cartoon.

Tonight, I'm standing in the drained shallow end of McCarren Park

Pool, a former public swim-center dug and christened in the summer of 1936, the eighth of eleven city pools powered by FDR's Depression-fighting Works Progress Administration. Situated on the southern edge of Greenpoint, on the precipice of neighboring Williamsburg, the pool was emptied in 1984 but has since been (contentiously) adopted by the radio monolith Clear Channel, which donated $250,000 to the City Parks Foundation to allow for basic structural improvements (and, depressingly, the whitewashing of graffiti) and outfitted the pool with a big, fancy stage. The pool cuts a massive valley; it was originally intended to float nearly seven thousand swimmers. I will later read on Shadow lands.net—a "ghosts and hauntings" website, the entry to which requires clicking on a graphic of a sword jammed into a stone—that a little girl drowned in the pool and is still "seen roaming the area at night, calling for help." For me, the fog of haunting hangs thick over much of north Brooklyn, although it seems to have less to do with paranormal schisms and more to do with too much change, too fast, by young people culturally predisposed to celebrate grit. Williamsburg and Greenpoint are spared the flower boxes and refinished exteriors of equally (if differently) gentrified neighborhoods like Park Slope, and here, dirty vinyl siding and rusted tin awnings are reminders of a past that's been consumed and commodified by the present. I can't decide which revolution—the one that erases all ugliness or the one that anoints it—is creepier.

Along the exterior edges of the pool, the Brooklyn Brewery has set up tents, selling local lager by the cup, while women from fellow Brooklyn venue Warsaw (located inside the Polish National Home, which has served as a meeting hall–performance space for north Brooklyn's considerable Polish community for nearly a century and has turned its first floor into a hipster-enticing indie-rock ballroom, complete with colossal oil paintings, Polish and American flags, chandeliers, and a disco ball) dish out kielbasa platters and plates of pierogi, complete with sautéed onions, apple sauce, and sour cream. I am eating a vanilla ice cream cone with chocolate crunchies, bought from a Mister Softee truck parked poolside, and waiting for Iron and Wine to take the stage. Studying the crowd, I check off rote signifiers of twentysomething Brooklyn hipster-dom: star tattoos, oversize sunglasses, studded belts, canvas bags with woodland animals (squirrels, deer, and finches, especially) patched in place, scads of rubber bracelets, American Apparel T-shirts, too much jewelry, choppy haircuts, skinny waists. We all look the same.

Iron and Wine is the pet project of former community college professor Sam Beam, a South Carolina native whose voice still harbors a tiny bit of drawl, even filtered through eight solid inches of beard. Beam recorded his debut album, *The Creek Drank the Cradle*, on a shoddy four-track in his Miami home (whispering into the microphone, indie-legend goes, so as not to wake up his sleeping daughters). Comprised solely of scratchy, barely there vocals, acoustic guitar, and a bit of banjo, *The Creek Drank the Cradle* is an intensely personal record, tackling faith, fidelity, and human catharsis with urgency. It is the kind of record that gets passed between friends like dog-eared copies of Rilke or Robert Lowell, pressed into hands, slipped into mailboxes, tucked under pillows. It's impossible not to think that we would all be a little better off if it came standard in hotel drawers.

The Creek Drank the Cradle was put out, mostly untouched, by Seattle's famed Sub Pop Records in 2002. (Nirvana released its lo-fi debut, *Bleach*, on Sub Pop in 1989, initially selling somewhere around six thousand copies—but *Bleach* went many times platinum after Nirvana's major label breakthrough, *Nevermind*, ushered in a flannel-shirted revolution, inadvertently making Sub Pop America's most prominent—and probably wealthiest—independent record label, 49 percent of which is now controlled by Warner Bros.) The record was instantly adopted by indie-rock fans, mostly because it was so easy to be tugged into the quasi-escapist, heavily idealized portrait of Beam-as-basement-troubadour—a bearded, southern father of two with a cardboard box full of shitty equipment and an unassuming shoulder shrug. Listening to *The Creek Drank the Cradle* felt like accidentally digging up a diamond, clutching it briefly in a soil-streaked palm, and then shoving it deep into your front pocket, eyes shooting around suspiciously. Nobody who found it could ever believe their luck. The vague sense that the composition and realization of *Creek* were just as unexpected and accidental as the record's eventual celebration lent Beam's work an edge of serendipity. Which seems especially profound (and jarring) in the face of all this hipster ornament.

Beam followed up his debut with a string of increasingly better-recorded, slightly more raucous releases, beginning with 2004's *Our Endless Numbered Days*. Now, when Iron and Wine tours, Beam plays rock clubs, not coffeehouses, threading his dulcet murmurs through giant, buzzing stacks of speakers, shot into sticky black boxes with NOFX stickers plastered to the floor, long frozen in place by hundreds of coats of beer-and-spit shellac. In its truest forms, folk music has always been progressive, audacious, fearless—and when Beam shuffles onstage, commanding reverent silence in a room better known for fist-pumping and beer-hollering, his moves are just as brave, just as revolutionary.

The last time I saw Iron and Wine perform, following the release of 2005's *Woman King* EP and *In the Reins*, a collaboration with Arizona's mariachi-infused folk-rockers Calexico, his set was largely electric, and Beam's signature hush had been exchanged for a thin, clear yelp. Although his electric presentation was rich and complete, it also felt protected and distant, insulated from the audience by towers of amplifiers and speakers. Looking around at all the sloping concrete, empty space, and open air, I'm presuming that Beam will be plugged in tonight, too, and I think about how in some ways, going louder is also a way of pulling back.

Chicago's Califone is opening for Iron and Wine tonight, and they amble onstage to light applause. Formed by Tim Rutili in the late 1990s as an antidote to Red Red Meat, Rutili's previous (and heavily experimental) band, Califone has since produced eight long-players, each with a slightly different lineup of musicians. Listening to Califone's sweaty, blues-heavy scrap-rock is not an entirely stable sensory experience: devious, fertile, and dangerously pretty, it sounds as futuristic as it does ancient, synthesizing mountain and Delta traditions with contemporary technology, marrying organic instruments with otherworldly blips—and reimagining Americana for a nation more reliant on machines than the grace of God. Lyrically, the frontman Tim Rutili favors tiny vignettes over narrative arcs, and his songs usually read more like prose poems than stories—which, given the hyperfragmented sound-collage of Califone's instrumentation (banjos and synthesizers, acoustic guitars and loops of found sound), makes a certain kind of sense. The disparity of sounds feels broken, nonlinear, and imagistic.

Months later, when I talk to Califone about its music, we're crouched in the basement of Brooklyn's Southpaw, where the band is scheduled to perform a sold-out show, their second in as many nights. "It's all instinct," Rutili says, explaining his band's distinctive clatter. "There's not a lot of talk about theory or anything."

Rutili and bandmate Jim Becker, who plays banjo and violin, certainly consider early Americana records an influence, although they're more interested in recreating the intangible grit and grain of rural music, rather than mimicking its sound. "I remember when I first heard Robert Johnson—it blew my head off," Rutili says. "The way we use that old stuff in Califone is more as a texture—a feel that we tried to lift. It's hard to relate to [on a literal level] because it's not 1912."

Both Rutili and Becker are well versed in early American folk and blues. "When people ask me 'So, what were your favorite recordings of this year?' it's all fiddle music from the 1920s and '30s. Mississippi string band music—that's just from outer space—it's great. North Carolina, West Virginia fiddlers—I've had the opportunity to play with some of these guys. I've always listened to country blues, fife and drum, Cajun music. It's endless." Becker nods.

"When I was like, seventeen, in high school, I used to go to the Town Hall pub and play open mics," Rutili recounts. "And there was a woman there, she was maybe fifty years old, and I started dating her daughter. But the mom had a record collection that fucking killed me. That's where I first heard the Harry Smith folk anthology. She was from that generation, she had all those records . . . and I was thinking, OK, I really like this part of it, but I really like Black Flag a lot, too, and I really like Hüsker Dü. But that stuff always stayed with me, so it's interesting to hear [newer, younger artists] discovering that stuff now," Rutili explains. "The thing about those old records," he continues, "is the way [they were] recorded with one microphone—the scratches, hearing someone's foot tapping on the ground. I think to approach those songs you need to use your own aesthetic to destroy them. And that's the thing about the people doing folk music now—they're trying to make records that sound as if they were made in the 1960s. And in a lot of ways I love it, but there's something to be said for originality—to take those things and put it through your own filter, and not be slavishly devoted to that one sound."

Tonight at McCarren Park, Califone rolls through tracks from their most recent release, *Roots and Crowns*; the crowd is appreciative, but Califone seems better suited for a smaller, more intimate venue, where their twitters and gasps are more audible. Here, every chord and shout fights for ear-space with casual conversation, beer lines, and bloggers scrolling through their digital cameras, comparing photographs. By the time Sam Beam walks onstage, the crowd is thicker, the sun is dipping below the horizon, and everyone seems better prepared to stand still and listen to songs. Beam, joined by a full band (including his sister on backing vocals), plays a mostly plugged-in set, save a handful of acoustic cuts, and the crowd grows weirdly rowdy, screaming incomprehensible requests at the stage. This is not the folk show of yesteryear.

Beam is part of a new—if difficult to effectively delineate—

movement in folk music. In the last decade and a half, a slew of avant-folk players have inched into the indie-rock market, nudging aside power-pop trios and noise ensembles to make quiet, meditative acoustic music as much a part of the indie aesthetic as Converse sneakers. Starting in New York in the mid-1980s with anti-folk—a punk-folk hybrid that mocked the mushiness of 1960s folk revivalists, revving up folksy songs with snotty asides and irreverent lyrics—and continuing through myriad permutations, folk music has been consistently reimagined for younger, hipper audiences.

In August 2003, the U.K. music magazine *The Wire* published a cover story titled "Welcome to the New Weird America," wherein the Scottish scribe David Keenan jets to Brattleboro, Vermont, to detail "a groundswell musical movement" drawing on "an intoxicating range of avant garde sounds, from acoustic roots to drone, ritualistic perfor- mance, Krautrock, ecstatic jazz, hillbilly mountain music, psychedelia, archival blues and folk sides, Country funk, and more." Keenan attends the Brattleboro Free Folk Festival, organized by Matt Valentine (who currently performs with Erika Elder as half of MV & EE with the Bum- mer Road and is generally considered the founding father of the east coast arm of the free-folk movement), and speaks with festival perform- ers, trying his best to isolate and describe the heartbeats behind this new, beguiling strain of American folk music.

Following Keenan's article, most of the artists and albums included in his piece were tucked under the umbrella of "New Weird America," which flowed into the slightly more descriptive "free-folk," which be- came "freak-folk," and subsequently devolved, as more and more diverse artists were swept up in the wave, into the catchall "indie-folk"—even though the differences between psych-infused free-folk like MV & EE and acoustic indie-folk like Iron and Wine generally seem profound enough to warrant at least two distinct, hyphenated prefixes.

In his article, Keenan talks about how contemporary free-folk artists are writing an "alternative American narrative," which makes sense, seeing as how this particular branch of American folk is, in some ways, antithetical to its predecessors. Although most free-folkers cite early American folk and blues among their most significant influences, the genre is largely experimental: its melodies and narratives operate outside of standard folk paradigms and its stories are not linear or universal in a way that's immediately self-evident, making the music feel, at times, inaccessible. The songs are often unstructured and long (think Grateful Dead meets Captain Beefheart) and thus less likely to be repeated around a campfire or sung to children. Meanwhile, their creators are intellectual eccentrics, removed from the working-class everyman-ness of more "down-home" acts like the Carter Family or Woody Guthrie.

Still, these songs and records are concerned with social change, created without much commercial ambition (releases are often hand-pressed in limited numbers), and facilitate a sense of community (plenty of free-folk artists seem to record and play mostly for one another, self-referentially, collaboratively, and, in some cases, exclusively). There is also a New Age–retro-hippie mysticism inherent to free-folk that, while inviting ridicule from plenty, harkens back to (as Keenan points out) the metaphysical mystery of Harry Smith's Celestial Monochord. And although free-folkers' unchained, improvised noodling and stream-of-consciousness structure doesn't lead to songs that sound like traditional folk songs, there is a common element of total spontaneity and truth: as Keenan writes, "they have stripped improvisation of its jazz-informed reputation as a cerebral discipline and rebirthed it as the original, primal musical gesture, reminding it that it was always folk music's most natural mode of expression."

Free-folk is also heavily influenced by British folksingers from the latter half of the twentieth century, mirroring, however inadvertently, the exact origins of *all* American folk music, which itself was inspired by Celtic, Scottish, and English folk songs in the early 1800s. British bands and artists like Bert Jansch and Pentangle, Comus, Shirley Collins, the Incredible String Band, Donovan, Vashti Bunyan, Fairport Convention, Roy Harper, and loads of others peaked in Britain in the 1960s and '70s, cranking out high, disorienting songs, marked mainly by the ways in which they weaved ancient Celtic traditions with world music flourishes (the Incredible String Band incorporated Middle Eastern instruments like sitar, oud, and tamboura), or added elements of jazz, progressive rock, psychedelia, and, occasionally, earlier California alt-country (think Gram Parsons–era Byrds). The resulting records were both traditional and strange, highly stylized, and consumed, for the most part, by niche rock fans and never folk music purists.

But ultimately, free-folk is as equally inspired by early Americana as it is by modern British folk, and the genre pays considerable homage to Harry Smith's *Anthology of American Folk Music* in particular. The former musician–music journalist–music executive Howard Wuelfing, who operates the public relations company Howlin Wuelf Media and represents the majority of emerging free-folk artists, emphasizes the *Anthology*'s influence on his clients' sound: "Its CD release in the nineties was vastly influential on the new generation of folks turned on by the Old, Weird America. But I'd say that different artists working in this sort of music draw on different percentages of [British and American folk], varying from artist to artist. Just as important, [free-folk artists] are also influenced by [contemporary] avant-garde musicians like Current 93's David Tibet and Genesis P-Orridge's later work with Psychic TV, not to mention a whole generation of quirky American singer-songwriters from the late sixties, like Biff Rose, Linda Perhacs, Jesse Winchester, Ruthann Friedman, Michael Hurley, Karen Dalton, Randy Newman, Van Dyke Parks, and others."

Free-folk is also sold (when it's sold at all) to fans of avant-garde or experimental music (Wuelfing describes his target audience as "people who are attracted to innovation and the unusual") and, with its meandering structure, unrecognizable instrumentation, and jam-band atmospherics, would likely seem wholly foreign to most Ramblin' Jack Elliott fans.

Regardless, the genre is gaining in commercial viability: in the early 1990s, Will Oldham, a singer-songwriter from Louisville, Kentucky, began recording bleak, folk-tinged music under various guises, most fronted by the word *Palace* (see Palace Brothers, Palace Music, Palace Songs, or just Palace), before releasing one full-length and two EPs under his given name and a slew of records as confounding alter-ego Bonnie 'Prince' Billy. Oldham's dark (and occasionally bizarre) records earned him considerable underground success and proved that indie-folk could be perverse and emotional at the same time. Oldham's songs, much like Califone's or Freakwater's, are a mishmash of broad American influences, pulling in and synthesizing everything from punk to blues to folk to classic country (in 2000, an aging Johnny Cash even recorded a duet with Oldham—a cover of Oldham's chilling "I See a Darkness"—for one of Cash's Rick Rubin–produced comeback albums, *American III: Solitary Man*). Oldham rarely gives interviews, but in 2002 he endeavored to explain his sound to the UK newspaper *The Observer*: "Too much emphasis is put on American roots music when people try and place me," Oldham insisted. "You know, I grew up listening to punk: Hüsker Dü, Dinosaur Jr. I'm steeped in a lot of stuff. Led Zeppelin as much as Bukka White. Miles Davis as much as Merle Haggard. It all goes in and some of it stays there, and some of it comes back out."

In 2002, Devendra Banhart, a Texas-born folksinger raised in Venezuela, released his debut, *Oh Me Oh My . . .* , on Young God Records, an independent label founded by Michael Gira, formerly of acclaimed experimental rock band Swans. *Oh Me Oh My . . .* laid the groundwork for Banhart's sophomore breakthrough, 2004's *Rejoicing in the Hands*, a collection of beguiling acoustic songs, each anchored by Banhart's otherworldly falsetto (eerily reminiscent of Emmett Miller and

John Jacob Niles) and fairy-tale lyrics. Banhart is an unabashed disciple of modern British folk: he recently trilled on former Pentangle frontman Bert Jansch's solo record, *The Black Swan*, Vashti Bunyan sings on *Rejoicing*, and Banhart appears on Bunyan's latest, *Lookaftering* (if one is predisposed to believe Internet rumors, Banhart also writes Bunyan's name on his arm before every show). But in many ways, Banhart's creaky, whimsical folk songs seem just as informed by the wily antics of Woody Guthrie and, later, Bob Dylan.

Around the same time Banhart began slinking onto college radio charts, Joanna Newsom, a California-born, classically trained harpist, released her debut, *The Milk-Eyed Mender*, on Chicago's Drag City Records (following a successful tour with fellow Drag City–signee Will Oldham). Newsom's chirpy, overarticulated vocals were an enticing accompaniment to the record's sparkling melodies, and Newsom became an underground pop star of sorts. Other bands and artists, with notably diverse approaches to the free-folk sound—see CocoRosie, Vetiver, Six Organs of Admittance, No-Neck Blues Band, P.G. Six, Sunburned Hand of the Man, Dredd Foole, White Magic, Wooden Wand and the Vanishing Voice, Faun Fables, Animal Collective, Espers—promptly followed, united, at times, by only the fanciful capriciousness of their names.

The relatively elevated profile of free-folk owes a considerable amount to the viability and visibility of indie-folk musicians like Banhart, Newsom, Oldham, and Beam, who, despite being far from the mainstream, represent the more commercial end of the sound. Free-folk was emerging as a valid (if still slightly confused) subgenre of independent rock, and it wasn't terribly long before journalists began trying to nail down the specifics of the movement. In a 2004 article for *The New York Times*, Alec Hanley Bemis defines Banhart, Newsom, and their peers as being part of "a highly idealistic pack of young musicians whose music is quiet, soothing, and childlike, their lyrics fantastic, surreal, and free of the slightest trace of irony." Two years later, the *Times* published another story about the phenomenon, this time by the music critic Will Hermes, who declared free-folk "one of the most creatively vigorous strains of underground music." In 2005, the *San Francisco Chronicle* called free-folk's primary players "the new flower children," citing influences ranging from "the British Isles folk of Davey Graham, Bert Jansch, and just about anything produced by Joe Boyd, through the Delta and country blues of Lead Belly and Reverend Gary Davis to Fred Neil's bluesy folk-jazz and Tim Buckley's rococo improv-folk-rock." Later that year, the British author Simon Reynolds was more skeptical (and I suspect his prose is tongue-in-cheek), writing about the movement in *The Village Voice*: "These tracks either dissipate into oxbow lakes of abstraction or gradually accumulate disparate jetsom [*sic*] into tripnotic juggernauts . . . the only truly folky aspect is a slight bias toward sounds of acoustic provenance."

While the indie/free-folk scene can hardly be called cohesive (unlike crunk or grunge or, say, New York punk, it's not geographically determined, which makes it far more difficult to demarcate), there are still enough connections and cross-references to build a pretty decent color-coded map. Aside from squabbling over the last dented Fender Rhodes at the local Salvation Army, indie/free-folk artists tend to share producers, labels, friends, tours (Devendra Banhart thanked Beam in the liner notes to his third full-length, *Nino Rojo*, even though at the time of the record's release, they had never met). Old or new, folk is, after all, still an exercise in community. And even though indie/free-folk isn't geographically based in any real, encompassing sense, a few distinct communities—San Francisco, Chicago, Brooklyn—do exist. I'm most compelled by the homespun scene Keenan infiltrated, in the areas surrounding Brattleboro, Vermont. It's where the term *free-folk* first came into use, when Matt Valentine orchestrated the first (and, so far, last) Brattleboro Free Folk Festival in May 2003.

Brattleboro is tucked in the southeastern corner of the state, in a green, brambly valley between the Connecticut and West Rivers, and is best known for its kayaking, ice skating, art galleries, and the fact that public nudity, if not "done to promote sexual gratification," is entirely legal within its borders. When I chug up Main Street and into town, arriving slightly after midnight on a blustery mid-January Friday, the air temperature is hovering around seven degrees, and no one appears to be capitalizing on the city's relaxed notions regarding nakedness. Streets are barren, dusted with snow, and dark. I've rented the only room at the Artist's Loft, a local art gallery topped by a two-room apartment and leased to out-of-towners by the weekend. I park, tug my wool hat down over my ears, grab my duffel bag, and sprint upstairs. The interior of the loft is decorated with classic Vermont kitsch: loads of oil paintings and watercolors, stacks of books, a blanket with cross-stitched pictures of herbs, a library of VHS tapes, quilts, a shelf full of mugs, a crystal punch bowl with eight glasses, a water pitcher shaped like a toad, a lamp made out of a clarinet, baskets, pillows, ceramic bowls, and, on a shelf overlooking the bed, a series of nesting Russian dolls. The bathroom features a flamingo shower curtain and a collection of antique wooden combs, culled from a variety of global cultures. The living room window looks out over the frozen Connecticut River. Periodically, throughout the night, freight trains roar past, horns blasting to scatter, I'm told, vagrants and cats; I'm fairly certain I don't get more than ten consecutive minutes of sleep before the sun rises and sharp, white light starts beaming through the windows. It is a cold and unforgiving morning.

Waddling through town—my body swathed in four layers of fleece, legs wrapped preemptively in tights, long johns, and jeans—I decide Brattleboro contains all the necessary components for a neo-hippie paradise: a friendly, well-stocked cooperative supermarket packed with fresh organic produce, textile shops with names like Save the Corporations from Themselves, at least two bookstores, a record shop, a brewery, and a nice spot to go ice skating. I buy a cup of coffee from Mocha Joe's, get into my car, and follow Route 9 west to the Royal Chelsea Diner, just outside of town, where I order a bowl of oatmeal, brown sugar, and locally produced maple syrup. The waitress calls me "Hon," coffee is poured (and poured often) into a thick, ceramic mug, and my entire breakfast—even after I order a homemade cranberry nut muffin, on the side, with Cabot Creamery butter—costs me less than six dollars.

Everyone I've ever talked to about the free-folk scene in southeastern Vermont suggests I should try my very best to meet up with Byron Coley, famed record collector, musician, and writer for *Forced Exposure*, *Spin*, and *The Wire*, among other outlets. (When I interned in the editorial department at *Spin* as a student, I remember reading Coley's pivotal columns in back issues of the magazine from the 1980s, sneaking copies to my desk when I should have been transcribing interviews.) After breakfast, I finally meet up with Byron in the café of the Brattleboro Food Co-op, where we talk about the origins and nuances of free-folk as a genre—Coley, as far as I can tell, has a better, more thoughtful handle on the specifics of the genre than anyone else I've met.

"It's record collector music, in a way," Coley muses. "I first knew Matt [Valentine] as a record collector. I would sell him weird folk stuff, British and American primitive stuff, weird homemade acoustic guitar music . . . records with a real mysterious vibe. So it was very record collector in that it was about getting records and looking and seeing, OK, who wrote these songs? Same as the guys discovering blues in the sixties—you'd get a Cream album, and look, and be like 'Who's Robert Johnson?' It was largely guys, sitting alone in their rooms, at night, looking at liner notes.

"[Free-folk] isn't part of the folk tradition," Coley explains. "[These records] are all creations of, and re-creations of, folk tradition. [It] isn't something that's being passed down through generations—it's being learned, and it's being learned from records," he continues. "So it's like a fabulous simulation. But that doesn't mean that it's not heartfelt, and it doesn't mean that it's not true, contextually, for the people who are doing it. And it doesn't mean that [the artists] have sold themselves a bill of goods by doing it. But there are people who are fabricating something interesting, and people who are fabricating something much less interesting, and a lot of that has to do with the models that they choose to structure themselves after. And that's where the record collector thing really becomes important. The more you've heard, the better chances you have of creating an interesting model."

For Coley, I surmise, free-folk is—much like rock 'n' roll—an inherently derivative exercise. What saves it, as a genre, is that its influences are so obscure and far-reaching that the resultant sounds seem entirely new and unusual. "All contemporary culture is a collage of stuff that's been done, sometimes to death. So it's a matter of finding an interesting way to represent it, and to do it in a way where, if it's not exactly new, it resembles newness," Coley declares. "It's something I think Matt [Valentine] is extremely successful at. I can sit down and listen to his stuff and pick apart where this stuff is coming from, but it's such a weird quilt of elements, and I recognize that that's his tongue, that's the way he speaks, that's his vision."

Coley has lived in the Connecticut River Valley for nearly twenty years, and he recognizes the region's significance in the origins of the free-folk revolution. "In the Internet era, it's very difficult to maintain any kind of a regional style for any appreciable period. There's too much seeping, too much back and forth between stuff." Coley shrugs. "A place like Brattleboro has always been kind of a land out of time. It's a liberal enclave with a weird history. And that's where you'll see this [music] happening—you'll never see it happening in opposition to something."

I ask Coley what he thinks about new, more mainstream indie-folk, like Iron and Wine. "I reviewed *The Creek Drank the Cradle* in *The Wire*. People were like, 'What is this, I've never heard this, how can this be on Sub Pop?'" Coley laughs. "I wrote [Sam Beam] and was like, Yeah, there's all these people up here [in Vermont] doing this stuff, and he was like, 'What? I have no idea what you're talking about. I've never heard of any of that stuff at all.' He was just off doing his thing, in some kind of isolation."

So is it possible, then, to draw a line from Sam Beam to Matt Valentine? I ask. "Oh yeah. There's really an aesthetic—it's qualitative, in a way, but it has to do with . . ." He trails off. "OK, now I've said it, but is there really a line?" Coley laughs.

I think of what Beam told me, in a 2004 interview for *Paste* magazine: "I honestly don't feel like I'm part of a scene. But at the same time, it's hard to deny it—the sound is similar, there are so many common people. I think people are always playing acoustic music, but public attention tends to crest. It cycles," he admitted. "Like the whole sixties into the seventies, when people suddenly wanted to hear something more synthetic. It goes back and forth."

"There should be," Coley finally finishes. "That was the first thing that Sub Pop did that was really not a rock thing. I was really surprised when I first heard it. And something led Sam Beam to send in that tape." We pause. Neither of us is ready to presume precisely what that impetus—an inevitable cultural moment? a series of social and political clues that spurred a whole new generation of free-thinkers to latch on to acoustic guitars? a sudden, nationwide sense that it was finally time for folk music to reemerge in the underground?—may have been.

Later, when I ask Eric Johnson of Chicago's Fruit Bats—a fellow Sub Pop–signee who plays remarkable electronics-infused folk music— whether or not he thinks there is a viable, if broad, freak-folk scene, he seems optimistic. "I'd like to think there's a sense of community. That's not such a bad thing, y'know? I've toured with Iron and Wine and played with Califone, who sort of gave me my start and are my musical godfathers. I feel like there's a lot of crossover and respect on all ends." Johnson nods. "Fruit Bats has always been pretty independent, even though it's been seen alternately as an extension of Califone, or Sub Pop, or [Johnson's current collaborators] the Shins or whatever. I'd like to try and dip my toe into all that stuff, really. Devendra, I love him as a person and an artist. Those Animal Collective records have consistently blown my mind, though I've never once met those dudes. There's all kinds of stuff going on that makes me feel like there must be some sort of collective consciousness happening, but it seems to be unfolding in a pretty organic way. And [the music being made] is all really different."

Johnson also confirms Coley's theory that free-folk is, in many ways, the inevitable by-product of record collecting. "I'd always been into folk with psychedelic elements. I got really into that stuff in my early twenties, y'know when you get to that age where you become an obsessive studier of genres, figuring out that the Byrds lead to the Burrito Brothers lead to the Dillards, and then I got into the British stuff: Nick Drake into Fairport Convention and then the slightly weirder stuff like that Mayo Thompson solo record, or the Incredible String Band. All those old bands were taking elements of traditional music like blues and American country and Celtic music, or whatever, and infusing the drug culture into that. At least that was how I saw it. Then I figured with technology like samplers and synths, you could take it a step further. When I was getting Fruit Bats going in the mid- to late-nineties, I had this weird vision of what I wanted to call Log Cabin Spaceship Music—even with this vision of a rocket made out of logs hurling through space. Sort of like that idea that Gram Parsons came up with—'cosmic American music,' this slightly contradictory name for something that didn't have a totally clear concept, just a mix of shit I really liked, really. It wasn't until a little bit later that I found out that the Incredible String Band had a song called 'Log Cabin Home in the Sky.' Anyway, so yeah, it made perfect sense to fold in futuristic stuff into this folky music. It seemed like the next step," Johnson finishes.

Byron Coley is at his most comfortable when talking about records, and we chat for more than an hour before he leaves to pick up his son. I spend the rest of the afternoon roaming Brattleboro, driving north to the longest covered bridge in all of Vermont, eating lunch at the Townshend Dam Diner, buying farm-fresh eggs, watching ice fishers and hockey players on the backwater lake behind the Brattleboro Retreat, a nonprofit mental health and addiction recovery center founded in 1834 and previously known as the Vermont Asylum for the Insane. When my toes go numb, I stumble back to the roadside and curl into the backseat of my car, turning the heat up as far as it will go, and playing CDs from Iceland's Sigur Rós (the coldest music I know), listening to my teeth click together.

Early in the evening, I arrange to meet Matt Valentine and Erika Elder at McNeill's Brewery, a former firehouse–police station–jail with a dozen artisan beers on tap and gaggles of burly locals competing in some sort of wall-mounted ring toss. McNeill's smells old and wintry, like chili and sweat and flannel and beer. I find a table near the back, by the dartboard, and watch Valentine and Elder wander through the door, side by side. Valentine, with a dark, bushy beard, copious black hair, and little round glasses, bears an unsettling resemblance to a young Allen Ginsberg; Elder is petite and pretty, with long dark hair and gentle eyes. I wave. We procure cold pints, and talk for a while about Vermont.

Valentine began recording at Tower Recordings in New York in 1994, when there was little to no acoustic music present in the city's underground. "When [Tower Recordings] did our first album in 1994, no one was doing folk." Valentine shrugs. "It was the heyday of Nirvana. We were playing acoustic guitars, a very DIY setup, and everyone else had a really big sound, while we were doing much more lo-fi things. And to me, that was the start of the acoustic underground. Up until then, not much was happening in an avant-garde-meets-acoustic-music way. And ultimately, if I had to classify free-folk as a genre, that's what it would mean to me. That's how I see it."

Elder grew up in a small town outside of Lynchburg, Virginia, and Valentine is from New York's Hudson Valley; the duo moved to Brattleboro in 2002, after playing together—mostly instrumental, heavily improvised psych-folk—in New York for several years. "The Connecticut River here is really strange. There's a centrifuge forming. So there's this folklore that people in Brattleboro never leave, because it's always spinning. You get sucked in. There's an energy here."

"It's very Aleister Crowley." Elder laughs. "When we started playing together in 1999, we found ourselves coming up here to play more often than we played in the city. [The free-folk artist] Dredd Foole came to Brattleboro, and he and his wife were really instrumental in us coming up here—they gave us maps, circled stuff in the paper for us. And then there was Byron [Coley] and Thurston [Moore, guitarist for Sonic Youth and owner of Ecstatic Peace, Valentine and Elder's current record label] and the whole scene down in Northampton, which was really accessible."

Like Coley suggested, both Valentine and Elder seem supremely inspired by their record collections. "[The *Anthology of American Folk Music*] is a massive influence. I got into the Harry Smith stuff through [the 1960s Americana label] Yazoo Records and [the American singer, guitarist, and former Folkways artist] Michael Hurley. Hurley did songs directly off the *Anthology*."

"Right, and with my family, in the mountains—we weren't hillbillies or anything, but they would always sing those songs," Elder adds.

"We sit around the piano with Erika's family on the holidays, and we all sing songs." Valentine smiles.

Although their work together (and Valentine's early Tower releases, in particular) significantly predates the sudden free-folk explosion of 2003, neither Valentine nor Elder seem especially miffed that a slew of younger, more urban artists are lapping up all the credit for a genre they were so instrumental in pioneering. "A lot of the artists now, they're younger—people in their early twenties or even teens. In a way it's a really positive time," Valentine muses. "When we first started playing, it was a lot harder to find the music, to find the source material. Before the *Anthology* CD reissue came out, before the Internet and downloads and all that. The way that the whole thing has gone, I'm really happy that this music is in vogue now, and is actually reaching more people. But I also think that the way some people take it, it's like the seventies, where a lot of it is just pop—it's not really folk. There are some people who are really beautiful at it, like Will Oldham. But then there are people post-Will, post–what we're doing. And it's so watered down." Valentine shrugs. "It's really amazing how popular it is right now. We're amused by it."

In grand folk tradition, Valentine and Elder harbor few commercial ambitions, although the swell in free-folk awareness certainly hasn't hurt their chances at pushing a few more crates of albums. "Our aim was never to obfuscate. The idea is that the music should be heard," Valentine explains.

"We're so excited about this new record [2007's *Green Blues*] because we actually think people are going to hear it. From the beginning, we wanted people to hear it," Elder adds. We finish our beers and order more and keep talking about records until Valentine and Elder have to leave for a show—their friends'—in nearby Northampton.

It's not difficult to understand how what Valentine and Elder and all free-folkers are accomplishing mirrors what Americana musicians have been doing for decades—like Elvis Presley or Waylon Jennings or A. P. Carter or Woody Guthrie, free-folkers pillage the past for scintillating bits of sound, simultaneously pulling from and tweaking a century's worth of song, folding in their own ideas and hopes, reimagining Americana for a brand new world. By circumventing traditional folk avenues—wherein songs are passed down from parent to child, neighbor to neighbor—and learning, instead, through scratchy old LPs and mixtapes and thrift store 78s, free-folk artists are reclaiming a past (and an oral folk tradition) that's been lost, at least in part, by suburban sprawl, technology, isolation, change. The strength of the free-folk community feels, by twenty-first-century standards, old-fashioned. Still, the music—futuristic in both scope and sound—is anything but.

The next morning, after another horn-riddled night at the Artist's Loft, I slide onto 91 South, gnawing on a chunk of Grafton cheddar I picked up at the Brattleboro Food Co-op and anxiously plotting a side trip to Amherst, Massachusetts, where I'll spend way too much time pillaging the two-dollar shelves at the outstanding Mystery Train Records, titillated by the prospect of a few hours of new music and a couple hundred miles of highway. Brooklyn looms, massive and demanding and filled with things I know. But for now, more mystery, the crux of my American wealth: new records and new roads.

A few weeks later, I'll see Valentine and Elder perform at Uncle Paulie's, a bar–lunch counter–music space on the northernmost outskirts of Greenpoint, Brooklyn, practically inaccessible by public transportation and directly across the street from the Newtown Creek Water Pollution Control Plant, the largest of New York City's fourteen wastewater treatment centers. The plant—a mesmerizing, rancid maze of colossal bulb-shaped water containers, tubes, and grim warehouses—sits on the south shore of the Newtown Creek channel, which separates Brooklyn from Queens. This particular plant, which covers thirty-six acres of overindustrialized waterfront, is fed by 180 miles of New York sewer, and walking from my car to the front door of Uncle Paulie's, I think I can smell every last inch: the air feels moldly, wet, green. Uncle Paulie's is typically packed with sanitation workers who've just hopped off shift, but tonight the room is filled with young people wearing thrift-store clothes and funny eyeglasses. When Valentine and Elder set up and begin playing in the front of the room, the crowd goes reverential, and Uncle Paulie's gets so quiet I think I can hear dirty water swishing through pipes across the street, circling, pushing, working hard and coming out clean.

Epilogue

The late Justin Tubb, son of the country legend Ernest Tubb, once defined Americana as "the music of the working man, the farmer, the trucker, the factory worker." I think that's a pretty good place to start, although if I've learned anything in the process of writing this book, it's that Americana is more complicated than any lone platitude—however pithy or appealing or clever—could ever manage to describe. And after eighteen months of eagerly trawling American roads, yapping with all willing parties, buying concert tickets, devouring books, watching movies, sneaking into academic archives, rasping desperate, late-night notes into my own voice mail, coveting souvenir shot glasses, chomping biscuits in roadside diners, trying to learn how to play musical saw, spending all my spare cash on records, ignoring my friends and cowering in my apartment, unshowered and unchanged, for horrifying expanses of time, mulling and typing and listening—I've finally established, for myself, a working understanding of how and what Americana means, what it sounds like, where it lives.

It hasn't been easy. As far as I can tell, Americana is inherently nebulous, destined to change its meaning with each subsequent generation, as unfixed and malleable as the décor at the Shack Up Inn. It's inherently fluid: a state of mind, a romantic notion, a mirage, a joke, a dream. It is worshipped, loved, and reinvented three hundred times a day. It is whatever songs, objects, recipes, dances, or prayers best reflect broad, varied American ideology at a specific point in time.

For some, that means Americana is a vapid marketing cliché, convenient for trying to sell tin lunch boxes with the cast of *Hee Haw* on the front, or overalls, or cookie jars festooned with dried flowers and bits of fraying red-checkered cloth. For others, it's a reminder that we're all still staring down the same sets of problems this particular country has always faced—racism, bigotry, poverty, and too much close-mindedness. Sometimes it sounds like the music being played by revivalists like Alison Krauss and Gillian Welch and Steve Earle. Sometimes it's more like the million-selling tracks piping out of car radios and retail store stereos and cell phones (as Ray Raposa, the frontman for the San Diego free-folk outfit Castanets, once asked me: "Are R. Kelly or Eminem or Hillary Duff any less American than [alt-country acts like] Dock Boggs or Whiskeytown or Old Crow Medicine Show?"). At all times, it is all of these things.

It seems worth noting that commercial hip-hop and Nashville country—both genres with considerable debt to classic Americana music—currently sell by the boatload, moving more units than almost all other kinds of pop music. Yet neither genre jibes particularly well with old-fashioned notions of what Americana should sound and look like, which means that definition must be, on some level, faulty. Early folk, blues, and country records are gritty and underproduced, concerned with exposing the plight of the workingman, offering empathy, hollered by everyday-looking people as a way of retaliating against perceived injustice. But most mainstream country and hip-hop albums are excruciatingly produced (part of this is obviously attributable to advances in recording technology), narcissistic, alienating, and more concerned with escapism (certainly, escapism is a more viable coping mechanism now than ever before—the ubiquity of television sets and movie theaters means a chance to forget about our shitty jobs and scummy apartments and canned-soup dinners) than authenticity. Country and hip-hop artists may occasionally lament impoverishment, but more frequently celebrate absurd extremes—see the squirmy sappiness of a Faith Hill ballad or the excessive wealth and debauchery in a Nelly song. Still, there are plenty of compelling crossovers: bluster-and-boast has been a mainstay in popular music since early rock 'n' roll (see, also, Outlaw country), and both classic Americana and modern hip-hop draw heavily on their predecessors' work, retooling and reinterpreting tracks that have long been a part of public consciousness. All three genres have roots in working-class or impoverished communities. But only two are big sellers at Wal-Mart.

Aside from a handful of rural enclaves, what most people think of as Americana music—acoustic, folksy, quiet songs—now lives in cities and coffeehouses, admired by upper-middle-class, well-educated people, and collected and fetishized by academics and/or record store clerks. With more and more frequency, it is being re-created and reimagined by independent musicians and blasted into the underground, sometimes to enormously compelling ends. For example, shape-note singing, a church-based southern song system rooted in four notes (sung as fa, sol, la, and mi) and initially designed as an all-inclusive, participatory choral tradition, has, curiously, recently reemerged in indie-rock, first with Portland, Oregon, garage-punks the Joggers—who belt shape-note melodies mid-song—and then elsewhere: when Brooklyn drone-rockers Stars Like Fleas partner up with a fifteen-piece shape-note choir for a thirty-minute performance at the now shuttered Lower East Side club Tonic, the results are both disjointed and miraculous.

Meanwhile, bands like Fruit Bats or Gainesville, Florida's Holopaw are reinterpreting "Americana" as a more open-ended aesthetic decision. "I think at this point the word 'Americana' has aged to a point where it's a pretty general term," Fruit Bat Eric Johnson muses. "There's plenty of space between the Byrds, Will Oldham, and Uncle Tupelo, sonically speaking, but they've all probably been referred to as Americana music at one point or another. I guess the dictionary term would be 'modern pop music that directly nods to early American music,' and that's a pretty perfect way to look at it. As far as Fruit Bats go, I much prefer the Americana tag than, say, indie-pop. It has a more noble, classic ring to it. As a musician, sometimes of course I have the standard, clichéd knee-jerk reaction to classification, but I guess you gotta call it something."

"Maybe Americana is wearing a certain type of shirt and playing an acoustic guitar while someone moans over it," Holopaw drummer Michael Johnson offers, when I ask him about the term in late 2003. "Or maybe it doesn't have the finger picking, but you still see a genuine American oddball putting his heart and soul into sound." In 2003, Holopaw released its eponymous debut on Sub Pop; lyrically, *Holopaw* is teeming with old American imagery, all KOA maps and clipper ships, shortwave radios and Appaloosa horses. Musically, the record offers a seamless blend of plugged-in diddlings and warm acoustic strums, mandolin and pedal steel rubbing noses with broken synthesizers and dim percussive loops. Johnson (whose solo outing, the fantastically clever *Nonsense Goes Mudslide*, features mostly electronic instruments) embraces Holopaw's hybrid mission. "A little fuzz bass here, a sixteen-track vocal loop there—that's the fun part of it for me. How can we take this three-chord ballad and skew it a bit? Oh yeah, I'll whistle out of tune in the third verse!" Johnson says. Blending 1970s country rock rowdiness with gentle, lo-fi flourishes, *Holopaw* nods to an impressively wide spectrum of influences. "For Holopaw, it's becoming less of an obvious division," Johnson continues. "The traditional elements have gravitated toward the weird, and the weird has moved slightly closer to the traditional. Because [the record] is rife with unconscious references, *Holopaw* is somewhat palatable in the current audio climate—but I don't think it's gonna make us huge or anything. We're still a little too weird for that."

Red Heart the Ticker, a husband-wife indie-folk duo from Philadelphia by way of Marlboro, Vermont, also understands the challenges inherent to fusing old with new. Vocalist-guitarist Robin MacArthur's song-hunting grandmother, Margaret MacArthur, recorded for Folkways in the early 1960s and is still considered one of Vermont's most beloved folklorists (in 2002, the Vermont Arts Council granted her a Lifetime Achievement in the Arts award). When I first meet Robin MacArthur and her partner, Tyler Gibbons, a few hours before their show at New York's now defunct Mo Pitkin's, MacArthur humbly recounts her paternal heritage: "My grandmother had two babies when she moved into a house [in 1948] with no running water, no electricity, no telephone, and no insulation. The windows were shot out; the floors had been eaten by porcupines. But [Margaret] was just a really energetic, motivated person, and almost immediately went out trying to find music. It was hard, because other than church music, there wasn't a lot of music around, and she had to go digging." MacArthur continues: "She had five kids, and almost all of them stayed there, on that land, and built little houses of their own. So I grew up in this weird little pocket of music and woods and homesteading. My dad makes guitars, my uncle makes mandolins, and my family performed at folk festivals all over the country. My brother and I spent a lot of time in the van."

Now, MacArthur and Gibbons play their own strange, otherworldly folk songs, as influenced by the ephemera of Will Oldham as by the earnestness of Loretta Lynn; for their self-released debut, they recorded their work on a laptop computer in a two-hundred-year-old timber-frame barn. The resulting songs were a fusion of old and new folk technique, and inextricably tied to their Vermont roots. "We're both working on creating a language of place that's not cheesy, that's not cows and Ben and Jerry's," MacArthur explains. "I'm always trying to find a really authentic regional voice that's not a cliché but actually belongs to a place and reflects that place."

It's possible that there is no single way to identify what anyone really means when they call something Americana (although MacArthur's notion of "belonging to a place" is certainly a persuasive start). There is too much useless vocabulary available for defining the already clichéd idea of what it means to be an American in the twenty-first century. As the author Hampton Sides writes in his essay collection *Americana*, "The United States is such a glorious mess of contradiction, such a crazy quilt of competing themes, such a fecund mishmash of people and ideas, that defining us is pretty much pointless." Appropriately, Americana music is as perplexing and mottled and gripping as the people cranking it out— whether they're washboard players or rappers or DJs or pop singers or jug bands.

One thing I'm certain of is that all American music reflects the landscape from which it springs—and as that landscape changes, chewed up by the developments and industry and environmental disasters, as the air we heave in and out of our lungs is filled with new particles, as the water we drink gets its fluoride levels regulated and mineral content tweaked, it makes perfect sense that American music becomes slicker, more machinated, and less like reality. We are all subject to our environs, fashioned and chiseled and sanded into shapes. We have highways for arteries and clouds for brains and sticks for bones. The sounds we make are Americana.

SELECTED BIBLIOGRAPHY

INTRODUCTION: GOODBYE, BABYLON

Author's interview with: Jeff Green.

ONE: AIN'T IT A PITY, I'M IN NEW YORK CITY!

Cribb, John. *A Field Guide to Interstate 95: The Traveler's Companion to the History, Geography, and Trivia That Lie Beneath the Nation's Busiest Highway.* Lanham, MD: Madison Books, 1989.

Frazier, Ian. *Gone to New York: Adventures in the City.* New York: Picador, 2006.

Heat-Moon, William Least. *Blue Highways: A Journey into America.* New York: Little, Brown, 1983.

Kerouac, Jack. *On the Road.* New York: Viking, 1957.

Kunstler, James Howard. *The Geography of Nowhere: The Rise and Decline of America's Manmade Landscape.* New York: Touchstone, 1993.

McMurtry, Larry. *Roads: Driving America's Great Highways.* New York: Simon & Schuster, 2000.

The National Cooperative Highway Research Program website. www.trb.org/CRP/NCHRP/NCHRP.asp.

Orski, Kenneth. "Beyond the Interstate Highway System: It May Be Time to Re-think the State-Federal Relationship." *Innovation Briefs* 16, no. 3 (May–June 2005).

Stuever, Hank. *Off Ramp: Adventures and Heartache in the American Elsewhere.* New York: Picador, 2005.

The U.S. Department of Transportation, Federal Highway Administration website. www.fhwa.gov.

Wolfe, Charles and Kip Lornell. *The Life and Legend of Leadbelly.* New York: DaCapo Press, 1999.

TWO: BLUESLAND

Cheseborough, Steve. *Blues Traveling: The Holy Sites of Delta Blues.* 2nd rev. ed. Jackson: University Press of Mississippi, 2004.

Daniel, Pete. *Lost Revolutions: The South in the 1950s*. Chapel Hill: University of North Carolina Press, 2000.

Deep Blues. DVD. Directed by Robert Mugge, written by Robert Palmer. Oil Factory/Radio Active: 1991.

Gordon, Robert. *It Came from Memphis*. New York: Pocket Books, 1995.

Guralnick, Peter. *Feel Like Going Home: Portraits in Blues and Rock 'n' Roll*. New York: Little, Brown, 1999.

Lomax, Alan. *The Land Where the Blues Began*. New York: The New Press, 2002.

Palmer, Robert. *Deep Blues*. New York: Penguin, 1981.

THREE: YOUNG AND LOOSE AND FULL OF JUICE

Escott, Colin, with Martin Hawkins. *Good Rockin' Tonight: Sun Records and the Birth of Rock 'n' Roll*. New York: St. Martin's, 1991.

Gordon, Robert. *It Came from Memphis*. New York: Pocket Books, 1995.

Guralnick, Peter. *Careless Love: The Unmaking of Elvis Presley*. New York: Back Bay, 2000.

———. *Feel Like Going Home: Portraits in Blues and Rock 'n' Roll*. New York: Little, Brown, 1999.

———. *Last Train to Memphis: The Rise of Elvis Presley*. New York: Back Bay, 1994.

———. *Lost Highway: Journeys and Arrivals of American Musicians*. Boston: David R. Godine, 1979.

Hamm, Charles. *Yesterdays: Popular Song in America*. New York: W. W. Norton, 1979.

Lomax, Alan. *The Land Where the Blues Began*. New York: The New Press, 2002.

Palmer, Robert. *Deep Blues*. New York: Penguin, 1981.

Tosches, Nick. *Hellfire: The Jerry Lee Lewis Story*. New York: Dell, 1982.

U2: Rattle and Hum. DVD. Directed by Phil Joanou. Midnight Films/Paramount Pictures: 1988.

FOUR: I'M GOING TO GRACELAND

Guralnick, Peter. *Careless Love: The Unmaking of Elvis Presley*. New York: Back Bay, 2000.

———. *Last Train to Memphis: The Rise of Elvis Presley*. New York: Back Bay, 1994.

Marling, Karal Ann. *Graceland: Going Home with Elvis*. Cambridge, MA: Harvard University Press, 1996.

Nash, Alanna. *The Colonel: The Extraordinary Story of Colonel Tom Parker and Elvis Presley*. Chicago: Chicago Review Press, 2003.

Presley, Priscilla. *Elvis and Me*. New York: G. P. Putnam's Sons, 1985.

U2: Rattle and Hum. DVD. Directed by Phil Joanou. Midnight Films/Paramount Pictures: 1988.

FIVE: TRAIL OF THE HELLHOUNDS

Author's interviews with: George Booth II, Greg Johnson, Daddy Rich, Erika Wennerstrom.

Cheseborough, Steve. *Blues Traveling: The Holy Sites of Delta Blues*. 2nd rev. ed. Jackson: University Press of Mississippi, 2004.

Gordon, Robert. *Can't Be Satisfied: The Life and Times of Muddy Waters*. New York: Back Bay, 2002.

Guralnick, Peter. *Searching for Robert Johnson*. New York: Plume, 1998.

Gussow, Adam. "Where Is the Love? Racial Violence, Racial Healing, and Blues Communities." *Southern Cultures* 12, no. 4 (Winter 2006).

McInerney, Jay. "White Man at the Door." *The New Yorker*, February 4, 2002, 54–63.

Palmer, Robert. *Deep Blues*. New York: Penguin, 1981.

Raban, Jonathan. *Old Glory: A Voyage Down the Mississippi*. New York: Simon & Schuster, 1981.

Titon, Jeff Todd. *Early Downhome Blues: A Musical and Cultural Analysis*. Urbana: University of Illinois Press, 1977.

SIX: MUSIC CITY, USA

Author's interviews with: Bobby Bare, Jr., Chuck Eddy, Edd Hurt.

Dawidoff, Nicholas. *In the Country of Country: A Journey to the Roots of American Music*. New York: Vintage, 1998.

Doggett, Peter. *Are You Ready for the Country: Elvis, Dylan, Parsons, and the Roots of Country Rock*. New York: Penguin, 2000.

Hemphill, Paul. *The Nashville Sound*. Atlanta: Neverthemore, 2005.

Jennings, Waylon. *Waylon: An Autobiography*. New York: Warner, 1996.

Malone, Bill. *Country Music, U.S.A.* 1968. 2nd rev. ed. Austin: University of Texas Press, 2002.

Peterson, Richard A. *Creating Country Music: Fabricating Authenticity*. Chicago: University of Chicago Press, 1997.

Tosches, Nick. *Country: The Twisted Roots of Rock 'n' Roll*. New York: DaCapo Press, 1985.

SEVEN: I'M GOING WHERE THERE'S NO DEPRESSION

Author's interviews with: Grant Alden, Bobby Bare, Jr., Janet Beveridge Bean, Chuck Eddy, Edd Hurt, Catherine Irwin, J. D. Wilkes.

Doggett, Peter. *Are You Ready for the Country: Elvis, Dylan, Parsons, and the Roots of Country Rock*. New York: Penguin, 2000.

Fallen Angel: Gram Parsons. DVD. Directed by Gandulf Hennig, written by Sid Griffin and Gandulf Hennig. BBC Music Entertainment: 2006.

Hinton, Brian. *South by Southwest: A Road Map to Alternative Country*. London: Sanctuary, 2003.

Joulie, Laurie. "A Conversation with Bill Malone." *Take Country Back*, January 2003. www.takecountryback.com/malone1.htm.

Malone, Bill. *Country Music, U.S.A.* 1968. 2nd rev. ed. Austin: University of Texas Press, 2002.

No Depression magazine, various issues.

Rockpile magazine, various issues.

Tharpe, Jim. "Hank Williams' Last Ride: Driver Recalls Lonesome End." *The Atlanta Journal-Constitution*, December 30, 2002.

EIGHT: I-64 WEST

Paumgarten, Nick. "Annals of the Road: Getting There." *The New Yorker*, April 24, 2006, 86–101.

NINE: COUNTRY ROLLS ON

Author's interviews with: Angela Hammond, Loyal Jones.

Malone, Bill. *Country Music, U.S.A.* 1968. 2nd rev. ed. Austin: University of Texas Press, 2002.

Tosches, Nick. *Where Dead Voices Gather*. New York: Back Bay, 2002.

TEN: AIN'T THAT A PRETTY OLE MOUNTAIN?

Associated Press. "Poisoned Air Killed 3 Miners, Tests Suggest." *The New York Times*, May 22, 2006.

Harlan County U.S.A. DVD. Directed by Barbara Kopple. Cabin Creek: 1976.

Johannsen, Kristin. "Dirty Money: The Economy of Coal." From *Missing Mountains: We Went to the Mountaintop but It Wasn't There*. Nicholasville, KY: Wind Publications, 2005.

Jones, Judy, and Karen Pratt. "OxyContin: A Prescription Painkiller." *Kentucky State Office of Rural Health Newsletter*. Hazard, KY, 2001.

Kaushik, Sandeep. "Valley of the Dolls: How the Media Built the Oxy-Con Scare." *Ace Weekly*, June 21, 2001.

Kentucky Department for Natural Resources. Mine Substance Abuse Task Force. *Final Report*, December 2005.

Malone, Bill. *Country Music, U.S.A.* 1968. 2nd rev. ed. Austin: University of Texas Press, 2002.

Rosenberg, Debra. "How One Town Got Hooked." *Newsweek*, April 9, 2001.

United States Department of Justice. National Drug Intelligence Center. *Kentucky Drug Threat Assessment*, July 2002.

Williams, John Alexander. *Appalachia: A History*. Chapel Hill: The University of North Carolina Press, 2002.

Zwonitzer, Mark, with Charles Hirshberg. *Will You Miss Me When I'm Gone?* New York: Simon & Schuster, 2002.

ELEVEN: THE LITTLE OLD COUNTRY GENERAL STORE FROM LEBANON, TENNESSEE

Author's interview with: Larry Singleton.

Cracker Barrel Old Country Store website. www.crackerbarrel.com.

TWELVE: A MATTER OF SONG!

Author's interview with: Jeff Place.

Cantwell, Robert. *When We Were Good: The Folk Revival*. Cambridge, MA: Harvard University Press, 1996.

The Celestial Monochord. "Einstein and Folkways Records." November 3, 2005. www .celestialmonochord.org/2005/11/einstein_and_fo.html.

Cohen, Scott. "Bob Dylan: Not Like a Rolling Stone." Interview. *Spin*, December 1985, 36.

Corliss, Richard. "Bob Dylan at 65." *Time*, May 24, 2006. www.time.com/time/arts/ article/0,8599,1197784,00.html.

Dylan, Bob. *Chronicles: Volume One*. New York: Simon & Schuster, 2004.

Elridge, Michael. "Remains of the Day-O." Interview with Harry Belafonte. *Transition Magazine*, www.transitionmagazine.com/remains.htm.

Goldsmith, Peter. *Making People's Music: Moe Asch and Folkways Records*. Washington, D.C: Smithsonian Institution Press, 1998.

Wolfe, Charles, and Kip Lornell. *The Life and Legend of Leadbelly*. New York: DaCapo Press, 1999.

THIRTEEN: MAKING FAMILIAR STRANGE

Author's interview with: Jeff Place.

Cantwell, Robert. *When We Were Good: The Folk Revival.* Cambridge, MA: Harvard University Press, 1996.

Christgau, Robert. Review of the *Anthology of American Folk Music. Spin*, October 1997.

Goldsmith, Peter. *Making People's Music: Moe Asch and Folkways Records.* Washington, D.C.: Smithsonian Institution Press, 1998.

Marcus, Greil. "The Old, Weird America." Liner notes to the *Anthology of American Folk Music* (reissue). Washington, D.C.: Smithsonian Folkways Recordings, 1997.

Smith, Harry. Liner notes to the *Anthology of American Folk Music* (original). New York: Folkways Recordings, 1952.

FOURTEEN: YOU WON'T FIND IT SO HOT IF YOU AIN'T GOT THE DO RE MI

(All quotes from Woody Guthrie's private letters, journals, and scrapbooks were taken from material maintained and controlled by the Woody Guthrie Archives, New York, New York.)

Author's interview with: Ramblin' Jack Elliott.

Cantwell, Robert. *When We Were Good: The Folk Revival.* Cambridge, MA: Harvard University Press, 1996.

Christgau, Robert. "Coney Island Okie." *The New York Times*, April 11, 2004.

Cray, Ed. *Ramblin' Man: The Life and Times of Woody Guthrie.* New York: W. W. Norton, 2004.

Dylan, Bob. *Chronicles: Volume One.* New York: Simon & Schuster, 2004.

Goldsmith, Peter. *Making People's Music: Moe Asch and Folkways Records.* Washington, D.C.: Smithsonian Institution Press, 1998.

Klein, Joe. *Woody Guthrie: A Life.* New York: Alfred A. Knopf, 1980.

Surviving the Dust Bowl. DVD. Produced and written by Chana Gazit for *The American Experience.* PBS Broadcasting/WGBH Educational Foundation: 1998.

FIFTEEN: THE NEW, WEIRD, HYPHENATED AMERICA

Author's interviews with: Sam Beam, Jim Becker, Byron Coley, Erika Elder, Eric Johnson, Tim Rutili, Matt Valentine, Howard Wuelfing.

Bemis, Alec Hanley. "Freak Folk's Very Own Pied Piper." *The New York Times*, December 12, 2004.

Hermes, Will. "Summer of Love Redux." *The New York Times*, June 18, 2006.

Keenan, David. "Welcome to the New Weird America." *The Wire*, August 2003, 32–41.

Reynolds, Simon. "Free Schtick." *The Village Voice*, October 31, 2005.

Richardson, Derk. "Freak Folk Flies High: A New Generation of Flower Children Keeps Psychedelic Folk Alive." *SFGate.com*, April 14, 2005. www.sfgate.com/cgi-bin/article.cgi?f=/g/a/2005/04/14/derk.DTL.

EPILOGUE

Author's interviews with: Tyler Gibbons, Eric Johnson, Michael Johnson, Robin MacArthur, Ray Raposa.

Hinton, Brian. *South by Southwest: A Road Map to Alternative Country*. London: Sanctuary, 2003.

Sides, Hampton. *Americana: Dispatches from the New Frontier*. New York: Anchor, 2004.

ACKNOWLEDGMENTS

Tremendous, unspeakable thanks to all those directly or indirectly fundamental to the creation of this book:

Grant Alden; Bobby Bare, Jr.; David Barker; Sam Beam; Peter Blackstock; the Brooklyn Writers Space; Califone; the Charlottesville Writing Center; Ben Chasny and Six Organs of Admittance; Byron Coley; Pete Daniel and the Smithsonian Institution; Chuck Eddy; Erika Elder; Ramblin' Jack Elliott; Fat Possum Records; Freakwater; Jeff Green and the Americana Music Association; Nora Guthrie, Hillel Arnold, and the Woody Guthrie Archives; Hatch Show Print; Heartless Bastards; Edd Hurt; Eric Johnson and Fruit Bats; Greg Johnson and the Blues Archive at the University of Mississippi; Michael Johnson and Holopaw; Loyal Jones and Berea College; Sam Kashner and Nancy Schoenberger at the College of William and Mary; Andrew Kesin, Thurston Moore, and Ecstatic Peace Records; Lance Ledbetter and Dust-to-Digital Records; Steve Manning and Sub Pop Records; Will and Ned Oldham; Ron Pen, Angela Hammond, and the John Jacob Niles Center for American Music at the University of Kentucky at Lexington; Jeff Place, Daniel Sheehy, and Folkways Recordings; Ray Raposa and Castanets; Red Heart the Ticker; Daddy Rich; Gaynell Rogers; the Shack Up Inn; Leslie Sharpe, Richard Locke, Honor Moore, Patty O'Toole, and Anna Peterson at Columbia University; Super Chikan; Th' Legendary Shack-Shakers; Matt Valentine; the Virginia Discovery Museum.

My editors, past and present, for making me a better writer: Ryan Schreiber and Scott Plagenhoef at Pitchforkmedia.com; Marc Smirnoff at *Oxford American*; Julia Cosgrove and Shoshana Berger at *ReadyMade*; Chuck Eddy at *The Village Voice*; Caryn Ganz, Charles Aaron, and Steve Kandell at *Spin*; and Yancey Strickler, Michaelangelo Matos, Michael

Azerrad, and Joe Keyes at eMusic.com. Extra special thanks to Josh Jackson, Jason Killingsworth, Reid Davis, Tim Porter, Kate Kiefer, and Steve LaBate at *Paste* magazine for their expert advice and for being brave enough to let me write exactly what I wanted to write: an essay about driving around, listening to records made by people with beards.

Andy Beta, Clarke Boehling, Adam Daniel, Andy Downing, Grant Hunnicutt, Marisa Jefferson, Kim Langford, Emily Manley, Sam Polcer, and Rod Waterman: I was duly warned that writing a book means slowly alienating everyone in your life, so double thanks for bringing me records and cupcakes, putting up with lapsed e-mails and broken dates, and being all-around aces, even when I didn't deserve it.

Richard Lucyshyn, for single-handedly bringing a sense of hope back to poetry and rock 'n' roll.

Jennifer Shotz, for scribbling genius bits all over my pages, talking me down from various precipices, and making my life better, easier, and more fun.

John O'Connor, for slogging through these chapters a million times each, offering wise, wise council over takeout from Chip Shop: this would have been a different book without your help. And by "different," I mean "probably still not finished" and "definitely not very good."

Dan and Mary Lou Stetka, for unbelievable generosity and kindness.

Karen Rudnicki, for unerring guidance and, most important, for getting it from the start.

Chris Parris-Lamb at the Gernert Co., for his enthusiasm, infinite wisdom, and unfailing appreciation for the Hold Steady.

Angus Carhill at Faber and Faber UK, for understanding all the complicated and compelling ways Americana translates abroad.

Denise Oswald and everyone at Faber and Faber (Jessica Ferri, Chris Peterson, and Charlotte Strick, in particular), for having not only impeccable taste in music, but for having real faith in this project and for allowing me to tell this story, this way.

Alexandria Petrusich, for twenty-eight years of unconditional love and encouragement, for zipping up my wedding dress, for scads of unassailable advice, for always being nearby with a sack of Smarties and a joke about Dad.

Bret Stetka, the love of my life, for far too many things to bother writing down: you are the best person I know. This is as much yours as mine.

And finally, to my parents, the incomparable John and Linda Petrusich, for their pipeline of support. Thank you for having the foresight to feed your kid candy and books at the very same time, so that she would always associate sweetness with stories.

INDEX